I0414120

Asian Ethnology

Asian Ethnology (ISSN 1882–6865) is a semi-annual, peer-reviewed journal published by the Nanzan Anthropological Institute, Nanzan University, Nagoya, Japan. It is produced in cooperation with Boston University's Department of Religion. *Asian Ethnology* is an open access journal and all back numbers may be viewed through the journal's website.

http://nirc.nanzan-u.ac.jp/en/publications/asian-ethnology/

Asian Ethnology publishes formal essays and analyses, research reports, and critical book reviews relating to a wide range of topical categories, including

- narratives, performances, and other forms of cultural representation
- popular religious concepts
- vernacular approaches to health and healing
- local ecological/environmental knowledge
- collective memory and uses of the past
- cultural transformations in diaspora
- transnational flows
- material culture
- museology
- visual culture

Editorial correspondence should be addressed to

Editors, *Asian Ethnology*
18 Yamazato-cho, Showa-ku
Nagoya 466–8673, Japan

TEL: (81) 52–832–3111
email: dorman@nanzan-u.ac.jp

INFORMATION FOR CONTRIBUTORS

Manuscript submissions should be sent as email attachments, in either Microsoft Word or Rich Text Format, to the address above. The author's name, which will be deleted for peer review, should appear only on the first page. All submitted manuscripts should be double-spaced throughout and limited to 10,000 words, including notes and references. Please include an abstract of up to 150 words, along with 5 key words that most effectively evoke the article's content. If a submission is accepted the author will be asked to provide a short biographical statement of up to 75 words.

The format should follow the articles contained in the present volume. For more detailed information, please consult the style guide found on the journal's website:

http://nirc.nanzan-u.ac.jp/en/publications/asian-ethnology/

Please be advised that submissions accepted for publication are subject to editorial modification. Submitted manuscripts should not have been published elsewhere nor currently be under consideration by another journal. Unsolicited book reviews will be considered, though there is no guarantee of publication. In principle, book reviews should not exceed 1500 words.

Asian Ethnology is indexed in: Arts & Humanities Citation Index; ATLA Religion Database; Bibliography of Asian Studies; Current Contents/Arts & Humanities; International Bibliography of Book Reviews; International Bibliography of Periodical Literature; International Bibliography of the Social Sciences; Religion Index One Periodicals; and Scopus.

Asian Ethnology

Volume 76, Number 1 · 2017

Interpreting Sinitic Heritage:
Ethnography and Identity in China and Southeast Asia

Articles

Reviews

Films

BOOKS

Anne E. McLaren
University of Melbourne

Editor's Introduction

Interpreting Sinitic Heritage
Ethnography and Identity in China and Southeast Asia

This special issue seeks to explore shifting dimensions of implicit, adopted, or imposed Chinese ethnicity with regard to contemporary ritual and performance traditions in China and Southeast Asia. The introductory article addresses recent issues within the framework of scholarly debates known as "critical Han studies" and "Sinophone studies," which seek to deconstruct conventional understandings of "Chineseness" within China and the diaspora. Ritual and performance traditions are often overlooked as factors in the formation of ethnic identities. However, they offer a rich domain for examining local inflections of being "Chinese" or, in some cases, resisting being "Chinese." Conventional views have maintained that oral and performance traditions are simply variants of a common "Chinese" culture or are marginal to national discourses about Chinese identity. It is argued here that a range of local players are seizing new opportunities to revive or reconstruct traditional performance culture in unexpected ways. Commerce, globalization, and state heritage agendas are dramatic factors in the transformation of non-elite or even formerly stigmatized cultural forms into iconic items of cultural heritage that engage with notions of "Chineseness" in ways both various and contestable.

KEYWORDS: ritual—performance—ethnicity—ethnography—Chinese—cultural heritage—identity

Asian Ethnology Volume 76, Number 1 · 2017, 1–18
© Nanzan University Anthropological Institute

> "Chinese history has always been written from the point of view of the center..." (FAURE and HO, 2013, xi)

RECENT SCHOLARSHIP has attempted to de-center notions of a monolithic China through the exploration of Sinitic languages and cultures beyond the borders of the Chinese state and in areas formerly considered marginal or peripheral.* This is evident in the work of historians and anthropologists such as David Faure and Ho Ts'ui-p'ing (cited above) and also in the emergence of new sub-disciplines that seek to deconstruct notions of a monolithic Chinese identity. We refer here to scholarly dialogues now known as "critical Han studies" and "Sinophone studies." Critical Han studies takes its name from the title of a major volume in this field (MULLANEY et al., eds. 2012). The critical Han scholarly dialogue offers an illuminating critique of the supposed unified ethnicity of the majority Chinese population, known as the Han people. It specifically critiques the conventional conflation of Han-ness with Mandarin speech and foregrounds instead the fact that so-called Han communities are divided into eight broad language groupings. In this collection we examine issues of folkloristics, ethnography, and identity in the case of two communities regarded as Han Chinese; one speaking a variety of western Mandarin, and the other a non-Mandarin speech form within the Wu language group. In recent decades, the song traditions of both regions have undergone distinctive reconstructions to emerge as valued heritage items of "Han Chinese" culture. A third case examined here deals with an ethnic minority in south China who do not identify as Chinese. In spite of this, their distinctive song forms are now construed as part of the culture of greater China.

Sinophone studies challenges notions of "Chineseness" in the case of the migratory communities in Asia. Conventionally, these "Chinese" attributes hinge on a Mandarin-speaking culture and the conventional written script. According to Shu-mei Shih, the author of influential studies in this field, the term "Sinophone" is used "to designate Sinitic-language cultures and communities outside China as well as those ethnic communities within China, where Sinitic languages are either forcefully imposed or willingly adopted" (SHIH 2013, 30). To date, Sinophone studies has dealt mainly with the influence of the Chinese written script and culture beyond Chinese national borders. In this special issue we will extend notions drawn from Sinophone studies to examine the ritual and theatrical culture of two Southeast Asian communities, one in Singapore and the other in Indonesia.

The collection of five studies presented here is the result of collaborative work on the part of scholars based in Asia and in the West. Some of the articles were originally presented in a panel entitled "Scripts and Oral Traditions in the Sinophone" at the Asian Studies Association of Australia Biennial Conference, University of Western Australia, 8–10 July 2014. Others were commissioned from scholars in Singapore and the United States. Two are coauthored by Western and Chinese scholars who engaged in joint fieldwork in their respective regions. Our intention here is to draw from scholarly frameworks that critique notions of a unitary "Chinese character" in order to explore issues of identity in oral traditions, folk performance, and the ritual arts of communities in China and beyond. Each case study reflects different types of engagement with ethnic and nationalist agendas in their respective communities. As a whole, these studies illuminate the dilemmas of "Chinese" heritage transmission in an era when China is gaining a stronger profile in world affairs and notions of "Chineseness" are becoming more fraught and contested.

The first two articles in this collection (McLaren and Zhang; Gibbs) deal with a folk performance form in a non-Mandarin and a Mandarin-speaking community respectively. Both communities are regarded as "Han Chinese" in current state classification in spite of very considerable differences in language and customs. As discussed here, the folk performances of these two regions, one coastal and one in China's western hinterland, undergo a process of refinement in order to measure up as examples of "Chinese" heritage. One even plays a role in international economic exchange (Gibbs). The third article (Ingram and Wu) is an example of a culture regarded as outside "Han Chinese-ness" but one that is capable of being co-opted into the greater cause of Chinese civilization. However, as demonstrated by Ingram and Wu, many compromises need to be made for this transformation to be effected. The population's own response is ambiguous, depending largely on education, generation, and economic opportunity. The fourth article deals with the dual ethnic identity (Javanese and Chinese) of a particular folk form still used in shamanistic rituals in contemporary Indonesia. The author (Chan) takes issue with contemporary Sinophone studies for seeming to elide issues of "Chineseness" with regard to folk performances and calls for greater recognition of Sinitic derivation. The final article (by Chia) deals with the survival strategies of a puppet troupe speaking a regional non-Mandarin language in contemporary Singapore. Chia focuses on the troupe's attempt to sustain the support of its own community (Henghua speaking), to engage with other Chinese communities (Hokkien and Mandarin speaking), and even to "negotiate" with the state, in the promotion of state-sponsored multilingual, multicultural events.

The latter-day transformations of the song traditions, rituals, and theatrical forms examined here are somewhat unexpected, in that each stands in an equivocal position with regard to China's traditional elite civilization. Orally-transmitted genres belonging to the common people have been historically ignored, marginalized, or stigmatized in the pre-contemporary period. Often they have been transcribed or recreated in writing only in recent decades. One example is the Wu-language songs of secret love affairs, sung throughout the Yangzi Delta by rice paddy farmers. Before the advent of socialist China, the genre in question was a cherished part of rural popular culture. Nonetheless, it was at the same time a source of embarrassment for its perceived "vulgarity" or even "obscenity." This case is reminiscent of Michael Herzfeld's notion of "cultural intimacy," that is, "the recognition of those aspects of a cultural identity that are considered a source of external embarrassment but that nevertheless provide insiders with their assurance of common sociality" (HERZFELD 2005, 3).

None of the genres discussed here were heralded as quintessential examples of Chinese civilization in the pre-contemporary period but, for reasons discussed in this special issue, many have become important cultural markers of regional identity in the twenty-first century. In the process of gaining recognition, these folk forms have become more visible within their own local regions, although the tradition requires modification to meet the needs of new audiences. This is particularly true for the cases from Mainland China. The two case studies dealing with Chinese cultural forms in Southeast Asia (temple puppet theater and spirit mediumship) have a more complex and less "visible" ethnic identity in their home contexts. In this special issue we will assess the reasons for variable rates of ethnic visibility and hence "Chineseness" in a range of oral and ritual genres. Levi Gibbs's study explains how songs from a once impoverished region became transformed into a regional "treasure," playing a role in international exchange. Catherine Ingram and Wu Jiaping examine the choral singing of the non-Chinese Kam people of south China and the process that led to the inscription of Kam songs in UNESCO's list of World Intangible Cultural Heritage. The once obscure songs of the Kam are now understood to add luster to the "Chinese" musical tradition. The Wu language song-cycles discussed by Anne McLaren and Emily Yu Zhang have undergone the elimination of "embarrassing" elements in their transition from a purely local tradition to a regional icon of Chinese heritage. Carol Chia describes how the temple theater of Singapore's Henghua-speaking population, a diasporic Chinese community, has been adapted to meet the needs of secular, modernizing Singapore. In this historical shift, the new form of Henghua puppetry that is performed to multicultural audiences is construed as representing "Chinese" culture in general, although it is still performed in the Henghua language. Meanwhile, in Indonesia, a remarkable form of spirit mediumship is implicitly understood within its receptive community to possess a dual identity as both Indonesian and Chinese. Understandings of "Chineseness," as negotiated by local players, receiving communities, and ethnographers, have been central to the renewed transmission of these cultural forms in recent times.

The first topic to be addressed here will be the reevaluation of Chinese ethnicity in recent scholarship. The Chinese state lists fifty-six ethnic groups on Chinese soil, of which the majority group, known as Han Chinese, comprises over 90 percent.[1] The arbitrary and "invented" nature of these categorizations and the absurdity of the assumption of unity for the massive Han majority have become clearer due to recent scholarly analysis. Stevan Harrell, known for his study of ethnicity in China's southwest, observes that governments "actively hide the fluidity and changeability of identity and group membership" (HARRELL 1996, 5). Melissa J. Brown has

demonstrated the malleability of ethnic classifications in her study of shifting ethnic identifications, both towards and away from Han Chinese ethnicity, in the case
of Taiwanese plains aborigines and the Tujia people of Hubei (BROWN ed. 1996;
BROWN 2004). Thomas S. MULLANEY's book (2010) is a fascinating exploration
of the process of ethnic classification carried out by state-commissioned ethnographers in 1950s China, a classification that remains the bedrock of ethnic taxon-
omy in China today. His chief finding is that Chinese ethnographers went beyond
static Stalinist models of ethnic classification to develop frameworks based around
"ethnic potential." In other words, the classifying ethnographers sought to assess
whether a particular community could, with state encouragement, develop into a
fully-fledged *minzu* 民族 or major ethnic grouping (MULLANEY 2010, 11).[2] He further states that "the Chinese state would be free, and indeed required, to intervene
and oversee the actualization of these 'potential' *minzu* in the post-Classification
period" (MULLANEY 2010, 12). In order to realize "ethnic potential," the ethnographers, the state, and the potential *minzu* group had to engage in a sustained project of consolidating ethnic identities. Far from being fixed or innate, ethnic identity
in China is thus based on "perpetual management by the state and the continued
participation by the people" (MULLANEY 2010, 135).[3] During the chaotic years of
the Cultural Revolution (1966–1976) there was a general hiatus in state policy to
promote ethnic diversity.[4] During this period of revolutionary zealotry the attempt
to "realize the potential" of ethnic groups was in abeyance. However, after Mao's
death in 1976 the reformist state led by Deng Xiaoping sought to restore previous policies of encouraging multiculturalism and accommodating ethnic diversity.
At the same time there were large-scale attempts to revitalize Han Chinese traditions. Folklore studies was reinstated as a recognized discipline and thousands
of career folklorists, culture cadres, and amateur ethnologists were mobilized
to collect and record folklore genres across every province and region of China
(TUOHY 1991, 205–10; MCLAREN 1994; 2010). Among the beneficiaries of this
policy were the Wu-speaking communities of the lower Yangzi Delta discussed by
McLaren and Zhang, the Yulin Folk Arts Troupe in northern Shaanxi discussed by
Gibbs, and the Kam community examined by Ingram and Wu in this special issue.

Three decades of active promotion of selected items of "tradition" has left a
somewhat ambiguous heritage, as will be discussed by the contributors here. The
economic and social transformation of rural China and of the non-Han borderlands has inevitably led to the same sort of dilemmas in heritage preservation and
revitalization that one finds throughout global developing societies. One of the
most significant changes has been the progress towards almost universal school-
ing at primary level, coupled with an intensification of the use of Mandarin as a
medium of instruction. This factor, designed to promote economic growth and
national unification, has severely undermined the transmission of the language and
cultural forms among many ethnic groups.[5] The market economy of the reform
period has led to a higher standard of living, but when "ethnicity" becomes commodified and sold in the marketplace it risks being transformed into a hybrid form
of dubious "authenticity." Ingram and Wu, in their contribution to this special
issue, discuss the impact of the marketization of folk culture in the case of the

southern Kam people. As Dru Gladney noted two decades ago, non-Han Chinese in the borderlands are easily objectivized and eroticized as the Orientalized "Other" appreciated by Han Chinese and international tourists (GLADNEY 1994; 2004).[6] Now that China's urbanization has reached approximately half of its 1.4 billion population, it is rural China that is now exoticized for the benefit of urban Chinese, who increasingly seek out eco-tourist or nostalgic theme park sites to remind them of their cultural roots (CHIO 2011; MCLAREN 2011).[7]

As noted by numerous scholars, the Chinese state, while accommodating ethnic diversity, also aims to ensure that the realization of "ethnic potential" never be allowed to come into conflict with the primary goal of promoting "the nation-state as the primary source of emotional transference and personal identification" (JANKOWIAK 2008, 91). In response to these two somewhat contradictory goals, the state tends to "oscillate" between "soft" policies on the one hand, designed to promote affirmative action for minorities, and on the other hand, repressive policies designed to intimidate any ethnic resistance to the unified nation (JANKOWIAK 2008, 93). This can lead to a sense of divided loyalty on the part of some ethnic groups. The consequence of this divided loyalty is that communities tend to promote the "local attributes" of their traditions while making suitable adaptations to ensure the receiving audience can accept the revised form as "Chinese." Many communities have been happy to accommodate state agendas of multicultural harmony, seeing this as a way for regional folk forms to attain national prominence. One example is the Man or Manchu communities studied by Chih-yu Shih who take part enthusiastically in national patriotic activities (SHIH 2002, 101–13). Another example is the Yulin Folk Arts Troupe investigated by Levi Gibbs, which has welcomed its new role as a "bridge" in establishing commerce between the home province and The Dow Chemical Company, based in the U.S.. In the latter case, the folk genre concerned is perceived not as the expressive art of a remote rural community but rather as representing an originary form of "Chinese" culture. In the case of Kam big song, the "reform" of traditional song forms in the contemporary period is seen as a loss by some members of the community; for others the reforms offer a career opportunity and national prestige (see the article by Ingram and Wu).

CRITICAL HAN STUDIES

Critical Han studies offers fresh insights into the constructed nature of Han Chinese ethnicity and allows us to see more clearly the complexity of ethnic identification within the vast population that we conventionally view as "Chinese." As Mullaney observes in his "Introduction and Prolegomenon" to *Critical Han Studies*, the Han Chinese comprise 1.2 billion people living within Chinese state boundaries (MULLANEY et al., eds. 2012, 1). They speak many different languages, which are often mutually unintelligible, and reside across vast tracts of space in very diverse geographic zones. As he points out, the term "Han" is not so much "a coherent category of identity" as "an umbrella term encompassing a plurality of diverse cultures, languages and ethnicities" (MULLANEY et al. 2012, 2). The term "Han," while an ancient term used from time to time to indicate the people of north and central China, came into prominence in the late nineteenth century as a way of identifying and mobilizing those Chinese who did not belong to the Manchus, the ethno-group who ruled China from 1664 to 1911. In the nineteenth century, under the influence of imported notions of Social Darwinism, the term "Han Chinese" came to be interpreted rather as a bio-racial category within the so-called Yellow Races (DIKÖTTER 1992, 82–83). Building on the work of other scholars working in Chinese ethnicity, and on Fredrik BARTH's (1969) notions of "ethnic boundaries and boundary maintenance," Mullaney puts forward a stimulating new way of understanding the constructed nature of contemporary Han ethnicity (MULLANEY et al., eds. 2012, 16). In this new framework, contemporary Chinese self-identification as "Han" becomes a historically contingent process whereby diverse peoples arrived at a notion of common ethnicity in relation to other groups in their shared space. In other words, notions of "Han-ness" relate to constructions of the Other, which in this case are those considered not to have the cultural attributes of the dominant race. Han Chinese populations define non-Han populations within their state boundaries as "more and less civilized, more and less dangerous, more and less exotic, and so forth, establishing a hierarchy in which each group is defined relationally to the Han apex" (in MULLANEY et al., eds. 2012, 3, citing BLUM and JENSEN eds. 2002).

The critical Han hypothesis can be fruitfully applied to the Wu-language folk epics studied by McLaren and Zhang in this volume. These long song-cycles relating tales of love and passion from the lower Yangzi Delta have been transmitted orally over many generations. They were traditionally sung by nonliterate rice-paddy farmers while toiling in the fields or journeying along the waterways that crisscross the delta. In pre-contemporary times this genre was regarded as vulgar at best and obscene at worst. In the nineteenth century, provincial governors and local magistrates attempted to ban the publication of printed booklets based on these popular songs. During the early socialist phase in China, traditional Wu songs were either repressed or rewritten to reflect new ideological content. It was not until the reform era (post 1978) that Wu songs came to be regarded as a cherished part of the regional tradition and were inscribed as items of national-level Intangible Cultural Heritage (MCLAREN 2011). However, the transition from marginalized genre to regional treasure was not an easy one. In order to promote Wu songs to national recognition, local ethnographers first needed to resolve issues related to the nature of Han Chinese ethnicity and Marxist historiography.

When lengthy sung narratives were elicited by ethnographers in the 1980s from rural communities in the lower Yangzi Delta, the scholarly world in China was shocked and amazed. Conventional Chinese thinking was influenced by Marxist frameworks that associated the emergence of epic poetry with preliterate societies, whereas the Han Chinese, who developed the writing system thousands of years ago, were believed to have entered a state of civilization in ancient times. For this reason, in Chinese scholarly thinking, sung epics found on Chinese soil are associated with non-Han peoples such as Tibetans, Mongols, Kazaks, the Yi people, and so forth, but not with the category designated as Han. Placing

Wu song-cycles on a par with the epic production of non-Han populations thus required rethinking conventional Marxist historiography. More fuel was added to the fire by other Chinese scholars who saw the edited transcripts as an artificial assemblage put together by local folklorists seeking a reputation. In the end the scholarly controversy was resolved largely in a consensus that Han Chinese communities could indeed possess verse narratives of epic length, even if this meant placing Han Chinese people on a par with "less advanced" minorities.

Another point of contestation was the intrinsic value of vernacular material regarded as vulgar or pornographic and its suitability to be included in ongoing heritage projects. This study examines one of the more famous of the song-cycles to explore issues of ethnicity in non-Mandarin speaking Han Chinese communities, the place of formerly stigmatized genres in Chinese cultural heritage, and newly emerging constructions of "Chineseness" in the contemporary period. Were these songs of illicit love worthy of a niche in the civilization of the Han Chinese? Through a comparison of original and later transcripts and enriched by fieldwork with ethnographers and singers, McLaren and Zhang explore the dilemmas faced by those seeking to promote once stigmatized cultural forms as regional icons of "Han Chinese" culture.

In the article by Levi S. Gibbs, "Culture Paves the Way, Economics Comes to Sing the Opera," we turn to a more mainstream Han Chinese community residing in China's ancient western heartland at the intersection of the Yellow River and the Great Wall. However, the villagers in this part of northern Shaanxi Province, while speaking a local version of Mandarin, suffered a form of "invisibility" based on remoteness and poverty. Today the region of Yulin has a vibrant cultural existence in the songs of its master-singer, Wang Xiangrong, who is the main performer examined in this study. The song repertoire of this area, comprising love songs, drinking songs, spirit medium tunes, and Mongol-Han ditties, drew little attention in premodern times and perhaps would not have survived into the contemporary period without the extensive efforts of singers, ethnographers, and local administrators. In 2009 the broader regional genre of "northern Shaanxi folk songs" was listed as a national-level item of Intangible Cultural Heritage. Gibbs's study profiles the imbrication of contemporary folk performance and economic aspirations in this locality. This is not a new subject. Historically, the ritual and folk arts have often played a strong role in regional economies. Helen F. Siu, for example, in her study of the Chrysanthemum Festival in the Pearl River Delta (1990), has demonstrated the concentration of interests shared by powerful lineage groups and the local governing elite in pre-socialist China. In the post-Mao period, the Chrysanthemum Festival was revived by the state specifically to attract overseas Chinese investors and build business confidence (Siu 1990, 785–86). Other coastal regions underwent a similar revival of ancient material and intangible culture. The discovery of an ancient trading junk in the waters of Quanzhou was profiled in a new maritime museum to not only celebrate past heritage but also to signal openness to trade and foreign investment (Wang 2006, 10–11). While earlier studies of the economic impact of folk revival have focused mostly on the deployment of "folk" culture in tourism, or to attract overseas Chinese people nostalgic for their "homeland," Gibbs's study is possibly the first to specifically treat the role of folk performance in the negotiations of major global players, in this case, China's largest coal company and the multinational giant, The Dow Chemical Company. Gibbs makes two innovative contributions to the discussion of issues of Han Chinese identity and folk culture. The first is to develop a paradigm, based on notions of relationship and reciprocity, in which one can understand an exchange of cultural forms as a form of "ritualized relationship" essential for the development of positive personal economic outcomes. The second contribution is to understand how this complex form of "gift exchange" is interpreted in the case of a key individual folk song performer called Wang Xiangrong. Wang's apparent goal is to render his marginalized local region visible to the outside world: "I only want [...] that outsiders can get to know Fugu, to see our northern Shaanxi" (see Gibbs in this special issue). However, when the Yulin troupe performs on the international stage, Wang's songs from his hometown become transformed into something understood as authentic "Chinese" culture. In this way, Gibbs's study testifies to the convergence of individual, business, and diplomatic interests in the case of a northern Shaanxi locality.

The reification of a Han Chinese culture that one often finds in the contemporary revival of folk performance is reminiscent of earlier projects where non-Han minority cultures were used as a form of international exchange. Ralph A. Litzinger, in his discussion of an exhibition of Yunnan Nuosu culture held at a museum in the United States in the year 2000, draws out the dilemmas of U.S. anthropologists who organized this exhibition: "How to work against the grain of the standard ethnological representation of minority nationality otherness in China, in which ethnic minority culture is often viewed as a remnant of the social evolutionary past of the Chinese nation?" (LITZINGER 2001, 90). But on interviewing Nuosu scholars involved in the exhibition, Litzinger realizes that their objective was to "give the viewer a sense of what they see, and not incorrectly so, as the sheer and indisputable beauty of Nuosu cultural life" (LITZINGER 2001, 95). The Nuosu people had suffered greatly during the socialist decades and were proud and delighted that their culture could now be the object of aesthetic appreciation by an international audience. In this case obtaining international recognition was a crucial step in gaining national recognition. Nor did the Nuosu elders wish to erase the impact of modernity in order to parade an artificial "authenticity" for their cultural forms. Rather, they attempted to assert the "dignity" of the minority culture and to escape from the paradigm of ethnic primitivity, where the minority is forever fossilized in the pre-contemporary period (LITZINGER 2001, 95).

In the case of the Han Chinese population of northern Shaanxi, the elevation of a folk song genre to become part of diplomatic exchange, together with the famous terracotta warriors, implies a similar elevation of the status of the people in this once marginalized and impoverished rural community. In this curious "ritual exchange" we see The Dow Chemical Company learning how to play the diplomatic game "Chinese-style." They declare they wish to "share some of China's important heritage with the people of this region (that is, the Midwest)" (see Gibbs in this special issue). Gibbs concludes that this cultural dance, superimposed against the hard business of negotiations between two energy giants, opens up a "liminal space" in which both sides can realign their economic relations with public opinion. This finding demonstrates that it is not just "minority" folk culture that can be used for economic gain as a cultural signifier; a reified version of Han Chinese folk culture can be used to the same end.

The study of Catherine Ingram and Jiaping Wu examines the impact of state-led research into the discovery and transformation of a folk performance genre of the Kam people of Guizhou Province, south China. The Kam speak a Tai-Kadai language and are a non-Han Chinese people. Known as "Dong" in Mandarin, the Kam belong to a designated ethnic minority group (*shaoshu minzu* 少数民族).[8] In the early 1950s Chinese cadres visited remote Kam villages and investigated the community's language, folk customs, and expressive culture. They took a particular interest in a form of singing known as "big song," a form of polyphonic choral singing. As Ingram and Wu explain here, this ethnographic intervention of the 1950s was to radically alter the future of this people. Until then Chinese music had been considered to lack polyphonic singing. In fact, Westerners had earlier critiqued Chinese music for its "monotonous" quality in comparison with the more advanced and "complicated" forms of European polyphonic singing. The serendipitous discovery of polyphonic singing in the Kam community was warmly welcomed by Chinese folklorists who were now able to point to the existence of polyphonic music on Chinese soil. It is ironic that the Kam people, who do not belong to the Han Chinese majority, were used to fill this perceived "gap" in the "Chinese" musical repertoire, thus enhancing the status of this non-Han minority by recognizing their contribution to greater Chinese civilization.

Ingram and Wu argue that the ethnographic engagement with the Kam people represents "one particular stage in a long-standing and complex interrelation among notions of ethnicity, culture, and Chinese nationalism or identification" (see Ingram and Wu in this special issue). However, this process was not without its sacrifices and compromises. Ingram and Wu explain in detail the modifications made to the traditional genre under the influence of new social and economic trends of the reform era. Big song had traditionally been performed in pagoda-shaped buildings known as *dare low*. Big songs were significant within the Kam tradition because they were used to transmit "history, philosophy, and other local knowledge" (McLaren et al. 2013, 63). However, once identified as a remarkable type of choral singing, big song was promoted as a stage performance for a local public and in this way became "entirely divorced from its original cultural context" (see Ingram and Wu in this special issue). This gradually led to its latter day transformation into a form suitable for the entertainment of national and international audiences. In 2009, Kam big song was inscribed on UNESCO's Representative List of Intangible Cultural Heritage of Humanity as "Grand Song of the Dong Ethnic Group." Once canonized in this way, Kam big song could not escape engagement with shifting paradigms of Chinese ethnicity. Although clearly non-Han in origin, this once local genre has now been naturalized as a form of "Chinese" singing.

This case study adds strength to the hypothesis put forward recently by Tim Oakes that China heritage projects are viewed by the Chinese state "as powerful tools of modernization and development; that cultural display implies a project of 'improvement' and of building 'quality' among the 'backward' rural population" (OAKES 2013, 381). This offers a bleak prognosis for the agenda behind Chinese attempts at "preservation" (*baohu* 保护), which too often are simply blunt tools of development. However, Ingram and Wu also discuss the simultaneous existence of what they call the "village tradition," where villagers interested in transmitting their own songs in the form they please to future generations continue to do so, although often in different forms and with different participants. In Kam communities it is now mostly married women, formerly prohibited from Kam singing, who carry on the tradition. This phenomenon of an officially-recognized ethnic culture and an unofficial one carried out in private domains is known elsewhere in China.[9] The ongoing Kam "village tradition" is not entirely the same as in the past but rather illustrates that some Kam people have seized the initiative to carry on aspects of the past in spite of the pressures of commercialization and modernization.

SINOPHONE STUDIES

The newly emerging sub-field of Sinophone studies extends scholarly dialogue about shifting ethnicities by highlighting the complexity of notions of Chinese identity in the migratory communities of Southeast Asia. Shu-mei Shih points out that the term "diaspora" to describe Chinese-origin communities residing outside China is increasingly problematic as Chinese populations have undergone a process of localization and hybridization over the generations (SHIH 2013, 38). The conventional notion of the Chinese diaspora was one based "on a unified ethnicity, culture, language, as well as place of origin or homeland" (SHIH 2007, 23). She observes further that the term "Chinese" is too often reduced to the Mandarin-speaking Han Chinese. The reality of the diaspora is somewhat different. Chinese-speaking communities in Asia speak mostly non-Mandarin Chinese languages, or may speak Mandarin with a non-standard accent. She points out the historically contingent nature of languages spoken by these migratory communities, which combine the language of the site of origin with the languages of the settlement community, resulting in hybridized forms of expression. The resulting "Sinophonic culture" may well be quite distinct from the culture of its home of origin. Some communities have assimilated to the extent that they no longer speak any Chinese language (SHIH 2007, 29). Shih concludes that "Chineseness is not an ethnicity but many ethnicities" (SHIH 2007, 24).[10] Sinophone studies, with its focus on the non-Mandarin speaking groups of Asia and critique of the "colonialism" of the Mandarin-speaking Han Chinese, offers fresh insights into the condition of China-derived cultural forms in Southeast Asia. However, to date Sinophone studies has concentrated principally on written forms used in the diaspora. In this special issue we seek to critically evaluate the potential contribution of Sinophone studies to areas of oral and ritual culture among diasporic communities.

Margaret Chan is a specialist in theater anthropology who has authored a monograph on spirit mediumship in Singapore (CHAN 2006). As a second-generation

Singaporean of Hokkien descent, she explores the intriguing dual ethnicity of a form of spirit mediumship in Indonesia. In her study of Nini Towong, Chan explores the rarely-acknowledged affinities between a divinatory ritual performed in Indonesia and a parallel ritual form known in China. It has been said that the most ancient basic substrate of religious experience in China is ritual activity to propitiate the spirits (Poo 1998, 3 and 207). Chan's major contribution here is to highlight the importance of recognizing ethnic origins and affiliations that have been elided for political reasons in indigenous and Western scholarship. In this way, she calls for greater understanding of the interconnected nature of ritual expression across ethnic lines, and greater public recognition of historic Sinic influences within Indonesian society. Chan's major objective is not so much to establish historical links, although the argument here is persuasive, but rather to understand how it came about that probable non-indigenous origins have been obscured in the construction of this spirit-basket divination ritual as an iconic Javanese cultural treasure.

Drawing on extensive fieldwork carried out in Java, Yogyakarta, Kebumen, Cirebon, and West Kalimantan between 2008 and 2010, she presents a richly-textured study of the practice of Nini Towong in modern day Indonesia. Nini Towong is a spirit possession ritual featuring a doll-like effigy. The movements of the doll when shaken by participants were used to make predictions on matters important to the village such as the coming harvest. One of the more puzzling attributes of the effigy in Indonesian practice is that the doll can be devised as either male or female, and the choice of sex also determines the choice of ethnicity. The male form has slanted eyes and is considered to be Chinese, whereas the female form is regarded as Javanese. The ritual form is given two different names: Nini Towong refers to the Javanese type of effigy and *jailangkung* to the Chinese type. Nonetheless, in spite of the dual names and two types of effigy, the likely Chinese origin and attributes of this spirit-doll practice have been obscured in scholarship and public opinion. One important factor was the animosity felt by indigenous populations towards the Chinese ethnic community in the colonial period, a state of affairs that carried over into the New Order era. In contemporary Indonesia even Chinese whose forebears arrived centuries ago bear the label of "non-indigenous" and are still considered "outsiders." Understandably many seek to put aside Chinese identity (REID 2009). This "outsider" status contributed to the general denial or ignorance of possible Chinese origins for what were seen as embedded indigenous culture and customs. Another issue is the focus of Western scholarship on Indic as opposed to Chinese influences. The monumental material culture of Indic culture fascinated early European scholars, who tended to underplay the role of Chinese merchant communities in the cultural formation of the Indonesian archipelago. Drawing on models of "social encounters" in "contact zones," Chan concludes that, whatever the ethnic origin of Nini Towong and *jailangkung*, both can be considered complementary cultural artefacts belonging to contemporary Indonesia. In this line of analysis, Chan takes issue with the focus of Sinophone studies on eliding Chinese distinctiveness in the diaspora, preferring instead the notion put forward by Wang Gungwu that individuals choose to draw from a range of cultural inheritances.[11]

Carol Chia's study deals with the attempt of a non-Mandarin Han Chinese community to maintain their tradition of ritual puppet theater as a marker of identity in contemporary Singapore. The ancestors of the Henghua-speech community in contemporary Singapore migrated centuries ago from the Putian region in Fujian Province. Like other Chinese communities in Southeast Asia, they formed temple associations to offer social and ritual protection in their host country. Temple puppet theater aims to bring down blessings from guardian deities to the temple community. Henghua people commission temple puppeteers to entertain the gods with plays in order that their families may prosper and that their children succeed in exams; also, the passing of the soul ceremonies provide ritual closure at death. In modern, contemporary Singapore, the puppeteers and temple custodians have to navigate their way between the perceived need to propitiate traditional guardian deities on the one hand, while on the other hand they must present a nonreligious "face" as entertainers in the public domain. The Singaporean state, concerned about national cohesion in this multiethnic society, is cautious about drawing attention to ethnic and religious divisions. For this reason, the ritual activity of sub-ethnic groups in Singapore has often been elided or rendered invisible in regular discourse. As noted in Sinophone studies, non-Mandarin-speaking Chinese communities tend to be marginalized in a diaspora that equates "Chineseness" with Mandarin. Chia draws on contrasting frameworks of "state-regulation" and "state-toleration" to explain both the resilience of temple theater into the present day and the modern-day adaptation of puppet theater into a form of public entertainment. She demonstrates that the Henghua-speaking group in Singapore is a distinctive example of a community that has managed to preserve cherished religious rituals in the private space of their own temples, while at the same time adapting their performance art into a more public form that can be used to entertain a multiracial audience. In this way the tiny Henghua-speaking community can play a visible role in state-promoted demonstrations of racial harmony between the three major racial groups of Singapore (Chinese, Malay, and Indian). In order to play this dual role of being both Henghua and "Chinese," the community needs to develop a new, secular, and multilingual performance mode.

Chia's findings can be read in conjunction with the work of Beng Huat CHUA who has observed the importance of public celebrations of ethnicity in modern-day Singapore (2009). He notes the anomalous use of the term "Chinese" to describe the majority population "when the overwhelming majority of the contemporary *Huaren* are local born and for whom Singapore is home" (CHUA 2009, 240). He favors the adoption of the historic self-identifier, *Huaren*, over the newer term, Chinese, to describe this majority. As in Mainland China, the Singapore state tries to promote Mandarin as the lingua franca of this majority group: "Dialects were abolished in all public broadcast media, with the aim of uniting the *Huaren* through *Huayu*" (CHUA 2009, 240). In any case, English became the dominant primary language of education in the 1970s (CHUA 2009, 241). This leaves the city-state's mother tongues pushed to the margins of social and economic life, especially the non-*Huayu* (non-Mandarin) language forms of the polyglot Chinese population. In modern-day Singapore, Chua claims, Asian identities are expressed primarily through language, culture, and art. These public performances of multiracial harmony are necessary to avoid "cultural erasure" and provide a bulwark against the perceived corrosive effect of Western culture (CHUA 2009, 246). Chua argues that "vernacular" culture allows *Huaren* to vent anxieties about the quotidian: "Family, making a living, financial problems, (un)employment, children's growing up pains and education, death, and ghosts and deities" (CHUA 2009, 247). This is exactly the provenance of the temple puppet theater of the Henghua-speaking community, a cultural expression that offers blessings and consolation amid the trials of everyday living.

CONCLUSION

This special issue seeks to draw on recent scholarly paradigms in Chinese ethnicity, critical Han studies, and Sinophone studies to investigate specific oral and ritual traditions in the case of different types of "Chinese" communities both within China and beyond. In general, folk song genres, vernacular rituals, and theatrical traditions have been regarded as too localized to be a part of the national discourse about "Chinese" ethnicity or as simply variations of a common Chinese culture.[12] It is only in recent decades, particularly after the introduction of the global norms of Intangible Cultural Heritage, that selected folk genres have gained national and sometimes international recognition as a valued part of "Chinese" cultural heritage. As discussed here, the elevation from merely local appreciation to national or even international recognition has led to challenges to the transmitted tradition and various dilemmas for performers, receiving communities, ethnographers, and officialdom. In this special issue we have sought to set aside notions of preservation and authenticity to acknowledge that change and transformation is inherent in any oral or performance tradition. The performers of the cultural forms discussed here have lived out different types of modernity and their performances have embraced different types of visibility as ethnically-marked items of cultural heritage. This analysis goes beyond notions of cultural and ritual activities "as remnants or survivals of traditional, archaic or pre-modern modes, thus ignoring the contemporaneity of ritual activities," in the words of Ken DEAN and Thomas LAMARRE (2004, 257). As Dean and Lamarre point out in their study of Daoist rituals in Chinese Fujian, "It is simply impossible to submit that there exists a stable spatial and temporal divide between ritual activities and modernizing or globalizing forces" (DEAN and LAMARRE 2004, 262–63). Just as Dean and Lamarre's temple leaders "frame" ritual activities to honor both the communist state and their own guardian deities, so too do singers, ethnographers, and local bureaucracies in the cases examined here seek to "frame" their own performances in line with the perceived need for community acceptance and state tolerance or approval. As contemporary Asian societies confront rapid modernity, economic transformation, and the dominance of Western modes of living, the need to seek distinctiveness in inherited cultural forms becomes more acute. In particular, the promotion of selected vernacular forms as items of Intangible Cultural Heritage presents an image of cultural continuity in a world of constant change. The construction of cultural continuity offers reassurance to the citizenry and the outside world that an inner core of stable identity remains in spite of Western-style modernization. The discourse of "Chineseness," and its imbrication with the vernacular culture shared by the population at large, is an important part of this promised but possibly delusory cultural continuity.

NOTES

* The author wishes to thank the Chiang Ching-kuo Foundation for International Exchange Taiwan which provided financial support for work undertaken by Anne McLaren in this project.

1. The designated fifty-five "minority nationalities" reside in vast swathes of Chinese territory but tend to have a lower standard of living than the Han Chinese majority.

2. In an earlier study, Brown adopted the idea of "narratives of unfolding" to understand shifting ethnicities in China (BROWN 2004, 5).

3. One could add that this ethnic identification process was more "successful" in some cases than in others. Chih-yu Shih adopts the notion of "becoming minorities" to explain the strategies adopted by designated minorities in dealing with the state's ethnic agenda (SHIH 2002, 4). He also notes that the Tujia and Miao minorities of west Hunan have a relatively "weak ethnic consciousness" (SHIH 2002, 101).

4. During this period, both Han Chinese and minority group customs and traditions suffered catastrophically at the hands of the Red Guards.

5. Chih-yu SHIH gives many examples, including the case of the She people of Zhejiang and Fujian. The state promotes welfare and affirmative policies to assist people with She bloodline but it is becoming harder and harder to transmit the She language and unique cultural forms (2002, 114–28). Exceptions in the use of Mandarin are made in a few cases such as the singing of She folk songs ("mountain songs"; SHIH 2002, 126–27). State promotion of Mandarin is also having a negative effect on the transmission of Wu-language folk forms (LIU 2013, 66–71). The problem of Mandarin education is particularly acute among the Uyghur people of western China (SAFRAN 1998).

6. The same point has been made by Chih-yu Shih who notes the eroticization of folk arts when performed to outsiders, including officials and visiting ethnographers (SHIH 2002, 63–68).

7. See also the acerbic comments of Stephen Jones concerning a performance for officialdom by the Yulin Folk Arts Troupe, the same troupe discussed in the contribution of Gibbs in this special issue (JONES 2009, 211–12).

8. This collection focuses on performance culture in regional languages where different types of Chinese script are employed. For this reason, we have adopted simplified Chinese script in cases where the relevant scholars and practitioners have used this script (Mainland China) and traditional full-form script in cases where the scholars and practitioners have used this script (parts of Southeast Asia).

9. See the fascinating study by Sarah Davis into the Tai Lüe cultures of Sipsongpanna: "In Sipsongpanna, some elements of the unapproved, unofficial ethnic culture were also preserved underground" (DAVIS 2005, 7). In this case, the underground culture is religious and seen as subversive by the state. This is not the case with the unofficial "village traditions" of the Kam people.

10. While Shu-mei Shih concentrates on the distinctiveness of "Sinophone cultures" outside China, acclaimed scholar of the Chinese in Southeast Asia, Wang Gungwu, presents a

nuanced picture of a people experiencing different levels of being "bound" to Chinese identity as they adjust to the differing "history paradigms" of their host societies (WANG 2009).

11. In a recent study Chan has additionally investigated spirit mediums in West Kalimantan who channel multiracial spirits from Dayak, Malay, and Chinese culture at the Chinese New Year celebrations (CHAN 2013).

12. For a critical discussion of the latter point see LIU and FAURE (1996). In this line of thinking, local identity is necessarily subsumed within a greater "Chinese" identity. Liu and Faure argue this tends to overstate the supposed integration of the local region with the Chinese state.

REFERENCES

BARTH, Frederik
1969   *Ethnic Groups and Boundaries*. Boston: Little, Brown and Company.
        doi:10.1007/978-1-349-24984-8_18

BLUM, Susan D., and Lionel M. JENSEN, eds.
2002   *China Off Center: Mapping the Margins of the Middle Kingdom*. Honolulu:
        University of Hawai'i Press.

BROWN, Melissa J.
2004   *Is Taiwan Chinese? The Impact of Culture, Power, and Migration on Changing Identities*. Berkeley: University of California Press.
        doi:10.1525/california/9780520231818.001.0001

BROWN, Melissa J., ed.
1996   *Negotiating Ethnicities in China and Taiwan*. Berkeley: Institute of East
        Asian Studies, University of California Press.

CHAN, Margaret
2006   *Ritual is Theatre, Theatre is Ritual: Tang-ki Chinese Spirit Medium Worship*. Singapore: SNP International Publishing.
2013   The spirit mediums of Singkawang: Performing peoplehood. In *Chinese Indonesians Reassessed: History, Religion and Belonging*, Siew-Min Sai and Chang-Yau Hoon, eds., 138–58. London and New York: Routledge.
        doi:10.4324/9780203095362

CHIO, Jenny
2011   The appearance of the rural in China's tourism. *Provincial China* 3: 60–78.

CHUA, Beng Huat
2009   Being Chinese under official multiculturalism in Singapore. *Asian Ethnicity* 10: 239–50. doi:10.1080/14631360903189609

DAVIS, Sara L. M.
2005   *Song and Silence: Ethnic Revival on China's Southwest Borders*. New York:
        Columbia University Press. doi:10.7312/davi13526

DEAN, Kenneth, and Thomas LAMARRE
2004   Ritual matters. In *Impacts of Modernities*, Thomas Lamarre and Kang Naehui, eds., 255–92. Hong Kong: Hong Kong University Press.

DIKÖTTER, Frank
1992   *The Discourse of Race in Modern China*. Stanford: Stanford University
        Press.

FAURE, David, and HO Ts'ui-p'ing
    2013   *Chieftains into Ancestors: Imperial Expansion and Indigenous Society in Southwest China.* Vancouver and Toronto: UBC Press.

GLADNEY, Dru
    1994   Representing nationality in China: Refiguring majority/minority identities. *The Journal of Asian Studies* 53: 92–123. doi:10.2307/2059528
    2004   *Dislocating China: Muslims, Minorities, and Other Subaltern Subjects.* Chicago: University of Chicago Press.

HARRELL, Stevan
    1995   Languages defining ethnicity in Southwest China. In *Ethnic Identity: Creation, Conflict, and Accommodation*, Lola Romanucci-Ross and George A. De Vos. eds., 97–114. Walnut Creek, CA: AltaMira Press.
    1996   Introduction. In BROWN ed. 1–18.

HERZFELD, Michael
    2005   *Cultural Intimacy: Social Poetics in the Nation-State.* Second edition. Oxon: Routledge. doi:10.4324/9780203826195

JANKOWIAK, William
    2008   Ethnicity and Chinese identity: Ethnographic insight and political positioning. In *The Cambridge Companion to Modern Chinese Culture*, ed. Kam Louie, 91–114. Cambridge: Cambridge University Press. doi:10.1017/ccol9780521863223.005

JONES, Stephen
    2009   *Ritual and Music of North China, Volume 2: Shaanbei.* Surrrey, UK: Ashgate.

LITZINGER, Ralph A.
    2001   Beyond the museum complex: Minority culture and history at the *Mountain Patterns* exhibition. *Asian Ethnicity* 2: 89–96. doi:10.1080/14631360120018031

LIU, Jin
    2013   *Signifying the Local: Media Productions Rendered in Local Languages in Mainland China in the New Millenium.* Leiden and Boston: Brill. doi:10.1163/9789004259027

LIU, Tao Tao, and David FAURE
    1996   Introduction: What does the Chinese person identify with? In *Unity and Diversity: Local Cultures and Identities in China*, Tao Tao Liu, and David Faure, eds., 1–13. Hong Kong: Hong Kong University Press.

MCLAREN, Anne E.
    1994   Reconquering the Chinese heritage: Regionalism in popular Chinese culture studies in China. *Asian Studies Review* 18: 77–88. doi:10.1080/03147539408712982
    2010   Revitalising the folk epics of the lower Yangzi Delta: An example of China's intangible cultural heritage. *International Journal of Intangible Heritage* 5: 29–43.
    2011   Eco-sites, song traditions and cultural heritage in the lower Yangzi Delta. *Asian Studies Review* 35: 457–75. doi:10.1080/10357823.2011.628276

MCLAREN, Anne E., Alex ENGLISH, Xinyuan HE, and Catherine INGRAM
    2013   *Environmental Preservation and Cultural Heritage in China.* Champaign, Illinois: Common Ground Publishing.

MULLANEY, Thomas S.
   2010   *Coming to Terms with the Nation: Ethnic Classification in Modern China.*
          Berkeley: University of California Press.

MULLANEY, Thomas S., James LEIBOLD, Stéphane GROS, and
   Eric VANDEN BUSSCHE, eds.
   2012   *Critical Han Studies: The History, Representation, and Identity of China's
          Majority.* Berkeley: University of California Press.

OAKES, Tim
   2013   Heritage as improvement: Cultural display and contested governance in
          rural China. *Modern China* 39: 380–407. doi:10.1177/0097700412467011

POO, Mu-chou
   1998   *In Search of Personal Welfare: A View of Ancient Chinese Religion.* Albany:
          SUNY Press.

REID, Anthony
   2009   Escaping the burdens of Chineseness. *Asian Ethnicity* 10: 285–96.
            doi:10.1080/14631360903189666

SAFRAN, William
   1998   *Nationalism and Ethnoregional Identities in China.* London: Frank Cass.

SHIH, Chih-yu
   2002   *Negotiating Ethnicity in China: Citizenship as a Response to the State.* Lon-
          don and New York: Routledge.

SHIH, Shu-mei
   2007   *Visuality and Identity: Sinophone Articulations Across the Pacific.* Berkeley:
          University of California Press.
            doi:10.1525/california/9780520224513.001.0001
   2013   Against diaspora: The Sinophone as places of cultural production. In SHIH,
          TSAI, and BERNARDS, eds., 23–42.

SHIH, Shu-mei, Chien-hsin TSAI, and Brian BERNARDS
   2013   *Sinophone Studies: A Critical Reader.* New York: Columbia University
          Press.

SIU, Helen F.
   1990   Recycling tradition: Culture, history, and political economy in the chrysan-
          themum festivals of south China. *Comparative Studies in Society and His-
          tory* 32: 765–94. doi:10.1017/S0010417500016728

TUOHY, Sue
   1991   Cultural metaphors and reasoning: Folklore scholarship and ideology in con-
          temporary China. *Asian Folklore Studies* 50: 189–221. doi:10.2307/1178190

WANG, Gungwu
   2009   Chinese history paradigms. *Asian Ethnicity* 10: 201–16.
            doi:10.1080/14631360903189674

WANG, Mingming
   2006   "Great Tradition" and its enemy: The issue of "Chinese culture" on the
          southeastern coasts. In *Southern Fujian: Reproduction of Traditions in Post-
          Mao China*, ed. Tan Chee-Beng, 1–34. Hong Kong: The Chinese Univer-
          sity Press.

ANNE E. McLAREN
University of Melbourne

EMILY YU ZHANG
East China Normal University, Shanghai

Recreating "Traditional" Folk Epics in Contemporary China

The Politics of Textual Transmission

In the pre-contemporary period, farming communities living on the shores of Lake Tai in China's lower Yangzi Delta sang lengthy song-cycles about ancestral heroes, legendary figures, and amorous encounters while laboring in the fields. These folk songs, known as *shange*, were regarded as "vulgar" in the imperial era and repressed in the early decades of socialist China. However, in the contemporary period they have come to be regarded as gems of the Han Chinese folkloristic tradition. Leading examples are hailed as rare examples of epic-length sung narratives transmitted by Han Chinese communities, the majority population in China. Due to the economic transformations of recent decades, *shange* are no longer sung in their traditional rural contexts. They remain in the present day largely as textual recreations or as reconstructed performances on festival occasions. This study focuses on the contemporary textualization of one outstanding song-cycle in order to better understand the local dynamics at work in the written transmission of these folk epics. We will examine the treatment of material considered "immoral" or "feudal" in the recent past, controversy over the site of origin and composition of this folk epic, and the struggle to control the textual process at the local and national level. We will conclude by discussing the implications of this case for issues of Han Chinese identity and cultural heritage in the lower Yangzi Delta region.

KEYWORDS: folk epics—oral traditions—song-cycles—performance texts—Han Chinese identity

Asian Ethnology Volume 76, Number 1 · 2017, 19–41
© Nanzan University Anthropological Institute

CHINA COMPRISES a vast land space and a multitude of different peoples and languages.* Nonetheless, the majority group known today as Han Chinese is regarded as having a single cultural system transmitted by a written language that comprehends the considerable diversity of Han populations nationwide. As discussed in the introduction, critical Han studies has sought to deconstruct the notion of a monolithic "Han Chinese" identity on the grounds that this elides or renders invisible the considerable diversity that exists in the population known as Han Chinese. In this study we continue the debate by examining the situation of folk traditions in the case of China's Wu-language-speaking populations of the lower Yangzi Delta.

Once one turns to oral traditions, the distinctiveness of Chinese regional cultures becomes more obvious. However, scholars of Chinese civilization have focused on written works in classical Chinese (*wenyan* 文言), or on more popular works in a standard vernacular (*baihua* 白话), and only rarely on the so-called "regional cultures" (*difang wenhua* 地方文化) that reflect the actual lived experience of communities known today as Han Chinese. This relative neglect is particularly true of the rich folk culture of rural populations bordering Lake Tai and Lake Fen in the lower Yangzi Delta region, no doubt due to the geographic and linguistic complexity of the region. The Wu 吴 language grouping is complex and multiform. It prevails with numerous variants over large tracts of the provinces of Jiangsu and Zhejiang, together with the metropolis of Shanghai.

The discovery of the "folk," their languages, beliefs, and cultural forms, dates back a century. It began as part of China's early modernization movement of the 1920s but investigations came to an end during the ensuing period of foreign invasion, civil war, and political turmoil. Early socialist China (post 1949) saw a renewed interest in the popular culture of the common people, but scholarship in this field was aborted and largely destroyed during the Cultural Revolution (1966–1976). This situation began to change after party leader Deng Xiaoping came to prominence (post 1978). In the 1980s, the Chinese state began a massive effort to compile items of regional culture such as local opera, storytelling, songs, proverbs, and the like. In the case of the lower Yangzi Delta, folklorists collecting songs from villagers were surprised to discover song-cycles of epic length in the rural hamlets on the shores of Lake Tai and its tributaries. Chinese scholars were puzzled by the "anomalous" nature of their findings, which did not fit into existing paradigms about the historical development of Chinese civilization. Contemporary perceptions of the essential unity of the vast population designated as "Han Chinese" also obscured exploration into significant divergences among "Han Chinese," of which the most significant is the difference between people living north and south of the Yangzi River.[1]

Another thorny issue was how to deal effectively with stigmatized aspects of these songs such as "feudal superstitions" and erotic material. The local ethnographers were torn between two contradictory goals: on the one hand, the academic goal of accurately recording and publishing what the singers actually sang, and on the other hand, the perceived need to win approval from the political hierarchy. There were aesthetic problems as well. The ethnographers wished to develop exempla from oral culture that provided a satisfying reading experience and conveyed a clear message acceptable to the general public and the authorities (such as "an attack on the feudal marriage system"). However, the fragmented nature of the material did not easily lend itself to assimilation into the norms of written culture and the perceived need to arrive at a coherent narrative with an unambiguous message.

At a more practical level, ethnologists and local authorities found it difficult to record these Wu-language songs (*shange* 山歌, mountain songs or folk songs) in textual form because the Chinese character script has developed over the centuries to record primarily the language of the imperial court and the official examinations, as well as a standardized form of the vernacular used for entertainment literature. As a nonphonetic script, it was less accommodating of localized speech forms, including the Wu languages spoken in the lower Yangzi Delta. Song transcribers had to invent new orthographic conventions to record the words sung by singers in different parts of the delta.[2] Chinese ethnographers labelled the folk songs of their region as Wu songs (*Wu ge* 吳歌) in order to mark them as distinct from folk songs known elsewhere in China. The term "Wu" is redolent of historic associations. It refers to the ancient Wu kingdom of the delta (585–473 BCE), the ancestral founder, Wu Taibo 吳太伯, the Wu family of languages, and the people from the region. The reconstitution of the region's *shange* into Wu songs was not simply a matter of conserving a traditional but now virtually defunct oral performance art for future generations. The issue was rather whether the oral culture of commoner farming communities of the immediate past could become a standard bearer of valued tradition in the delta region of the present day.

The discovery of lengthy song narratives comprising thousands of lines, together with the consequent publication of a large number of transcripts, is a significant event in the field of Chinese popular culture. These long narrative song-cycles from the lower Yangzi Delta (here called "folk epics") are a new and largely unknown niche in China's rich oral tradition.[3] Unlike professional oral arts, such as storytelling and regional opera, which flourished in delta market towns and metropolises, the song narratives of villagers toiling in the paddy fields around Lake Tai circulated primarily in the scattered rural settlements hugging the shores of the water channels and major lake and river systems. While their zone of circulation was mostly limited to rural areas, the songs were enormously popular in their day. They offer unsurpassed insight into the everyday lives, supernatural beliefs, and folk ecologies of the farming populations of the Yangzi Delta in the immediate pre-contemporary period, and provide a rich storehouse of plots, themes, and motifs adapted by professional performers of operatic and storytelling genres and by writers and publishers of vernacular literature.

It was not until the early twentieth century that Chinese ethnologists began to collect the shorter form of Wu-language songs (WANG 1999); the longer narrative forms remained largely undiscovered until the 1980s.[4] The majority of Wu folk epics deal with events regarded by singers and their audience as "true stories" about actual people from the past. Many tales deal with the tragic fate of blighted lovers and focus on the social conflicts endemic to patriarchal society in pre-contemporary China. The ill-fated lovers contend with the disapproval of parents, a mismatch between the social classes, separation, sickness, persecution, and the wrath of local authorities. Their nights of "illicit" love are few; the stories linger rather on the stratagems of the lovers and the events that lead inevitably to the tragic end. Unlike the vernacular novels and stories about supernatural retribution that prevailed in the written culture of the last two dynasties, the Wu folk epics offer tales of lyrical intensity that, at least in their original state, do not seem to provide a definite "moral message" of the kind familiar to Chinese narrative traditions more generally. The most popular narratives contain powerful and moving song lyrics that were passed on by generations of communities bordering Lake Tai and Lake Fen.

Given the importance of the folk epics to delta populations and the relevance of these long song narratives to our understanding of oral-literate interactions in pre-contemporary China, the publication of volumes of Wu song-cycles in recent years is a welcome event. However, as with all attempts to capture in writing the elusive nature of an oral tradition, many questions remain. To what extent do these publications reflect the true state of these songs as originally sung in the paddy fields and along the waterways of the delta region? How were the original transcripts mediated in the process of editing and rearrangement? What compromises were made and what is the potential scholarly value of these transcripts? This study attempts to offer insights into the process of contemporary textualization of the Wu folk epics through detailed analysis of one well-known example, the song-cycle known today as "Fifth Daughter" (Wu Guniang 五姑娘). "Fifth Daughter" is regarded as one of the most outstanding of all the song-cycles discovered. Versions of the tale were sung all around the region of Lake Tai and Lake Fen and in the provinces of Jiangsu and Zhejiang. "Fifth Daughter" was one of the first of the lengthier songs to come to public attention and was one of the most contentious among scholars. Certain local folklorists still debate today whether "Fifth Daughter" is a genuine example of an orally-transmitted narrative or simply a number of separate short songs pieced together by contemporary folklorists to form an epic-length narrative. The controversial nature of the "Fifth Daughter" song-cycle and its significance as a now canonical example of Wu songs makes it a particularly revealing case study of the interaction between singer, ethnographer, and the Chinese state.

The collection of folk songs has long been an important cultural activity of the Chinese Communist Party. After the founding of the People's Republic of China in 1949, professional writers under party guidance drew strongly from existing folk culture to rewrite and recreate folk songs, storytelling, and regional opera into new cultural forms that embodied the socialist agenda of the "new China."[5] However, during the "reform era" (that is, post 1978) a new, avowedly more "scientific" interest in cultural heritage superseded earlier attempts to eradicate "feudal poison" from popular performance culture. Nonetheless, as discussed here, political considerations remained to vex the next generation of ethnographers. This case study will thus illuminate the dilemmas of contemporary Chinese ethnographers and local authorities in attempting to preserve performance arts that once played a central part in community life but now face extinction in what has become one of the most affluent and economically advanced regions of China. As observed in this study, issues of preservation and publication are closely bound to the type of identity that regions choose to project in the competition for "ownership" of their regional heritage. Notions of what constitutes Han Chinese identity was a debated issue in the case of the long folk narratives of the delta. An important conclusion to this study is that the process of textualization of the Wu folk epics failed to take into account significant aspects of the spiritual beliefs of the farming populations of the delta. Here we highlight these purely regional understandings, often elided in constructions of national culture, which arguably formed the "mental texts" or implicit assumptions of the singers.

WU SONGS IN THE LAKE TAI REGION

A thousand years ago, populations from north China fled war and disaster by migrating south to the marshy regions around the mouth of the Yangzi River. Here they intermarried with the indigenous population, known in ancient times as the Bai Yue 百越. Over the centuries, the original marshlands of the delta were laboriously converted into rice paddies, polders, embankments, and enclosed ponds, as a thriving agricultural economy was built around rice paddies, fish, and silk handicrafts.[6] However, the same period was also characterized by the pressure of a growing population, deforestation, low holdings per capita, and a greater incidence of periods of drought and flooding (SHIH 1981, 238–39; HUANG 1990, 33). Until the modernization of recent decades, this region was "a land of rice and fish." Even today in the regions bordering Lake Tai and Lake Fen, rivers and streams intersect each other in a chessboard pattern of interlocking waterways. Before the contemporary period, many townships and villages were almost completely surrounded by water. People travelled by boat or journeyed on foot along narrow paths bordering rivers or on narrow embankments above fields of rice paddies.

The Wu folk epics reflect the lives of the small landholders who eked out a precarious existence along the shores of Lake Tai and Lake Fen in the late nineteenth and early twentieth centuries. Usually all family members took part in the work in the fields. Women participated in the exhausting task of planting rice shoots, as well as threshing, weeding, raking, and operating the "dragon wheels" or pedal-operated irrigation wheel to water the rice paddy. These families also employed hired hands who went from home to home offering their services on a periodic basis.[7] Women of the family would bring the midday meal to the men toiling in the fields. In "Fifth Daughter," this is how the heroine, a young unmarried girl from a good family, happens to meet the hired hand, Xu Atian 徐阿天, who will become her lover.

As elsewhere in China, farming settlements were based around descent groups in the male line. Villages or groups of hamlets tended to have the same family name and identify as a kinship group. They formed tight-knit, self-governing communities. The family head was in charge of safeguarding the reputation of his family by enforcing a strict code of morality on the womenfolk in particular. In these remote water-locked villages, the operations of imperial governance appeared distant. For this reason it is only on rare occasions that one catches a glimpse of the institutions of imperial government in these folk epics. One example of this is the story about a doomed lover, Xu Atian, who is sent in chains to the Wujiang County *yamen* (office). A corrupt magistrate finds him guilty of a false charge of theft and condemns him to death. However, this song-cycle dwells primarily on the arbitrary power exercised by household elders and the brutal treatment they enact on their own flesh and blood. In the isolated settlements amid the wetlands of the delta region, one hears very little of the Confucian norms that, in theory, were meant to govern relations within the family and society at large.

In the original tradition, as reflected in original singer transcripts, the female protagonist is portrayed as the active initiator of the love-match. Original transcripts contain erotic segments depicting the young couple in the bath or in bed. It is precisely this that most offended gentry households in the pre-contemporary period and socialist authorities in more recent times. The story also contains a class aspect. In "Fifth Daughter," a girl from the home of a small landholder falls in love with a hired hand employed by her older brother. This transgression of both social class and sexual norms can only end in catastrophe. Nonetheless, although it is the young couple who violate the social norms, it is the weak and gullible older brother and his jealous and brutal wife who are seen to be the real villains of this tale.

By the 1980s, an elderly woman called Lu Amei 陆阿妹 (1902–1986) was the only singer who could recall a relatively full version of the tale of "Fifth Daughter." She came from the Fenyu Xiang region of Jiashan, on the southern banks of Lake Fen in modern-day Zhejiang Province. From a young age, her father, Sun Huatang 孙华棠, an acclaimed singer, taught her to sing mountain songs. By early adulthood, she became known for her talent at extempore performance. In the early 1950s she followed her husband north to Luxu, on the other side of Lake Fen. Lu Amei claimed to have first learned the song about Fifth Daughter from her father, who had in turn learned it from another singer of local fame, Yang Qichang 杨其昌, who lived during the *xianfeng* era of the last dynasty (1851–1861).[8] On the basis of this claimed genealogy, it appeared that Lu Amei's version has been in circulation in some form for around 150 years. The song transcripts sung by Lu Amei comprise some 2,800 lines, far more than any other singer of this song-cycle. During her lifetime, which bridged the republican era and the early decades of socialism, it was already difficult to sing songs about illicit love affairs. In fact, she became the butt of gossip precisely because of her skill in singing this tale:

People would say, "When Lu Amei sang the tale of Fifth Daughter/All her children will be carried away by Fifth Daughter." This startling rumor meant that Lu Amei as the singer was at the receiving end of innuendo and social pressure, to the point where fewer and fewer people dared to sing this tale and fewer and fewer people were familiar with the story.[9]

有人谣传说 '陆阿妹唱仔五姑娘哉， 生的小倌都被五姑娘领走了'。这些骇人听闻的流言， 使陆阿妹这样的歌手， 也受着诋毁与压抑， 以至后来， 传唱的人越来越少了，熟悉它的人 也越来越少了。

This statement implied that the spirit of Wu Guniang would punish those who sang of her scandalous life. Lu Amei herself became reluctant to continue singing "Fifth Daughter" as it was seen to lead to the premature deaths of her children. It was not until the early 1980s that, on the urgings of local folklorists, she agreed to sing her repertoire and allow recordings to be made. By this time she was an elderly woman, frail and somewhat deaf. Reports at that time indicate that she felt deeply embarrassed about some of the erotic material in the repertoire she had mastered as a young woman. This report comes from Qian Shunjuan, a female ethnographer who came to know Lu Amei in the 1980s.

> Lu Amei's own thinking became gradually liberated. At first she would not sing the segment "The brother's wife catches the couple in flagrante," which includes some "chaff" [explicit material]. It was not until Zhang Fanglan, Ma Hanmin [male folklorists], and others came to know her as if they were truly part of her family that she would first go secretly into her room to bow before the image of Guanyin [the Buddhist deity of compassion], and beg forgiveness from the bodhisattva. Only then would she come out from her room and sing this segment. (QIAN 1997, 22)

> 陆阿妹的思想也是逐步解放的， 她开头也没有唱 '五姑娘' 长歌中的 '嫂捉奸' 这样的包含有些糟粕成分的片断， 直到张舫澜， 马汉民等和她相处得真像自家人一样，她还要先悄悄跑到里间屋拜过观世音， 请菩萨宽恕， 再出来唱。

In the early 1980s folklorists in the Jiangsu town of Luxu, on the banks of Lake Tai, collected songs relating to the song-cycle of Fifth Daughter from local singers such as Lu Amei, Zhang Yunlong, Zhao Yongming, and Jiang Liansheng. Their songs were recorded on tape, transcribed in manuscript form, and then printed off in a mimeographed edition of two volumes in private circulation. It is this text, produced in 1983 and known as the *Wu Guniang ziliao ben* (here termed "Transcripts;" see JIANGSU SHENG MINJIAN WENXUE GONGZUOZHE XIEHUI: SUZHOU FENHUI BIAN 1983, hereafter JSMWGX), that provided the basis for all later printed editions. On a trip to Luxu in May 2011, the authors of this study were gifted with a copy of "Transcripts," and will be relying on this text to better understand the song-cycle as sung by Lu Amei and the later process of revising and editing.[10]

THE FIRST TEXTUALIZATION OF THE SONG-CYCLE, "FIFTH DAUGHTER"

The "Transcripts" comprise 87 separate songs of which 76 are by Lu Amei. Altogether there are 2,900 lines of sung material in 790 stanzas.[11] In order to retain the original flavor, the compilers adapted Chinese characters to record the Wu language expressions, although some compromises were made in the case of obscure Luxu idioms.[12] The songs were elicited by folklorists Zhang Fanglan, Ma Hanmin, and Lu Qun, who visited Lu Amei in her home between April 1981 and May 1982. It is evident from the dates on the transcripts of individual songs that Lu Amei did not sing the song-cycle in any particular "logical" narrative sequence. As the ethnographers asked her further questions about the plot she would call to mind further elements of the story. Given that she had a comprehensive mastery of the formulaic material of the Wu songs of her area, and well-developed views on the characterization of the central protagonists, it is also possible that she came up with new story elements to meet the demands of her scholarly audience for a fuller account of the tale. This would be in keeping with the usual conventions of epic singers who have mastered the repertoire and are able to compose the performance to meet the needs of the audience (HONKO 2002b, 338–39). One can thus assume that the Wu Guniang song-cycle sung by Lu Amei contained both material inherited and adapted from previous singers as well as material she composed extempore to meet the requests of the folklore scholars.

The "Transcripts" additionally contains a lengthy interview with Lu Amei where she explains in prose the story material of "Fifth Daughter" in her own understanding (257–74). Lu felt a deep sympathy for the tragedy that enveloped the central characters and a strong reluctance to "conclude" the tale with what her listening folklorists regarded as a satisfactory plot resolution. She told the folklorists in April 1981:

> You can never sing to the end of "Fifth Daughter." Even after ten nights and ten evenings you still can't sing right to the end. If you do wind up singing to the very end then you'll suffer misfortune. Fifth Daughter doesn't want people to tell her story because then she'll lose face. If you don't get chest pains then your belly will hurt. People who continue to sing this song are becoming fewer and fewer. I don't dare sing it rashly.[13]
>
> '唱无尽格五姑娘,'十夜十黄昏也唱勿完,　先底于说唱完要触霉头格,　五姑娘勿肯人家舒伊格事体才讲出来,坍台格,　旲寻,　吼事(坏事),　勿是心口疼,　就是要肚皮痛,　唱格人 越来越少了,　倨也不敢瞎唱格。

Selecting from the independent song segments in "Transcripts," Zhang Fanglan, Ma Hanmin, and Lu Qun arrived at what is now known as "the first arranged edition." According to Zhang's account, it took the three men three months to complete the task. The three of them divided up the allocated material, with Zhang providing the beginning, Lu Qun the middle section, and Ma Hanmin the ending. Zhang was then responsible for combining the three sections so that the text read as a coherent whole. This was not an easy task as the song excerpts were not necessarily mutually consistent. The singer would occasionally go off on tangents, providing more material that never came to a conclusive ending. The team of folklorists took it upon themselves to devise a "logical" sequence for the story, to form narrative linkages between individual songs, and to provide a "satisfactory" ending. They were pressed for time. The main goal of the folklorists was

FIGURE I. Zhang Fanglan (张舫澜), a resident of Luxu 芦墟, Jiangsu Province (江苏), has played an important role in the collection and editing of Wu song-cycles in the lower Yangzi Delta region. He is standing outside the Wu Song Pavilion 吴歌馆, built on the shores of Fen Lake 分湖, Luxu, to house an exhibit relating to Wu songs. May 2011. Photo by A. McLaren.

to exhibit the artistic qualities of "Fifth Daughter" in time for a conference on Wu songs run by the local cultural authorities in December 1981. Their arranged text of "Fifth Daughter" was presented at the conference and subsequently published in the literary journal *Zhongshan* in 1982. The text was later published as a separate monograph by the publisher Jiangsu Renmin Chuban.[14]

In interviews with the authors of this study in May 2011 and with Emily Zhang in March 2012, Zhang Fanglan explained the complex local politics of the time and how this influenced decisions made about how to edit the transcripts in order to provide a readable edition. Further correspondence from the early 1980s also lays bare the dilemmas of the ethnographers, publishers, and authorities. Below we discuss in turn three major issues that key players struggled with in the politics of the early reform era. The first problem was the "anomalous" discovery of lengthy song narratives belonging to a Han Chinese people as distinct from non-Chinese minority groups. The second issue was controversy over the authenticity of "Fifth Daughter" as a long song-cycle. The final issue was how to evaluate the "message" of this story of transgressive love and to render it into a form appropriate for a broad readership both within the delta and the nation.

DID HAN CHINESE POPULATIONS HAVE EPIC SONG TRADITIONS?

Chinese theorists, influenced by Marxist conceptions of the progress of history, held that Han Chinese communities had not produced long narrative songs of epic length. Qian Shunjuan is one of many local ethnographers who reported that the discovery of the long version of "Fifth Daughter" in 1981 "smashed the traditional view that the Han Chinese people have no long narrative poetry" (QIAN 1997, 3). The notion that epic poetry belonged to a specific pre-civilizational age was first advanced by Lewis H. Morgan (1818–1881). Morgan proposed three stages of human development, from savagery to barbarism and, finally, civilization (MORGAN 1985). Each stage was associated with a more advanced use of technology and more sophisticated modes of living. The second stage, barbarism, was said to include the emergence of poetry and mythology, analogous with the Greek Homeric age. Frederick Engels (1820–1895) took up Morgan's general analysis, which was then adopted by Chinese intellectuals in the twentieth century and became a fixture in later Marxist historiography.[15] In this line of thinking, epic songs were the provenance of "primitive" non-Han Chinese minority groups residing in the borderlands. Famous examples include the Tibetan epic "Gesar," the Mongolian epic "Jangar," and the Miao creation epic "Miluotuo." In other words, in the official discourse of the history of Chinese civilization, orally-transmitted epics belonged to the high tradition of nonliterate peoples. The Hua-Xia people, on the other hand, who developed into the group known today as Han Chinese, invented a literate culture at least three millennia ago. So, in this line of interpretation, the proto-Chinese population entered advanced civilization at an earlier date than the borderland tribes and had no need for an epic song tradition.[16] Closely related to this debate was the controversy over whether "Fifth Daughter" was really an epic length song narrative. To some it appeared to be rather the invention of enthusiastic ethnographers who had allegedly pieced together fragmentary song material to greatly extend the length and coherence of the original song. As we will discuss below, this controversy was ultimately resolved in favor of a consensus that songs of epic length were indeed indigenous to the Wu-speaking populations of the Yangzi Delta, even if this put them on a par with the "primitive" borderland populations. In the changed conditions of the 1990s it now became possible, indeed even a matter of pride, that the Han people had their own epic song tradition.

THE AUTHENTICITY OF "FIFTH DAUGHTER" AS A LONG SONG NARRATIVE

In 1981 the Luxu folklorists, Zhang, Han, and Lu, did their best to come up with a rendition of "Fifth Daughter" that met the needs of the time. As the first of the Wu long song-cycles to be recorded and published in a national publication, "Fifth Daughter" caused a minor literary sensation. Leading folklore scholars praised the lyric beauty of the songs and the heartfelt message of the suffering of the commoners in "the old society." But beyond Luxu, on the southern shores of Lake Fen, in the Jiashan region of northern Zhejiang Province, where Lu Amei had been born and raised, folklorists in her home region raised severe objections to the claim that the bundle of songs now associated with "Fifth Daughter" did in fact reflect an authentic tradition of an orally-transmitted song-cycle. These critics pointed out that in the Jiashan tradition of folk songs, there was indeed a narrative about "Fifth Daughter," but it was known only as a short song structured around the annual calendar (a poetic form known as Twelve Month Flower Names 十二月花名), comprising around one hundred lines. According to local legend, this song was first composed by the tailor who made a shroud for Fifth Daughter. He sang it as he went from door to door and in this way the song came into circulation (WANG 1993, 79). Jiashan singers interviewed in the early 1980s said they could not possibly remember a song two thousand lines long like the one produced from the transcripts of Lu Amei and claimed the longer story was not known locally (GAO and JIN 2003, 328). The short song version was, moreover, sung across a much wider geographic region in places such as Pinghu, Jiaxing, and Qingpu. Further, a lot of the song material in Lu Amei's rendition belonged to Wu songs of the area more generally and could have simply been added in by the singer to elaborate her song. Some critics went so far as to claim that the long version of Lu Amei published in *Zhongshan* had been pieced together from separate songs and substantially elaborated and revised by the folklorist editors in Luxu. In other words, it should not be considered an authentic example of a long narrative song (*changpian xushi ge* 长篇叙事歌) (GAO and JIN 2003, 328).

The Folk Culture Association of Suzhou, a major city in the delta, was keen to get at the truth of the matter and carried out an extensive investigation through visits to Wujiang, Qingpu, and Jiashan to meet and interview folk singers. When they listened to Lu Amei sing "Fifth Daughter" they were won over by the strength of her performance and concluded that the existence of a long, orally-transmitted song was indeed plausible. The emergence of an abundance of other long verse narratives in the delta region (close to forty) also convinced them of the veracity of the claim for the existence of "Fifth Daughter" in the long version.[17] Duan Baolin, a professor at Beijing University and Chairman of the Folk Arts Association, had been told that "Fifth Daughter" was a fraud and called for a copy of "Transcripts." Jin Xu subsequently sent off the mimeographed volumes, which then circulated among leading folklore scholars (GAO and JIN 2003, 332). After a period of discussion, senior Chinese scholars were won over to the view that "Fifth Daughter" existed in the long version, at least in the region of Luxu, where several singers could still sing this song-cycle in the early 1980s. Luxu was also the site of origin of numerous other long narrative Wu songs and historically had been a center of mountain song competitions in public forums. It was also known for its mountain song teams (*shange ban* 山歌班), comprising peasants with good voices who were hired by landlords to entertain the laborers toiling in the fields.[18] In addition, the volumes of "Transcripts" at least provided sufficient proof of the prevalence of the long version in the Luxu region. In this way a scholarly consensus was reached that, at least in the rendition of Lu Amei, "Fifth Daughter" could be considered a genuinely long narrative song-cycle.[19]

CONTROVERSY OVER THE TEXTUALIZATION OF "FIFTH DAUGHTER"

Although the authenticity of the long version of "Fifth Daughter" was more or less resolved, there still remained debate about the quality of the first

FIGURE 2. Two sisters born in the 1930s, Gu Youzhen 顾友珍 and Gu Xiuzhen 顾秀珍, are transmitters of the Jiashan version of the song "Wu Guniang." Photo taken by A. McLaren at the Cultural Center, Fenxiang cun (沉香村) Dingzha zhen (丁栅镇) in Jiashan (嘉善) County, Zhejiang Province, May 2011.

published text by the Luxu ethnographers. This text became known as "the first arranged (*zhengli* 整理) edition." The main reason was the perceived deficiencies of this version. Even scholars who agreed with the existence of the long narrative song held that the *Zhongshan* version had been edited and revised in such a way as to cast doubt on its claim to represent an oral text.[20] Subsequently, Suzhou scholar Jin Xu produced what is now known as "the second arranged edition" (*zai zhengli ben* 再整理本). The second arranged edition comprised 1,700 lines in 431 stanzas, about a quarter less than the first arranged edition. Care was taken to include original Wu-language expressions with annotations to make the text accessible to a national readership.[21] It was this edition that was included, with some pruning, in the important collection by JIANG (1989). Many years later, lengthy selections from "Transcripts" were published in another leading compendium of Wu songs (GAO and JIN 2003, 196–310). The latter included most of the material in the original "Transcripts" but left out some erotic material. Each song was listed separately and no attempt was made to knit the separate songs together as one finds in the first and second arranged editions. The disparities between these different versions of the song-cycle were now apparent to the scholarly observer who had access to all four versions.

The problem faced by all the editors and arrangers was how to present orally-transmitted song segments in a readable form for the purpose of scholarly preservation and also for the promotion of the longer Wu songs as a regional treasure. This involved more than just coming up with a coherent storyline. The editors had to work out how to evaluate the central protagonists, the true nature of the central conflict of the story, and how to resolve the conflict in a way that would be well received by both the political authorities and regional communities. In other words, a moral message was required. It seemed clear to these folklorists that "Fifth Daughter," in common with the other *siqing* 私情 type of narratives (tales of illicit love), conveyed a message about the evils of arranged marriage under the "feudal" system of pre-contemporary China. Virtually all Chinese commentators justify the publication of these narratives on the grounds of their denunciation of "anti-feudal marriage."[22] However, the original material also contained some troublesome scenes, such as the songs where the heroine took the initiative in seducing the hired hand, scenes of lovemaking that were deemed too graphic for publication, and, most troubling, an undeveloped plot resolution where the villains of the piece, the older brother and his unsavory wife, were not seen to be thoroughly punished for their evil deeds.

A comparison with "Transcripts" shows the scope of changes made by the editors of the first arranged edition. The 790 stanzas in "Transcripts" were compressed to only 583 stanzas. This edition also contained new material not found in "Transcripts", although the latter claimed to be the original recordings of the singers. In other words, the editors made insertions of their own, particularly to the ending. Song segments indicating what appeared to be alternative plot lines were excluded from the arranged edition. In other words, whereas "Transcripts" included the potential for multiple plot developments, even including elements that were mutually contradictory, the editors of the arranged text chose material from among disparate story material to form a single cohesive plot line.

One major point of difference lies in the treatment of the villainous sister-in-law. As recorded in "Transcripts," Lu Amei provides a much lengthier treatment of this character, including her reputation for promiscuity before marriage to Yang Jinda, her dominance of her hen-pecked husband, her interest in extramarital liaisons, and her cruel treatment of the two sisters.[23] Only a small portion of this material was included in later editions. Lu Amei's treatment of this theme opened up the potential for a plot line not explored by later editors. For example, in one song segment, Fifth Daughter voluntarily tells her sister-in-law that Atian has sent her a love token, presumably to seek her permission for her own affair. The sister-in-law urges her to accept and then spells out her own designs on Atian. This sets up scope to develop a consenting relationship between one man and two women, a not uncommon plot type in Wu songs.[24] Polygamy was a feature of pre-contemporary Chinese marriages, but a relationship between an unmarried man and two women who were sisters-in-law was regarded as abhorrent not least because it upset the hierarchies of seniority between the wife of the older brother (*saosao*) and his younger sister (*meimei*). In this case class was involved as well because the husband was a landowner and the offending male a hired hand.

Wu songs commonly treat the subversion of traditional kinship hierarchies. For example, a married man taking on the younger unmarried sister of his principal wife was a favored theme of several Wu song-cycles, and the phenomenon was not uncommon in historical practice.[25] In Wu songs dealing with a polygamous relationship, the focus of interest is on the competition between two women, one younger than the other, for the attention of the male. In the song sung by Lu Amei this conflict is expressed in terms of a choice between two types of common foods: "Of the wild flowers daubed with dew, only those fresh in bud are good to eat/But with sugarcane from Tangxi, it is the mature stalks that are sweet." The final couplet resolves the issue: "Atian rejected the mature stalk on the sugarcane/ He only wanted the red caltrop with the fragrant fresh stamen."[26] This song was not included in later print renditions, perhaps because it placed in jeopardy the perceived moral virtue of Fifth Daughter.

Another major point of difference is the plot resolution, particularly the issue of whether the villains are thoroughly punished. The songs recorded in "Transcripts" present little information about what happens to the major characters. One song by Lu Amei relates a story about the execution of Xu Atian by the local magistrate.[27] A brief four-line stanza further relates that the Yang homestead was burnt to the ground.[28] Finding this unsatisfactory, the editors of the arranged versions set up a version of the story that provided a more elaborate ending and punishment for the evildoers. The editors of the first arranged edition inserted sections that pointed the blame at the magistrate for condemning Atian to death and presented a tragic ending where both ultimately die. The editors of the second arranged edition set up an ending where the family accidentally sets fire to their own residence and the villainous older brother and his wife die in the flames. In other words, both sets of editors, finding "Transcripts" too skimpy and contradictory, borrowed from the tradition to craft an "appropriate" ending that punished the evildoers. From the song segments in "Transcripts," it appears that a singer could choose from one or another version as the occasion demanded, which accounts for numerous contradictions in the songs of Lu Amei.[29] In addition, there were personal reasons why Lu Amei was reluctant to provide an elaborate ending.

The open-ended nature of the original song-cycle reflects local beliefs about the powers of the spirits of those who die a violent death. Lu Amei told folklorists that it was unlucky to completely finish off the tale of Fifth Daughter because she did not come to a good end (*bu guangcai* 不光彩). The singer did not want to linger over the final events of her life in case the spirit of Fifth Daughter was offended and she herself met with ill fortune. In contrast, the editors of the later editions played down the role of the sister-in-law in bringing about the catastrophe, preferring to blame instead the patriarchal powers of the older brother and the venality of the legal system in the imperial era. In this way they could frame "Fifth Daughter" as less a story about an illicit love affair than an attack on "feudal marriage" in the "old society." However, in so doing, they distorted the understandings of the singers and their audiences, who preferred to frame disaster in terms of heavenly destiny, human frailties, and, as we shall discuss later, the need to appease the spirit of Fifth Daughter.

THE MENTAL TEXT OF THE SINGER

The numerous discrepancies between "Transcripts," representing the songs of actual singers at specific sessions, and the arranged editions compiled by folklorists, are readily explicable when one considers the differing nature of the oral and written epic form. These differences are well known in the history of the recording of oral epics and their later reshaping to form a literary tradition.

Here we will draw on the studies of Lauri Honko, noted for his studies on the textualization of epic forms. Honko stresses the importance of the creativity of particular individuals in the formation of long narratives. These can be illiterate singers who have outstanding ability to compose songs extempore and also literate editors immersed in the tradition who are at once scribes and creators capable of composing epic-length songs themselves. One example of the former is the illiterate singer, Anne Vebarna, who when provided with a "schematic plot" based on folklore was able to compose extempore a narrative song called "Peko" that came to be regarded as the national epic of her people, the Setu in Estonia (HONKO 2002b, 338). In another example of her versatility, Vebarna provided two radically different versions of a single story, one ending happily, and the other tragically (HONKO 2002b, 337). In the case of Lu Amei, she provided a suite of songs on the theme of "Fifth Daughter" for over a year to the folklorists who visited her. While many were indeed recalled from past performances and can be found in the songs of other singers, some may have been composed afresh based on her own imaginative adaptation of songs in that tradition. This does not render them less "authentic" than the songs she shares with other singers. Rather, one can see these songs as creative elaborations that demonstrate the potential of the repertoire to produce songs of epic length and power if circumstances permit (HONKO 2000, 22–23).

The case of the folklorist editors can also be considered as another act of creation, this time away from the oral epic to what Honko calls the written "traditional-oriented epic" (HONKO 2000, 7). Honko defines the latter as those "tradition-bound epics which have been molded, if not created, in the hands of performers, scribes, and editors. They possess 'anterior speech' in the form of oral epic registers internalized not only by their performers but also by their scribes and editors, but they are not direct documents from oral performances" (HONKO 2000, 7). The Finnish epic, *Kalevala*, is of particular relevance here. The written epic known today is largely the work of one man, Eric Lönrott (1802–1884), who collected narrative songs from eastern Finland, near the border with Russian Karelia, a region known for its epic poetry. Lönrott became immersed in the poetic tradition to the point where he was able to subordinate the collected material to his own internal vision and create what became an original folk epic that resonated with the Finnish public. As Honko puts it, Lönrott had a self-developed "mental text" that guided his own creation of the *Kalevala*. This "mental text" comprised "the storyline of the narrative in question, standard descriptions of events, repeatable expressions, phrases, and formulas familiar from the performances of other singers" (HONKO 2002a, 14). While the "mental text" contains many repeatable stereotypical elements shared by singers within a tradition, Honko is insistent that this "multiform" material "must be ordered by a single mind" to create a successful long epic (HONKO 2002a, 15).

Honko's idea of a "mental text" that must pass through the mind of an individual singer is relevant to both the oral composition of Lu Amei, who expanded on the tradition passed down to her to create her own unique version of a familiar narrative, and also to the reworkings of her recorded song-cycle by successive local ethnographers, who edited her text along the lines of their own particular "mental texts" of the narrative as a whole. In creating the *Kalevala*, Lönrott expunged obscenities, smoothed out localized expressions that would puzzle his readers, and filled in obvious plot gaps (Honko 2002a, 18). Similarly, the folklorists discussed here, Zhang Fanglan, Ma Hanmin, Lu Qun, and Jin Xu, exercised their own judgment in reshaping the material from the original singers to make a text that would pass muster with the cultural authorities and be deemed suitable for a national readership. It is the first edition that contains the most deviance from the original set of transcripts. This is no doubt due to the political exigencies of the time and reflects the difficulties of establishing that Han Chinese communities did indeed have narrative song traditions of epic length, and that these songs had "progressive" content that should be widely celebrated. The editors of the second edition were more aware of the pitfalls of an overly-enthusiastic adaptation. To avoid criticism of a lack of authenticity, they sought to return the written form of "Fifth Daughter" to one that was more firmly based on the original songs. Nonetheless, one could argue that both editions remain at some distance from the "mental text" that clearly existed in the mind of Lu Amei, with all its complexity and contradictions.

Of crucial importance is the "mental text" of the singer, Lu Amei, specifically the set of popular beliefs that lay behind her construction of the story of "Fifth Daughter." Our sources here are the song transcripts attributed to her and the lengthy oral interviews recorded in "Transcripts." There were several aspects that informed her "mental text": first, her belief in the historicity of the tale of Fifth Daughter and Xu Atian, and in her ongoing existence as an aggrieved spirit; second, her belief in the efficacy of mountain songs in mediating between the world of the living and the dead; and third, the way she associated a purely local incident with one of the master narratives told all over China.

Lu Amei and other Lake Fen locals strongly believed in the historical veracity of the story. Lu claimed: "When I was a child I heard the story from my grandmother and I myself have seen Fifth Daughter's combs and furniture."[30] Locals at Fenyu in Jiashan held that Fifth Daughter grew up in Fangjiabang on the shores of Lake Fen in the home of Yang Jinda. Descendants of the Yang family had continued to carry out ancestral rites using spirit tablets representing deceased family members in a side room of the original residence until the early 1950s. The Yang residence was eventually demolished in 1959 but some remnants could still be seen in 1981, including a boat shed, the ox herder's hut, and stone benches. Xu Atian was believed to have come from Yao'an cun, about 1.5 kilometers north of Fangjiabang. The original Xu family residence was not demolished until the 1980s. Descendants of the Xu family believed that Atian did indeed steal the spirit tablets of Fifth Daughter from the Yang residence and set them up in his own home. They claimed that Atian had his legs broken by the Yang family and ended his life as a beggar. His spirit tablet had been venerated by the family until the political movements of 1959.[31]

The belief in the historicity of the tale, the existence of sites relating to the couple for a period of over a hundred years, and the continuation of ancestral rites of veneration by descendants would have conditioned the reception of the song-cycle surrounding Fifth Daughter and Xu Atian and surely contributed to its longevity from the mid-nineteenth century to the present. This song, like many others in the

Wu song repertoire, deals with the premature and brutal death or disfigurement of one or both young lovers. In the context of delta life in the nineteenth century, scandals of this sort were the common substance of gossip and storytelling (MCLAREN 2017). However, premature and violent deaths were also a threat to the community because of the wandering souls of the aggrieved dead. Other folk epic traditions find their inspiration in striking acts of violence that disturb the social equilibrium. In Indian folk epics, for example, the spirits of those who died unnaturally are feared as a likely cause of misfortune. The community engages in ritual acts of propitiation, which in turn spurs the development of song- and story-cycles (KOTHARI 1989, 108–12).

Some claim that there is evidence of a cult to a woman whose situation paralleled that of Fifth Daughter close to the Lake Tai region in the early nineteenth century. In the neighboring region of Jinze in Qingpu a temple was erected to a woman from Luxu called Chen Third Daughter. She was said to have engaged in a secret love affair, and when this was exposed her father had her drowned in the river. When her spirit manifested itself after death, locals erected a statue of her, only to see it destroyed by a Qingpu official in 1826 (QIAN 1997, 18–19). Locals tend to link the story of Chen Third Daughter with the song-cycle of Fifth Daughter. While this cannot be attested, the existence of cults focusing on those who died with grievances is likely to have added further strength to the tale of "Fifth Daughter." These folk beliefs retained their persuasive power well into the twentieth century and help to account for the lack of an explicit ending of the song-cycle. Lu Amei herself felt a strong reluctance to "conclude" the tale with what the Chinese folklorists regarded as a satisfactory plot resolution. As mentioned previously, she told the folklorists she did not wish to offend the spirit of Fifth Daughter: "Fifth Daughter doesn't want people to tell her story because then she'll lose face."

While Lu Amei apparently tried hard to appease the spirit of Fifth Daughter by according her dignity through her singing, some of her neighbors believed she had indeed suffered adverse consequences due to her involvement in this story-cycle. At least one woman interviewed believed that unfortunate events in the life of Lu Amei could be attributed to her singing the tale of Fifth Daughter. In an interview in April 1982 a neighbor, Zhou Jiama, attributed the early deaths of Lu Amei's daughters to her involvement in transmitting the song-cycle of Fifth Daughter:

> If you sing of the scandalous events about Fifth Daughter she will be angry. At worst she could make you sleep for over a score of days, or at best, you could be sick in your heart. Of those who listen to the story of Fifth Daughter right to the end, there's not a single one who doesn't get heart pain. Why is that? It's because Fifth Daughter's angry *qi* 气 [life force] blows into the hearts of those listening to mountain songs.... Lu Amei raised seven girls, but all were taken away by Fifth Daughter. Amei now prays to the Buddha because she fears Fifth Daughter will cause trouble.[32]

As well as trying to accord "face" to the spirit of Fifth Daughter, another way that Lu Amei constructed her own version of the tale was through the lens of a famous narrative about the ill-fated lovers, Liang Shanbo 梁山伯 and Zhu Yingtai 祝英台, which enjoyed national as distinct from regional circulation. In one of Lu's songs, Fifth Daughter declares that she is just like Zhu Yingtai, who fell in love with the handsome Shanbo but whose affair with him ended in tragedy.[33] The association made here between Fifth Daughter and Zhu Yingtai allowed Lu Amei to relate a local scandal about a sexual transgression to the much-loved figure of Zhu Yingtai, who sacrificed her own life for that of her lover. It is also an example of how a tale known only to a particular region gathers strength and resonance from association with a national master narrative.

CONCLUSION

In the early twenty-first century the Wu songs, including "Fifth Daughter," were accorded national status as important items of cultural heritage. In 2004 China joined the UNESCO Convention for the Safeguarding of Intangible Cultural Heritage. In the following year the city of Suzhou won approval for Wu songs to be added to the Chinese national register (McLaren 2010b). The township of Luxu has set up a Wu Song Pavilion for the exhibition of Wu song artifacts and the teaching and performance of Wu songs (see FIGURE 1). In some schools, Wu songs have been added to the local curriculum. Yet, in this highly developed region of China, very few young people know of the rich cultural heritage of their farming forebears along the waterways of Lake Tai. The printed versions of the folk epics remain to be passed on to the next generation as examples of the oral traditions of the recent past. However, as discussed here, the true spirit of the original song-cycle can only be found after an intensive exploration of what the singers actually sang and the "mental text" that was their inspiration. This study thus delineates the limitations of the textualization of this particular song-cycle but more importantly points to the need for a detailed understanding of the social and political context shaping such "folk" re-creations in the contemporary period. In this case, controversy over what constitutes Han Chinese ethnicity played a role in shaping debate over the recognition of the song traditions of the region. Essentially, notions of Han Chinese as the "advanced civilization" gave way to a more nuanced assessment of the different ethnic and regional modalities that underlie the supposed unitary basis of the vast population designated Han Chinese. This is the major achievement of the local ethnographers and scholars of the region. In textual form, the Wu folk epics are the product of the efforts by local folklorists, in negotiation with the Chinese state, to transform a previously stigmatized regional genre into a cultural form worthy of national recognition as a cherished part of "Chinese" civilization.

NOTES

* Anne McLaren wishes to express her sincere appreciation to the Chiang Ching-kuo Foundation for International Scholarly Exchange for providing fieldwork and research assistance funding for this project ("The Cultural Heritage of the Lower Yangzi Delta"). Both authors wish to thank Chen Qinjian of East China Normal University for his inspiring influence on our projects in Chinese popular culture over many years. We also wish to express our gratitude to members of the Culture Bureau of Luxu, Jiangsu Province, and members of the Cultural Center, Fenxiang village, Dingzha, Zhejiang Province, for their assistance with this

project. Zhang Fanglan of Luxu provided us with his enthusiastic assistance during several visits to Luxu.

1. Traditionally, northerners were predominantly cultivators of grain and southerners cultivators of rice. Linguistic and cultural diversity is much more pronounced south of the Yangzi River than in the north. It is believed that southern Chinese populations have assimilated many of the customs and cultural forms of the originally non-Chinese peoples who resided south of the Yangzi in antiquity. This could potentially include song traditions (EBERHARD 1968). Archaeological finds in recent decades have proven the existence of multiple sites for originary proto-Chinese civilizations, including some predynastic civilizations in the lower Yangzi Delta. As Edward FRIEDMAN notes, these new findings challenge conventional understandings of a northern originary site of Chinese culture and call for the inclusion of what he calls a "southern narrative" in national reconstructions (2002, 42).

2. This is a similar problem to that faced by non-Mandarin communities of Chinese origin residing outside China. Shu-mei Shih notes the complexities of the "multiple orthographies" required to write down Sinophone literatures and argues that "Sinitic [written] languages … therefore pose important challenges to the fictive construction of Han ethnolinguistic homogeneity" (2013, 10). A famous early ethnologist, Gu Jiegang (1893–1980), writing in 1920, pointed out the difficulty of recording expressions in the Wu language: "There are truly so many words that one cannot explain or even write down and so many things one cannot verify" (preface to *Wuyu jilu*, republished in WANG 1999, 679). In order to publish his collections of Wu songs it was necessary to draw on unconventional vernacular forms in local circulation and provide glosses of local usages. The same dilemmas confronted delta folklorists in compiling the song collections of the 1980s.

3. We use the term "epic" here simply to refer to the narrative quality and length of these songs. The term should not be confused with epics on martial themes, such as Greek epics, or with the Chinese translation of "epic" as "poem on a historical theme"(*shishi* 史诗). Here we follow the broader definition of the term "epic" as defined by Blackburn et al. in the case of Indian village epics, where the term "heroic" is expanded "to include female and non-martial heroes" (BLACKBURN et al. eds., 1989, 5). Blackburn et al. use the term "romantic" to refer to the latter type of oral epic. The romantic epics deal with sexual relations that form a threat to the social order. They suggest that this "romantic" type of oral epic should be considered as "a cultural variant of an international genre" (BLACKBURN et al. eds., 1989, 5).

4. The only substantial Western study of delta folk songs is by the ethnomusicologist Antoinette SCHIMMELPENNINCK (1997). This work is based on recordings of songs conducted during fieldwork carried out between 1987 and 1992. It does not deal with the longer song-cycles discussed here although their existence is noted.

5. This phenomenon began in "liberated areas" well before 1949 but extended over the whole country in the early decades of socialist rule. An example much studied in the West is the tale of Liu Sanjie (LIU 2003).

6. For studies of the history and rural economy of the Yangzi Delta, see SHIH (1981), HUANG (1990), and LI (2003). Li stresses the interconnected nature of Lake Tai and its tributary systems and the need for constant waterworks to prevent drought and floods (LI 2003, 447–62).

7. Huang believes that around one third of the peasant population was engaged in some form of hired work from the fourteenth to the mid-twentieth centuries (HUANG 1990, 9).

8. See "Transcripts," vol. I, I (JSMWGX). For a fuller biography of Lu Amei see QIAN (1997, 14–38; 147–57).

9. See the postface by Jin Xu in JIN (2004, 206).

10. We would like to thank Zhang Fanglan for presenting us with this valuable set of transcripts, for his hospitality in inviting us to his home, and in taking us on a tour of the Wu Song Pavilion (Wuge guan) in Luxu. We are greatly indebted to him for his frank discussion about editorial and publishing decisions made in the 1980s.

11. For details on the performative aspects of Wu Songs see SCHIMMELPENNINCK (1997); ZHENG (2005, 92–100); JIN (2004, 4–5).

12. If no standard Chinese characters were available for an expression they would use homophonic characters based on the sounds of Mandarin; see "Transcripts," vol. 1, 6–12. Jin Xu notes that in some cases the transcribers substituted more standardized forms of the Wu regional language for obscure Luxu expressions; see postface in JIN (2004, 207). This was done for the sake of reader comprehension.

13. "Transcripts," vol. 2, 257.

14. It was also republished later in JIN (2004) on the grounds that while "flawed" it was of major historical significance. For these publication details see JIN (2004, 157).

15. For a discussion of the introduction of European notions of epic into China see YIN (2013). He notes that the perceived lack of European-style epic poetry in Chinese (actually Han Chinese) literature was seen as a sign of inferiority by famed intellectuals such as Liang Qichao (1873–1929), Wang Guowei (1877–1927), and Hu Shi (1891–1962); see YIN (2013, 132–33). Chinese scholars today accept the statement by Karl Marx that the epic form belongs to a less developed stage of the evolution of human society (according to YIN 2013, 136). In his reappraisal of the literature, Yin seeks to extend Western epic paradigms to include a wider range of themes beyond the heroic. Nonetheless, he limits his discussion of epics in China to the non-Han minority groups and does not include the long narrative songs discussed here.

16. In a parallel discussion, DE PEE (2001) has critiqued the adoption of the Morgan-Engels framework in Chinese scholarly understandings of kinship and marriage. He notes that in the attempt to arrive at "an objective, universal, linear development" for the Chinese race (DE PEE 2001, 560), Chinese scholars seek out signs of ancient primitivity in the marriage and kinship customs of contemporary non-Han minorities, which are thus deemed to be antecedent cultures to the dominant Han (DE PEE 2001, 575).

17. ZHENG (2005, 81–84) lists thirty-nine separate long narrative songs in his important study of the delta folk epic. Besides "Fifth Daughter," the Luxu region is known for a number of other lengthy song-cycles such as "Zhao Shengguan."

18. On *shange ban* and public song competitions see ZHENG (2005, 140–61). For Luxu song competitions see JIN (2004, 6–7). Singers who participated in these events acquired extensive skills in extempore composition. The prevalence of both song competitions and mountain song teams in Luxu greatly stimulated the development of the longer form of *shange*. By contrast, Jiashan was not known for its song competitions or singing teams and did not develop long narrative songs.

19. However, there are still cadres who express scepticism about the existence of a long version of "Fifth Daughter," as we found out on a visit to Taozhuang Culture Station on 26 May 2011 (interview with Zhang Songlin).

20. Not everyone was in favor of the bowdlerized version. WU Gongjian (1988) condemned the excision of erotic material, arguing that the original promoted a type of "modern" love based on personal choice. See also Qian's allusions to the inserted ending found in the first arranged edition (QIAN 1997, 36).

21. See the editorial notes on this tale (JIANG 1989, 265–66).

22. For an example see JIN, postface (2004, 206). He further explains that although the erotic sections were not considered to be as bad as that of the *Jin Ping Mei* (the famous erotic novel of the Ming period), nonetheless, it was difficult [impolitic] to include the more explicit material (2004, 206).

23. This is narrated in separate song segments such as "The matchmaker pays a visit" and so on; see "Transcripts," vol. 1, 22–31. One finds three times more material on this topic in "Transcripts" than in the edited versions.

24. Lu Amei spoke about this aspect of the story in an interview: "It is not that Xu Atian sought to have an affair with her, it was Yang Jinda's wife [the evil sister-in-law] who wanted to have an affair with him." See "Transcripts," 258.

25. This song type is categorized as "Going to get the younger sister" *jie ayi* 接阿姨; see McLaren (2010a).

26. "The sister and the *saosao* [older brother's wife] form an amour with the one lover" 姑嫂结识一个郎; "Transcripts," vol. 1, 123–24. Not included in other editions.

27. See "Transcripts," vol. 2, 223.

28. This is also by Lu Amei; see "Transcripts," vol. 2, 224. A song by Qian Afu included in "Transcripts" relates the whole story outline in around 113 lines. It presents a "happy" ending where the magistrate punishes the brother and his wife and allows the young couple to marry; see "Transcripts," vol. 2, 231–41. This highlights the flexibility of the tradition and the distinctiveness of the version presented by Lu Amei.

29. Lu Amei sang a song about Xu Atian's execution shortly after the affair was discovered. However, she also sang another song about how Atian comes to steal the spirit tablets of Fifth Daughter after her death, which means that he was still alive. In a "readerly" text these endings appear contradictory.

30. Interview with Lu Amei in 1981; see "Transcripts," vol. 2, 257 (Jsmwgx).

31. For reports on these sites see Wang and Zheng (1993, 78); Qian (1997, 17).

32. "Transcripts," vol. 2, 271 (Jsmwgx).

33. "Transcripts," vol. 2, 166–67 (Jsmwgx). Liang and Zhu were also held to be historical figures and reported grave sites can be found in various regions of China. One such site is at Ningbo, in coastal Zhejiang, within the Wu-speaking zone. For a study of this story-cycle over the centuries see Idema (2010).

References

Blackburn, Stuart H., Peter J. Claus, Joyce B. Flueckiger, and Susan S. Wadley, eds.
1989   *Oral Epics in India*. Berkeley, Los Angeles, and London: University of California Press.

De Pee, Christian
2001   Premodern Chinese weddings and the divorce of past and present. *Positions* 9: 559–84. doi:10.1215/10679847-9-3-559

Eberhard, Wolfram
1968   *The Local Cultures of South and East China*. Trans. from the German original of 1942 by Alide Eberhard. Leiden: E. J. Brill.

Friedman, Edward
2002   Symbols of southern identity: Rivaling unitary nationalism. In *China Off Center: Mapping the Margins of the Middle Kingdom*, S. D. Blum and L. M. Jensen, eds., 31–44. Honolulu: University of Hawai'i Press.

Gao Fumin 高福民 and Jin Xu 金煦, eds.
2003   *Wuge yichan jicui* 吴歌遗产集粹 [The essence of the heritage of Wu songs]. Shanghai: Shanghai Wenyi Chubanshe.

Honko, Lauri
2000   Text as process and practice: The textualization of oral epics. In *Textualization of Oral Epics*, ed. L. Honko, 3–54. Berlin and New York: Mouton de Gruyter. doi:10.1515/9783110825848
2002a   The *Kalevala* as performance. In *The Kalevala and the World's Traditional Epics*, ed. L. Honko, 13–25. Helsinki: Finnish Literature Society.

2002b Comparing traditional epics in the eastern Baltic Sea region. In *The Kalevala and the World's Traditional Epics*, ed. L. Honko, 327–41. Helsinki: Finnish Literature Society.

HUANG, Philip C. C.
1990 *The Peasant Family and Rural Development in the Yangzi Delta, 1350–1988.* Stanford: Stanford University Press.

IDEMA, Wilt L.
2010 *The Butterfly Lovers: The Legend of Liang Shanbo and Zhu Yingtai: Four Versions, with Related Texts.* Indianapolis and Cambridge: Hackett Publishing Company, Inc.

JIANG Bin 姜彬
1989 *Jiangnan shi da minjian xushi shi* 江南十大 民间叙事诗 [Ten long folk narrative poems from Jiangnan]. Shanghai: Shanghai Wenyi Chubanshe.

JIANGSU SHENG MINJIAN WENXUE GONGZUOZHE XIEHUI: SUZHOU FENHUI BIAN (JSMWGX)
江苏省民间文学工作者协会：苏州分会编 [Jiangsu Province folk literature workers association: Suzhou branch]
1983 *Wu Guniang ziliao ben* [Transcripts of Wu Guniang; "Transcripts" in text]. Mimeographed edition, 2 vols. Internal circulation.

JIN Xu 金煦
2004 *Zhongguo: Luxu shange ji* 中国芦墟山歌集 [Folk songs of Luxu, China]. Shanghai: Shanghai Wenyi Chubanshe.

KOTHARI, Komal
1989 Performers, gods, and heroes in the oral epics of Rajasthan. In BLACKBURN, CLAUS, FLUECKIGER, and WADLEY, eds., 102–17.

LI Bozhong 李伯重
2003 *Duo shijiao kan Jiangnan jingji shi* 多视角看江南经济史 (1250–1850) [Examining the economic history of Jiangnan (1250–1850) from multiple perspectives]. Beijing: Sanlian Shudian.

LIU, Lydia H.
2003 A folk song immortal and official popular culture in twentieth-century China. In *Writing and Materiality in China: Essays in Honor of Patrick Hanan*, J. T. Zeitlin and L. H. Liu with E. Widmer, eds., 553–609. Cambridge, MA: Harvard University Asia Center.

MCLAREN, Anne E.
2010a Folk epics from the lower Yangzi Delta region: Oral and written traditions. In *The Interplay of Oral and Written Traditions in Chinese Fiction, Drama and Performance Literature*, ed. V. Børdahl, 157–86. Copenhagen: NIAS Press. doi:10.1017/s002191181200162
2010b Revitalising the folk epics of the lower Yangzi Delta: An example of China's intangible cultural heritage. *International Journal of Intangible Heritage* 5: 29–43.
2017 Gossip, scandal, and the wanton woman in Chinese song-cycles. In *Wanton Women in Late Imperial Chinese Literature: Models, Genres, Subversion and Traditions*, Cuncun Wu and Mark Stevens, eds., 184–228. Leiden: Brill.

MORGAN, Lewis H.
1985 *Ancient Society.* Tucson: The University of Arizona Press. (Originally published 1877.)

QIAN Shunjuan 钱瞬娟
  1997   *Jiangnan minjian xushishi ji gushi* 江南民间叙事诗及故事 [Folk narrative poetry and stories of Jiangnan]. Shanghai: Shanghai Wenyi Chubanshe.

SCHIMMELPENNINCK, Antoinette
  1997   *Chinese Folk Songs and Folk Singers: Shan'ge Traditions in Southern Jiangsu.* Leiden: Chime Foundation.

SHIH, Chin
  1981   Peasant Economy and Rural Society in the Lake Tai Area, 1368–1840. PhD dissertation, University of California, Berkeley.

SHIH, Shu-mei
  2013   Introduction. In SHIH, TSAI, and BERNARDS, eds., 1–16.

SHIH, Shu-mei, Chien-hsin TSAI, and Brian BERNARDS, eds.
  2013   *Sinophone Studies: A Critical Reader.* New York: Columbia University Press.

WANG Fang 王仿 and ZHENG Shuoren 郑硕人
  1993   *Minjian xushishi de chuangzuo* 民间叙事诗的创作 [The creation of folk narrative poetry]. Shanghai: Shanghai Wenyi Chubanshe.

WANG Xuhua 王煦华, ed.
  1999   *Wu ge: Wu ge xiao shi* 吴歌—吴歌小史 [Wu songs: A brief history of Wu songs]. Reprint of original collection by Gu Jiegang 顾颉刚 et al. Nanjing: Jiangsu Guji Chubanshe.

WU Gongjian 吴恭俭
  1988   Lun "Wu Guniang" de xiandai xing 论"五姑娘"的现代性 [The modern significance of "Fifth Daughter"]. *Xiangtan daxue xuebao (shehui kexue ban)* 湘潭大学学报(社会科学版) 3: 57–62.

YIN Hubin
  2013   The paradigm shift of epic studies in China. In *Folk Traditions in Modern Society*, P. Hakamies, J. Sun, and V. Børdahl, eds., 126–39. Shanghai: Fudan University Press.

ZHANG Fanglan 张舫澜 and MA Hanmin 马汉民
  1983   *Wu Guniang ziliao ben* 五姑娘资料本 [Transcripts of Wu Guniang]. Mimeographed edition. 2 vols. Internal circulation.

ZHENG Tuyou 郑土有
  2005   *Wuyu xushi shange yanchang chuantong yanjiu* 吴语叙事山歌演唱传统研究 [Investigation into the performance tradition of narrative folk songs in the Wu language]. Shanghai: Cishu Chubanshe.

LEVI S. GIBBS
Dartmouth College

Culture Paves the Way, Economics Comes to Sing the Opera

The Rhetoric of Chinese Folk Duets and Global Joint Ventures

After economic decentralization policies were introduced in China during the late 1970s, the promotion of provincial cultural identities became a means to compete for comparative advantage to attract investment. Local cultural practices, often framed as uniquely Chinese, were sometimes portrayed as "windows" and "bridges" that would bring global attention to a locality. This article examines northern Shaanxi Province's use of song and dance to facilitate a joint project between the largest coal company in China and The Dow Chemical Company. Focusing on rhetoric surrounding a 2008 performance by the Yulin Folk Arts Troupe at a "Far East Meets West" event in Dow's global headquarters in Midland, Michigan, and reciprocal, Dow-funded performances by the U.S. National Symphony Orchestra the following year in China, I explore the symbolic role of reciprocal performances amid the forging of relationships between different localities in a global age.

KEYWORDS: folk songs—northern Shaanxi—Chineseness—cultural exchange—*guanxi*—gift exchange—provincial identity

Asian Ethnology Volume 76, Number 1 · 2017, 43–63
© Nanzan University Anthropological Institute

IN AN ERA of global capitalism, negotiations between localities, multinational corporations, regions, and countries involve contact between distant places and peoples, and one way of bringing them together is through cultural exchange.* This article looks at the rhetoric leading up to and surrounding an exchange of performances in the U.S. and China during negotiations for a joint venture between the Shenhua Group,[1] China's largest coal company, and The Dow Chemical Company, a U.S.-based multinational chemical corporation. In 2008, the site of the proposed venture, Yulin Prefecture, Shaanxi Province, sent the Yulin Folk Arts Troupe to perform at a "Far East Meets West" event in Midland, Michigan, Dow's global headquarters. Dow later reciprocated by funding the U.S. National Symphony Orchestra's 2009 Asia Tour, with performances in key cities in China. This exchange of performances amid the development of an economic partnership in many ways paralleled the use of gift exchange in the negotiation of interpersonal relationships. At the same time, the rhetoric surrounding the gift—a *regional* song and dance troupe's performance was described as offering an authentic *Chineseness*—ties in to recent trends in provincial self-promotion that blur the line between the local and the national.

In Marcel Mauss's classic work *The Gift*, he suggests that suggests that individuals develop relationships via three interlocking obligations: "to give," "to receive," and "to repay" (MAUSS 1966, 10–11). In the Chinese context, the reciprocal performances examined here can be thought of as "ritual object[s]"—Mayfair Yang's literal translation of the Chinese word for "gift" (*liwu* 礼物)—through which "one enacts a 'ritualized relationship'" (YANG 1994, 70). Yang suggests that "the ethics of gift-giving are extended to all human relationships," since gifts "require reciprocity, and so do relationships" (YANG 1994, 70). In the cultural exchange discussed here, the entities exchanging gifts were not individuals, but rather localities, governments, and corporations. Seen through the lens of Mauss and Yang, the presentation of a song and dance troupe performance from one place to another could be thought of as an attempt to establish a relationship between the two. At the same time, the receiving of the performance by the second locality and the arrangement of a reciprocal performance at a later date could be understood—like reciprocated gifts—as expressing a sense of mutual goodwill and a desire to affirm and strengthen that relationship.

When viewed as "ritual objects" (that is, gifts) in the negotiation of relations, these reciprocal performances bear certain similarities to "ritual objects" found in another type of social "ritual" discussed by Mayfair Yang—banquets (YANG 1994, 70). In Eric Shepherd's study on Shandong banquet culture, he suggests that in "the banquet context, *performance* reduces the gaps that exist between participants by integrating them into the group at the same time that it differentiates individual performers—when they perform, individuals contribute to the group atmosphere while displaying their unique styles and abilities" (SHEPHERD 2005, 28–29, emphasis added). It seems that a similar sort of dual objective—fusing together group integration with the display of unique individuality—was at play in the 2008 Midland and 2009 Asia Tour performances. While the goal of the exchange was to bring together "groups" at various levels—sharing "Chinese" culture with midwesterners and "American" culture with residents of Beijing, Shanghai, and Xi'an; bringing together Shenhua and Dow, Yulin and Midland, China and the U.S.—at the same time, the uniqueness of Yulin and Dow were emphasized through the performances and the rhetoric surrounding them. Just as the banquet participants in Shepherd's study perform songs, jokes, and poems to show devotion to the group through the vulnerability of performance while at the same time expressing their uniqueness in that group, the Yulin Folk Arts Troupe's Midland performance offered a cross-cultural presentation of "Chinese" tradition that simultaneously highlighted the unique individuality of Yulin within the larger group atmosphere. Thus, I suggest, through performances and the narratives that surround them, both individuals at a banquet and localities arranging a joint venture attempt to negotiate and renegotiate their relationships and assert themselves as unique members of new mergers.

In what follows, I begin by looking at some of the thinking behind Yulin Prefecture's decision to use culture to pave the way for economic development, as related by one of the region's star performers.[2] This sets the stage for my discussion of rhetoric surrounding the Yulin Folk Arts Troupe's performance in Midland, Michigan, in 2008 and the reciprocal set of performances by the U.S. National Symphony Orchestra in China in 2009. While the overall purpose of these reciprocal performances was to establish relations between the parties involved, given the size of the joint venture being negotiated, multiple players felt compelled to comment on the events, and each comment reveals distinct attempts by those players to position themselves in relation to the cultural exchange as a whole.

Although the case study discussed in this article relates to one locality in China, the rhetoric involved—using the exchange of "Chinese" culture to facilitate economic relationships—echoes many recent efforts by regions in China to advertise themselves both nationally and globally. My discussion will focus less on the events themselves, and more on how the various parties involved talked about those events. While it is beyond the scope of this article to show a direct connection between these cultural performances and the economic success enjoyed by Yulin in the following years, I argue that several recent events staged for the promotion of Yulin seem to have been driven by such rhetoric. Furthermore, Yulin's later economic success—it became known as "China's Kuwait" at one point—was used by some to validate the narrative of culture paving the way for economics (XINHUA 2012).

FIGURE I. Wang Xiangrong, "King of Northern Shaanxi Folk Songs." Photo by author.

CULTURE PAVES THE WAY

After economic decentralization policies were introduced along with market reform in China during the late 1970s, each province began to compete for comparative advantage to attract investment, and individual provinces found the need to promote provincial cultural identities (GOODMAN 1994, 4–5, 17; OAKES 2000, 674). With the expansion of global capitalism, the presentation of unique local cultures played a key role in bolstering provincial images (OAKES 2000). During the early 1980s, Yulin Prefecture, located in northern Shaanxi Province, decided to use folk culture to advertise itself through the establishment of the Yulin Folk Arts Troupe (*Yulin minjian yishu tuan* 榆林民间艺术团).³ One of its star performers, the professional folk songer now known as the "Folk Song King of Western China" and the "King of Northern Shaanxi Folk Songs," Wang Xiangrong 王向荣 (b. 1952) (FIGURE 1), described Yulin's use of northern Shaanxi folk songs as a "window" (*chuangkou* 窗口) through which other places could become familiar with the region.⁴

According to Wang,

First, you would become familiar with northern Shaanxi folk songs. Through a means of culture, [the people promoting Yulin] would first get close to you and set up an exchange. Then, they would get you to learn more about Yulin, and finally about Yulin's economy. The slogan at the time was "culture paves the way, economics comes to sing the opera" (*wenhua pulu, jingji changxi*). That means that culture first paves the road nice and good, and then the people who get things done, that is, the economic ... it means that culture serves as a kind of medium, yes, a weapon for exchange. First, it would be through song and dance. We would go to your Shanghai or your Xi'an, or Yunnan or Beijing. In order to advertise the region of Yulin, first we would bring songs and dances from Yulin. After that ... things from Yulin would gradually become more familiar and known by people in society, and the initial stages of this market would be set up.

先了解陕北民歌，先通过文化和你接近交流，然后让你了解榆林，然后了解榆林的经济，然后，当时的口号就说"文化铺路，经济唱戏"。诶，就是说文化把路铺好，然后真正搞事的，就是经济 ... 等于是文化作为一个媒体，嗯，作为一个交流的一个武器。嗯，首先就是通过歌呀舞呀，到你上海，或者是到你西安，或者到这个云南，到北京，就说为了宣传榆林这块儿地，那么，首先带着这个榆林的歌和舞。那么，这样以后 ... 等于榆林的东西在社会上在逐步被人们所了解和认识啦，才有了这个初步的市场。

The phrase "culture paves the way, economics comes to sing the opera" resonates with similar slogans popular across China, such as "trade (or economy) performing on a stage built by culture (*wenhua datai, jingmao changxi*)" (Li 2013, 86). Certain provinces have particular versions of this type of slogan based on local industries. For example, Guizhou Province, which relies more heavily on tourism, has used the phrase "trade performing on a stage built by tourism" (*lüyou datai, jingji changxi* 旅游搭台, 经济唱戏; OAKES 2000, 680). In addition, Wang's use of the term "window" (*chuangkou*) to describe the capacity of folk songs to place his region on the world's mental map is not unique. The use of terms like "window" and "bridge" are found elsewhere in recent discourse: initial joint ventures in areas of interior China have been referred to as "window enterprises," in that they highlight investment possibilities in a local area and may attract additional business ventures in the future (OAKES 1999, 45). A martial arts novel by the famous writer Jin Yong set in Dali 大理, Yunnan Province, has been described as a "bridge" bringing outside interest to that city, one that eventually led to the transformation of the place itself (NOTAR 2006, 4). Beth Notar cites a Chinese scholar who compared the novel "to a *spatial and temporal bridge*, between Dali and the outside, the local and the global, the underdeveloped and the economically developed," saying that this "literary text would allow the place and people of Dali to cross over into prosperity" (NOTAR 2006, 4, emphasis added).[5]

Like Yulin, many places in China have established song and dance troupes in order to advertise their localities.[6] The use of cultural performances to represent places naturally involves choices in repertoire, which are tied, in turn, to how the performing group wishes to present itself to a particular audience—be it in China or abroad.[7] When the Yulin Folk Arts Troupe performs in China, it presents a region-representing repertoire of songs that tie its locality to the national landscape.[8] In China, Wang Xiangrong performs pieces such as "The Infinite Bends of the Yellow River" ("Tianxia huanghe jiushijiu dao wan" 天下黄河九十九道湾) and "The East Is Red" ("Dongfang hong" 东方红), which evoke a sense of Chinese history and nationalism, while at the same time highlighting northern Shaanxi Province within that broader appeal to tradition (FIGURE 2).

However, when performing abroad, Wang said that he avoids singing songs with nationalistic symbols that might drive away foreign audiences, since the

FIGURE 2. Wang Xiangrong performing "The Infinite Bends of the Yellow River" at a televised Chinese New Year gala in central Shaanxi Province, 2012 (photo by author).

goal of such artistic exchanges is to bring people together. Instead, he often uses songs related to the theme of love—something that he views as fundamental to all cultures. In particular, he likes to perform songs from the "two-person opera" (*errentai* 二人台) genre popular at local temple fairs in his youth—songs that he characterizes as pure and folksy in their representation of love between men and women. Thus, in the 2008 Midland concert discussed below, Wang chose to perform a folk operatic duet called "The Flowers Bloom in May" ("Wuyue sanhua" 五月散花).[9] Featuring riddles about the types of flower that bloom in each month, Wang described this song as both locally authentic and imbued with the universally relatable theme of love.[10] One might add that an antiphonal song about love and courtship between a man and woman offered interesting parallels with the "courtship" of the joint venture at hand.

CULTURE AS A BRIDGE: YULIN, DOW, AND THE "HUMAN ELEMENT"

In early 2008, during the process of setting up a joint coal-to-chemicals project with the Shenhua Group in Yulin Prefecture, The Dow Chemical Company funded a four-month celebration of China's rich cultural heritage in Midland, Michigan—Dow's global headquarters—entitled "*A Celebration of China: Far East Meets West.*"[11] This included several performances and an exhibit of two terracotta warriors and other ancient relics on loan from Shaanxi Province. The exhibit, entitled "Timeless Warriors and Relics: 1500 Years of Ancient China" in English and "Yellow River Culture" (*Huanghe wenhua* 黄河文化) in Chinese, was put on display at the Alden B. Dow Museum of Science and Art, located at the Midland

Center for the Arts, from 20 January 2008 to 13 April 2008 (Dow 2008a). Dow's CEO Andrew Liveris and his wife Paula hosted the opening celebration for the exhibit, with the deputy director of the Shaanxi Provincial Cultural Relics Bureau, Zhang Wen, as their honored guest (Dow 2008c). The exhibition of Chinese relics was sponsored by the Shaanxi Provincial Cultural Relics Bureau, the Museum of Emperor Qin Shihuang's Terracotta Warriors and Horses, the Shaanxi Provincial Institute of Archaeology, the Shaanxi Cultural Heritage Promotion Center, The Dow Chemical Company, Northwest Airlines, Dow Corning Corporation, McKay Press, and local television and media (MCFTA 2008b). Northwest Airlines funded transportation costs for the forty-member Yulin Folk Arts Troupe, co-sponsoring the festival with its key corporate client, Dow Chemical (Dow 2008c).[12]

The festival's performance series included both Chinese and Western works. The Midland Symphony Orchestra held a concert of Verdi, Mozart, and Dvorak featuring two Chinese pianists, Angela Cheng and Alvin Chow (Dow 2008b). The Yulin Folk Arts Troupe performed at several regional public schools, leading up to "a special ticketed public performance" on 26 March 2008 (MCFTA 2008b). The various descriptions of the festival—the advertisement for the final performance, a speech given by a Yulin official during the closing ceremony, and articles produced by Dow—all pointed to the theme of culture as a bridge that brings people together, while at the same time emphasizing the unique resources that Yulin and Dow each brought to the table.

The final performance, entitled "Reflections of the Yellow River" in English and "Winds of the Yellow River: Sentiments of the Yellow Earth" (Ch. "Huanghe feng: Huangtu qing" 黄河风 · 黄土情),[13] was advertised on the venue's website as follows: "The Yulin Folk Art Troupe from the Chinese Province of Shaanxi will *transport you to a land of beauty and enchantment* through 'Reflections of the Yellow River,' a series of *traditional Chinese performances* featuring dance, acrobatics, and music" (MCFTA 2008a, emphasis added). Here, the performance was characterized as a bridge to the exotic, one that would "transport you to a land of beauty and enchantment"—it would take you to "China." Though performed by a *regional* song and dance troupe, the troupe's performances were billed as both "traditional" and "Chinese," suggesting that they were nationally representative and rooted in a long history of Chinese culture. Such notions of "Chineseness" and "tradition" are broad, familiar-sounding terms perhaps intended to facilitate audience engagement, since most Midwesterners would be unfamiliar with place names like Yulin and Shaanxi. While set in the context of bringing people together through cultural exchange, this advertisement also presented Chinese culture as a unique resource that the Yulin Folk Arts Troupe could provide.

This type of claim to Chineseness ties into the history of provincial attempts at self-promotion. According to Tim Oakes, "promoting Chineseness is part of a strategy whereby local elites attempt to promote a cultural identity attractive to the 'flexible accumulation' of global capitalism" (OAKES 2000, 669). Oakes suggests that this phenomenon of local claims to Chineseness is especially common in provinces "located *in China's interior*, ... relatively poor, with economies primarily dependent on agriculture and *natural resource extraction*" (OAKES 2000,

675, emphasis added).[14] He also suggests that the "identity-constructions offered … in each of these provinces claim a foundation on ancient, unique, and attractive regional cultures that, at the same time, can be called upon to spur a dynamic, innovative entrepreneurialism and sense of self-confidence" (OAKES 2000, 675). This rhetoric of an "ancient, unique, and attractive regional culture" serving as a resource for "dynamic, innovative entrepreneurialism" was particularly evident in a speech given by the party secretary of the Yulin Municipal Party Committee and director of the Yulin Municipal People's Congress Standing Committee, Li Jinzhu 李金柱, during the Yulin Folk Art Troupe's performance in Midland.

With officials from Dow and Northwest Airlines in attendance, Li framed the the Midland performance within the long history of U.S.-China relations—suggesting that the performance was representative of China—at the same time that he focused attention on Yulin's unique cultural and natural resources and its aspirations to use the relationship with Dow as a springboard foro future collaborations with the American business community. Here is an excerpt of the speech, translated from an article in the *Yulin Daily*:

> China and the U.S.A. are separated by vast oceans and have completely different historical backgrounds and social systems. However, for a long time, the people of these two countries have held deep feelings of mutual interest and friendship. *Yulin is situated in the northern part of Shaanxi. In addition to having a long history and a deep-seated culture, it also possesses abundant mineral products, energy sources, tourism and human resources, and is a national-level energy and chemical engineering base.* Our collaboration with The Dow Chemical Company has already drawn back the curtain, and we look forward to having more interest and participation from American businesses. At the same time, we also hope to develop a wide-ranging exchange with all walks of life in the U.S.
>
> …[C]ulture is a *window* that reflects a nation's historical heritage and inner, spiritual world. It is also the best *bridge* for promoting mutual understanding between different peoples and communicating the heart and soul of the people. Our presentation today for everyone, "Winds of the Yellow River: Sentiments of the Yellow Earth," is an artistic performance with rich, local color. Simple and unadorned, straightforward and uninhibited, bold and powerful—this is the folk song and dance of the plateaus in the northern part of Shaanxi province, which amply reflects the northern Shaanxi people's attitude of exerting oneself. The graceful, traditional ethnic music reflects the long-term accumulation of northern Shaanxi's long history and culture. This evening performance will help the American people to gain a deeper understanding of China, and promote exchange and collaboration between the two great nations of China and America.

> 中美两国远隔重洋，有着完全不同的历史背景和社会制度。但是，长期以来，中美两国人民一直相互抱有浓厚的兴趣和友好的感情。榆林位于陕西北部，历史悠久，文化底蕴深厚，并拥有丰富的矿产、能源、旅游和人力资源，是国家级能源化工基地。我们与陶氏化学公司的合作已经拉开帷幕，并期待着有更多的美国企业的关注和参与。同时也希望与美国各界开展广泛的交流。

> ……文化是反映一个民族历史文化和精神世界的窗口，文化也是增进不同民族相互了解和沟通人民心灵的最好的桥梁。今天为大家呈现的 《黄河风·黄土情》文艺演

出，是一台具有浓郁地方特色的文艺演出，质朴、粗犷和豪放的陕西北部高原的民间
歌舞，充分反映了陕北人民奋发向上的精神面貌，优美传统的民族乐曲反映了陕北深
厚的历史文化积淀。这台晚会将有助于美国人民加深对中国的了解，促进中美两个伟
大民族的交流与合作。　　　　　　　　　　　　　　(WANG 2008c, emphasis added)[15]

After beginning with the long history of "mutual interest and friendship" between
China and the U.S., Li immediately focused on the specific area of Yulin, situ-
ating it within China and outlining its history, culture, and natural and human
resources. His statement that the "collaboration with The Dow Chemical Company has already drawn back the curtain" for "more interest and participation from
American businesses" echoed Oakes' characterization of "window enterprises"
with their potential to attract further future investments to a region (OAKES 1999,
45). It appears that Li Jinzhu was already attempting to put this idea into action—
according to *Yulin Daily*, before Li's speech in Midland on 26 March 2008, he
had just finished spending two days leading a delegation from Yulin on a "goodwill mission" to establish sister city relations with Baytown, Texas, the home of
ExxonMobil and Chevron Phillips (WANG 2008a; 2008b). Interestingly, in Li's
speech to the Midland audience, he did not mention the Shenhua Group, the
coal company with which Dow was planning to collaborate, but instead framed
his address in terms of China's relationship with the U.S., Yulin's relationship with
Dow, and Yulin's potential relationships with other American corporations.

While Li Jinzhu's speech highlighted the unique resources that Yulin brought
to the cultural exchange, articles produced by Dow emphasized Dow's role as a
powerful force in facilitating cultural exchange, pointing to the positive impact
that economics can bring to local culture. Like Yulin, Dow foregrounded the
potential for such exchanges to increase understanding between nations, but here,
the focus was on Dow's ability to bring *Chinese* culture to the area surrounding
its global headquarters. In a public relations article posted on its website, subtitled "Dow Contributes to Cultural Exchange Between U.S. and China," Dow
was introduced as "a diversified chemical company that combines the power of
science and technology with the 'Human Element' to constantly improve what is
essential to human progress" (DOW 2008a). While briefly mentioning additional
support for the event from the Shaanxi Provincial People's Government, the article made no mention whatsoever of Yulin, the Shenhua Group, or the potential
coal-to-chemical joint venture. Although it briefly mentioned "a business forum"
as one component of the celebration, this appeared as almost an afterthought to
the "series of cultural activities" that preceded it (DOW 2008a). Instead, the article
focused on portraying Chinese culture as a scarce commodity—one the Dow was
able to bring to the Midwest. The article began:

> Two authentic Chinese terracotta warriors have arrived in Midland, Michigan,
> the global headquarters of The Dow Chemical Company, as the centerpiece of
> a four-month celebration of the rich heritage of China. The 2,200-year-old war-
> riors will spend their first Chinese New Year in the U.S., and will be cultural
> ambassadors, sharing stories of the rich history of China.　　　　(DOW 2008a)

Framing the terracotta warriors as "one of the greatest archaeological discoveries of the 20ᵗʰ century" and a link to "the ancient culture of China," the article suggested that by seeing them, visitors from all over the Midwest would have a chance "to come and learn about the mysterious Chinese culture first hand" (Dow 2008a). The terms "ancient" and "mysterious" point to a rare, exotic factor echoing the suggestion that the Yulin Folk Art Troupe's performance would "transport you to a land of beauty and enchantment" (MCFTA 2008a). At the same time, both the terracotta warriors and the Yulin Folk Arts Troupe were characterized in terms of their "authenticity" and "Chineseness." The terracotta warriors were referred to as "authentic" and "ancient treasures," while the Yulin Folk Arts Troupe performance was described as "an authentic Chinese art performance" (Dow 2008a; 2008c).

While presenting itself as a broker of cultural exchange, Dow described the benefits of that exchange differently depending on the audience. In the public relations article mentioned above, it stressed the benefits for the public at large, while another article in Dow's corporate newsletter pointed to the benefits that the cultural exchange would bring to Dow's business. In the former PR piece, "Terracotta Warriors to Spend Chinese New Year in the U.S.: Dow Contributes to Cultural Exchange Between U.S. and China," Dow CEO and Chairman, Andrew Liveris, was quoted as saying, "As a global company with growing operations in China, east is meeting west in many exciting ways. … We are pleased to be able to sponsor this cultural exchange as a way to share some of China's important heritage with the people of this region" (Dow 2008a). In the latter article published in *Around Dow*, entitled "Far East Meets West: Dow Celebrates Relationship with China," Liveris was quoted emphasizing the beneficial business relationship that the exchange would foster: "Building a strong relationship with China is a top priority for Dow, and the benefits of this relationship can't be measured. … That relationship is built as we share our strengths with each other. *This kind of cultural exchange, based on trust and goodwill, lays the groundwork for a valuable, long-term relationship*" (Dow 2008c, emphasis added). The former article pointed to the benefits to the public good that economics could bring to culture, while the latter article outlined the other side of the coin—how cultural exchange benefits business. While both Li Jinzhu and Andrew Liveris described the cultural exchange as bringing together the U.S. and China, just as Li's speech used that broader context to promote Yulin's direct relationship with the American business community, the subtitle of Dow's corporate newsletter article—"Dow Celebrates Relationship with China"—rhetorically placed the multinational corporation in direct connection with the People's Republic of China. This was different from its more "public" role as a facilitator of cultural exchange between the two countries, as evidenced by the subtitle of the PR article—"Dow Contributes to Cultural Exchange Between U.S. and China."

The Dow corporate newsletter article also included a photo of Li Jinzhu and a former Dow executive vice president shaking hands, with a terracotta warrior standing between them in the background (FIGURE 3). During Li's speech, he presented the Midland Center for the Arts with two full-size terracotta warrior replicas to "serve as a reminder of the unique cultural exchange that enriched Midland

FIGURE 3. "Far East Meets West: Dow Celebrates Relationship with China," p. 6 (courtesy of The Dow Chemical Company).

in 2008" (DOW 2008c). I would suggest that this highly stylized photo could be read in several ways.

To begin with, the handshake, while broadly signaling the beginning of a beneficial relationship between localities, corporations, and nations, could also be read as a symbol of specific relational aspirations between any of the players involved—Yulin and the American business community, Dow and China, Shenhua and Dow, and/or Yulin and Midland. At the same time, regardless of one's particular reading of the handshake, we have the lone terracotta warrior standing behind, looking on in approval—culture as a bridge. The Dow newsletter article concluded by discussing the next step in the budding relationship between Dow and Yulin: "The end of the Chinese festival actually marks the beginning of another cultural exchange. Party Secretary Li invited Dow to Shaanxi Province in 2009, to share U.S. culture with our Asian counterparts. It is too soon to say what that effort will be, but employees can be sure it will represent the company and the United States in true Dow fashion" (DOW 2008c).

Eventually, Dow decided to share U.S. culture with their Chinese counterparts by sponsoring the 2009 Asia Tour of the National Symphony Orchestra (NSO) of The John F. Kennedy Center for the Performing Arts, based in Washington, D.C. (KENNEDY CENTER 2012b). While funded by Dow partly in reciprocation for Yulin and Shaanxi's Midland performance and exhibit, the NSO tour was imbued with multiple levels of meaning as it gave concerts in Beijing, Xi'an, Shanghai, Macau, and South Korea (KENNEDY CENTER 2012b). While the 2008 Midland event had been *rhetorically* placed within the context of Sino-U.S. relations, the NSO's 2009 Asia Tour was given a more prominent *official* dimension—it was formally invited by the Ministry of Culture of the People's Republic of China to celebrate the thirtieth anniversary of the establishment of diplomatic relations between the P.R.C.

and the U.S. and "to further Sino-U.S. diplomatic relations" (KENNEDY CENTER 2009). The Asia Tour also marked the ten-year anniversary of the NSO's first tour to China in 1999, when Jiang Zemin had invited it after hearing the NSO perform during his visit to Washington, D.C., in 1997 (KENNEDY CENTER 2009). The NSO has a strong history of being associated with U.S. national affairs, including presidential inaugurations and diplomatic goodwill missions, and its Asia Tour was treated as a significant event by both China and the U.S. (KENNEDY CENTER 2009). The presidents of both nations sent congratulatory messages, with Hu Jintao pointing to music's ability to "promote communication between people's hearts of different countries" and to "enhance the mutual understanding between the two peoples," and Barack Obama describing music as "a common language of the world that builds up intercultural bridges, pushes forward relations among peoples and nations, strengthens our understanding of history and tradition, and enriches our lives and communities" (CHINA EMBASSY 2009).

Andrew Liveris, in speaking of the tour, pointed to Dow's important role in the relations between the two countries, saying, "This year not only marks the historic anniversary of engaged and positive Sino-U.S. relations, but also the 30th anniversary of Dow's operations in Mainland China. As a global company and as a long-standing member of the Chinese business community, Dow is pleased to be a supporter of this tour to showcase the strong cultural ties and increased understanding between China and the United States" (DOW 2009). While Shaanxi, Yulin, Shenhua, and the joint venture were not explicitly mentioned, the tour's destination cities included the capital of Shaanxi province, Xi'an. An article posted on a Shaanxi news site highlighted the business overtones of the NSO's Xi'an performance on 14 June 2009, citing numerous Shaanxi provincial officials who attended the performance and noting that earlier in the day, a member of the Provincial Party Standing Committee met with a delegation of Dow executives for its Asia Pacific, Middle East, and Africa regions, where the Shenhua-Dow Coal-to-Chemicals Project was described as a signature project for Shaanxi's energy and chemical engineering base, with all of the preparatory work moving along at a rapid pace (ZHANG 2009).[16]

Though Dow's sponsorship of the NSO's 2009 Asia Tour appears to have been inspired by Li Jinzhu's request for Dow to reciprocate for the Midland performance by sharing U.S. culture with Shaanxi Province, the official rhetoric surrounding the tour focused attention mainly on the music of the NSO and its ability to serve as a bridge between nations. Even the article from the Shaanxi news site discussed earlier focused primarily on the Xi'an concert, while relating the business dealings to the artistic event. It is interesting to note that the NSO has a history of performances used to facilitate relations: its first international tour in 1959 to "19 Latin and South American countries" was "undertaken as part of President Eisenhower's Program for Cultural Presentations, a project of the U.S. State Department, for the purpose of building goodwill throughout the region" (KENNEDY CENTER 2012a). The foregrounding of cultural events as a means of shifting public attention amid negotiations has been referred to in Chinese as the "artifying of politics" (*zhengzhi yishuhua* 政治艺术化), a term that Jing Li suggests "brings 'art' to the foreground on stage and endows 'art' with a seemingly apolitical position that officials hope will ease the crossing of boundaries and be identified with by all" (LI 2013, 88–89).[17] A similar idea is found in Danielle Fosler-Lussier's discussion of U.S. State Department-funded cultural exchanges involving musicians, where she cites a musician-turned-diplomat who suggests that the goals of such exchanges are to "create the conditions for understanding" (FOSLER-LUSSIER 2010, 62). One is reminded of Wang Xiangrong's description of the power of northern Shaanxi folk songs to help Yulin "gradually become more familiar and known by people in society." Wang, Li, and Fosler-Lussier all point to culture's ability to bridge gaps. They hint at the liminal space created by cultural exchanges—a liminality that offers the potential for a realignment of relations and public opinion—not unlike the liminality experienced in banquets when participants are able to align and realign their relationships with each other (TURNER 1969; SHEPHERD 2005; SCHECHNER 1988).[18]

RHETORIC PAVES THE WAY

The slogan "culture paves the way" appears to have been a driving factor in Yulin's self-promotion during recent years, with several large-scale events highlighting folk songs and folk singers as key cultural attractions for the region. In 2006, Yulin held an international conference and fieldwork project on northern Shaanxi folk music in conjunction with CHIME, the European Foundation for Chinese Music Research, followed by two televised singing contests (2006 and 2010) in search of the "Ten Greatest Northern Shaanxi Folk Singers" (HE 2006; ZHANG 2010). In 2007, the Second Yulin International Folk Songs Festival showcased northern Shaanxi folk songs as one of three major world song traditions, along with Russian and African American folk songs (CHEN 2007).[19] More recently, in 2009, northern Shaanxi folk songs were declared a national-level item of Intangible Cultural Heritage, and Wang Xiangrong was chosen as one of two national-level "representative transmitters" (*daibiaoxing chuanchengren* 代表性传承人) of the tradition.[20]

As for Dow, since its sponsorship of the NSO's 2009 Asia Tour, it has continued to fund NSO performances amid negotiations with various countries. Apparently pleased with the results that cultural exchange can bring to business, Dow sponsored another NSO tour in 2012 to Mexico, Trinidad and Tobago, Argentina, Uruguay, and Rio de Janeiro (KENNEDY CENTER 2012a). According to Andrew Liveris, "After the resounding success of the Asia Tour, Dow is pleased to continue our partnership with the NSO for the Americas Tour.... It is an honor to collaborate with Whirlpool to bring one of the great national treasures of the United States—the National Symphony Orchestra—to our employees, customers, and other community members throughout this region" (KENNEDY CENTER 2012a).

While it is difficult to gauge whether and to what degree Yulin's cultural exchanges contributed to its economic growth in the years following the Midland and Xi'an performances, by 2012 Yulin had become known as "China's Kuwait" and was "a major energy and chemical industry base with the exploitation of coal, oil and natural gas" (XINHUA 2012). On 24 May 2012, the chairman of the Shenhua Group, Dr. Zhang Xiwu, was appointed chairman of the World Coal Association (WCA)—the first time in almost thirty years that the WCA would be led by a Chinese coal producer (WORLD COAL ASSOCIATION 2012). Later that year, the mayor of Yulin presided over a meeting where it was announced that students "in Yulin ... [would] enjoy totally free education from preschool through high school starting in 2013" (CHINESE BUSINESS VIEW 2012). Though Yulin's economy slowed soon after, its massive growth at the time seemed to play into the narrative that culture paves the way for economics.[21]

During my fieldwork in 2011 and 2012 while Yulin's economy was still going strong, Wang Xiangrong would frequently incorporate the narrative of Yulin's economic rise into his onstage banter and tie that rise to the attraction of local culture. When speaking to his fellow classmates at a 2012 elementary school reunion in his hometown area of Fugu County (located in Yulin), Wang said, "What is greatness? What is uniqueness? The more local something is, the closer it is to the people, the more it belongs to the entire world.... I am a Fugu person. I only want to take my Fugu things and use them so that outsiders can get to know Fugu, to see our northern Shaanxi." Like others in northern Shaanxi, Wang saw the potential for local folk songs to become internationally recognized, bringing additional visibility to the region.[22] As I traveled with Wang from performance to performance, he would often introduce me onstage and have me sing a song or two I had learned from him, suggesting to the crowd that my fascination with these local songs *was compelling evidence for* their attraction to a global audience. Wang's elevation of the local to global status—sometimes speculating that Fugu songs would become "global songs" (*qiuge* 球歌)—paralleled the assertion that culture had paved the way for Yulin's economic rise. After all, it seemed, not only had northern Shaanxi folk songs attracted investments to Yulin—now they were beginning to attract foreign PhD students.

As this article has shown, Yulin's exchange of performances with Dow and Midland and the discourse surrounding that exchange attempted to forge relationships between the local and the global, while at the same time defining the parties involved in relation to one another (MAUSS 1966; YANG 1994; SHEPHERD 2005). The gifts of "Chinese" and "American" culture facilitated by Yulin and Dow provided a symbolic bridge connecting localities, corporations, and peoples. Within this exchange, the liminality of performance offered a space in which feelings, opinions, and representational images could be affected and transformed, and the rhetoric surrounding those performances attempted to seize upon the power of that liminality. When Yulin presented its regional song and dance troupe's Midland performance as representative of "Chineseness," it offered a "rare" and "unique" commodity—traditional "Chinese" culture—in the hopes of establishing and deepening a web of relations, while simultaneously focusing attention on Yulin's unique qualities. As Wang Xiangrong's discussion of repertoire has shown, such representations of "Chineseness" are carefully chosen in consideration of the audience at hand. When the performance is for a *national* audience, songs with nationalistic overtones tied to Chinese history and culture are used that simultaneously elevate northern Shaanxi's place on the national stage. On the other hand, when the goal of the performance is to build rapport with *international* audiences, a "simple" folk duet about love fuses "localness" and "Chineseness" into a rhetorical bridge that connects Yulin to a globalized world—culture paves the way.

NOTES

* A slightly altered version of this article will appear as a chapter in the author's forthcoming book to be published in the University of Hawai'i Press's Music and Performing Arts of Asia and the Pacific series, edited by Frederick Lau. See GIBBS forthcoming.

1. More specifically, its subsidiary, China Shenhua Coal Liquefaction Corporation Limited, also referred to as China Shenhua Coal to Liquid and Chemical Company Limited.

2. The interviews with Wang Xiangrong, the "King of Northern Shaanxi Folk Songs," were conducted during my fieldwork with the singer from 2011 to 2012.

3. For a brief history of the Yulin Folk Arts Troupe, see SHANG (1996); see also JONES (2009).

4. While my research and Wang's comments focus on the role of folk song performance in the Yulin Folk Arts Troupe, the troupe's dance performances deserve to be studied as well.

5. In addition to a bridge, the Chinese scholar also compared Jin Yong's novel "to a traditional matchmaker who arranges a marriage between locals and tourists" (NOTAR 2006, 4).

6. For a description of the growth of professional troupes, focusing especially on ethnic minority groups in China, see MACKERRAS (1984, 212–17). For a more recent study of tourism and musical performing arts in China, see MACKERRAS (2011).

7. Arif Dirlik notes a progression from earlier representations of the local in terms of "its contrast to the national" to later cases where "the local derives its meaning from its juxtaposition to the global" (DIRLIK 1999, 152).

8. This often involves building up such a repertoire from local sources. In Yulin, Wang Xiangrong remembered noting an initial lack of such representative pieces worthy of the big stage when he began working in the Yulin Folk Arts Troupe in the early 1980s, and having to adapt such pieces from local tunes.

9. The *errentai* genre is popular in parts of Yulin Prefecture as well as neighboring Shanxi Province and Inner Mongolia, but not so popular in other parts of northern Shaanxi, such as Yan'an. While described here as local, it is not exclusively local to Wang's home area.

10. For the lyrics and melody to a version of this song sung by Wang Xiangrong and Guo Yunqin 郭云琴, see HUO (2005, 32–33).

11. Andrew Watson, Yang Xueyi, and Jiao Xingguo note, "Shaanxi forms part of the Shanxi—Shaanxi—Inner Mongolia coal field, which holds over 50 percent of China's total coal reserves. The emphasis on the energy sector adopted as part of the revision of national industrial strategy in 1994 was seen as a significant gain for the province, and especially as an avenue of development for the poor north" (WATSON et al. 1999, 80). For background on the history of China's coal industry, see WRIGHT (2012).

12. According to Northwest Airlines's corporate newsletter, "Northwest co-sponsored the festival with key corporate customer Dow Chemical, investing in the communities we jointly serve" (NWA 2008). The newsletter also noted that demonstrating, "Northwest's support of this cultural exhibit, Steve Sear, vice president sales and customer care, attended 'Reflections of the Yellow River,' a program of traditional Chinese performances" (NWA 2008).

13. In Chinese, the characters *feng* 风 ("wind") and *qing* 情 ("feelings/sentiments"), when combined into the word *fengqing* 风情, can mean both "local conditions and customs" and "fine taste" or "refined feelings."

14. OAKES (2000) provides examples from Shanxi, Anhui, and Guizhou.

15. This article was entitled "The Yulin Folk Arts Troupe Attends the 'Chinese Music and Culture Festival' in the U.S.: Li Jinzhu Gives a Speech at the Closing Ceremony" (WANG 2008c). Another article with similar content, attributed to the same editor, and also in *Yulin ribao* (Yulin Daily), was entitled "Northern Shaanxi Culture in America" (WANG 2008b).

16. Early estimates suggested that the coal-chemical complex at Yulin could be operational by 2016, and it eventually achieved this goal, beginning production in December 2015 (ICIS NEWS 2009; SUN 2016).

17. In her article on minority folk song and dance performances from Yunnan Province at the 2007 Smithsonian Folklife Festival in Washington D.C., Jing LI (2013) notes that she heard the term "artifying of politics" (*zhengzhi yishuhua*) used by a cultural official from the Yunnan delegation.

18. While TURNER (1969) is discussing the liminal aspects of rites of passage and how they allow individuals to move from one social category to another (thus realigning their relationships with other people), I am suggesting that the liminal space of these cultural performances allows audiences to realign their impressions of and perceived relationships with the cultures represented onstage.

19. The "African American folk songs" section was represented by the American blues and R&B singer Bobby Rush.

20. The other "representative transmitter" for northern Shaanxi folk songs was He Yutang 贺玉堂 (1949–2013), who appeared in CHEN Kaige's film, *Yellow Earth* (1984). For an excellent description of China's efforts to preserve Intangible Cultural Heritage (ICH), see REES (2012).

21. Reports suggest that a slowing down of the coal industry that began in late 2012 contributed to a decline in Yulin's overall economy in recent years (LIU 2015; WONG 2016). Dow reportedly withdrew from the joint venture in 2013, although Shenhua and the local government decided to proceed with the coal-chemical project (ICIS NEWS 2014; XINHUA FINANCE AGENCY 2015). The Yulin plant began producing "coal-based low-density polyethylene" in December 2015, churning out an estimated 220,000 metric tons in 2016 (CCFGROUP 2016; SUN 2016).

22. Two academic conferences were held in 2009 and 2011 concerning the translation of northern Shaanxi folk song lyrics into languages including English, French, Arabic, Korean, German, and Italian (ZHONGGONG SHAANXI SHENGWEI XUANCHUANBU 2009).

REFERENCES

CCFGROUP
2016   Shenhua Yulin, first coal-to LDPE maker, gains its talk in PE market. 19 January. http://www.ccfgroup.com/newscenter/newsview.php?Class_ID=D00000&Info_ID=20160119099 (accessed 3 January 2017).

CHEN Kaige 陳凱歌, dir.
1984   *Huang tudi* 黄土地 (*Yellow Earth*). Guangxi Film Studio.

CHEN, Lin
2007   East and West to sing in Shaanxi. 15 August. http://www.china.org.cn/english/culture/221020.htm# (accessed 9 August 2014).

CHINA EMBASSY (EMBASSY OF THE PEOPLE'S REPUBLIC OF CHINA IN THE UNITED STATES OF AMERICA)
2009   President Hu Jintao and President Barack Obama send congratulatory messages to the United States National Symphony Orchestra (NSO) (06/12/09). 16 June 2009. http://www.china-embassy.org/eng/zmgx/t567959.htm (accessed 6 January 2013).

CHINESE BUSINESS VIEW
  2012   Local governments offer free education. *Global Times*, 23 December. http://www.globaltimes.cn/content/751746.shtml (accessed 4 January 2013).

DIRLIK, Arif
  1999   Place-based imagination: Globalism and the politics of place. *Review* (Fernand Braudel Center) 22: 151–87.

DOW (THE DOW CHEMICAL COMPANY)
  2008a   Terracotta warriors to spend Chinese New Year in the U.S.: Dow contributes to cultural exchange between U.S. and China. 30 January. http://www.dow.com/news/corporate/2008/20080130a.htm (accessed 14 September 2012).
  2008b   Event calendar. http://www.dow.com/greaterchina/en/events/calendar.htm (accessed 18 December 2012).
  2008c   Far East meets West: Dow celebrates relationship with China. *Around Dow* (June): 6–7. http://msdssearch.dow.com/PublishedLiteratureDOWCOM/dh_0132/0901b80380132224.pdf?filepath=news/pdfs/noreg/162-02418.pdf&fromPage=GetDoc (accessed 18 December 2012).
  2009   National Symphony Orchestra tour to celebrate 30th anniversary of U.S.-China friendship. 10 June. http://www.dow.com/greaterchina/en/news/2009/20090610a.htm (accessed 4 January 2013).

FOSLER-LUSSIER, Danielle
  2010   Cultural diplomacy as cultural globalization: The University of Michigan Jazz Band in Latin America. *Journal of the Society for American Music* 4: 59–93.

GIBBS, Levi S.
  Forthcoming *Song King: Connecting People, Places, and Past in Contemporary China*. Honolulu: University of Hawai'i Press.

GOODMAN, David S. G.
  1994   The politics of regionalism: Economic development, conflict and negotiation. In *China Deconstructs: Politics, Trade and Regionalism*, David S. G. Goodman and Gerald Segal, eds., 1–20. London and New York: Routledge.
  2002   Structuring local identity: Nation, province and county in Shanxi during the 1990s. *The China Quarterly* 172: 837–62.

HE Feng 何凤
  2006   Shaanbei minge dasai zongjuesai jiang tuichu "shi da Shaanbei mingeshou" 陕北民歌大赛总决赛将推出"十大陕北民歌手" [Northern Shaanxi folk song contest finals will present the public with the "ten greatest northern Shaanxi folk singers"]. 17 April. http://www.cnr.cn/2004news/whyl/200604/t20060417_504195235.html (accessed 9 August 2014).

HUO Xianggui 霍向贵, ed.
  2005   *Shaanbei minge jingxuan* 陕北民歌精选 [A choice selection of northern Shaanxi folk songs]. Xi'an: Shaanxi Lüyou Chubanshe.

ICIS NEWS
  2009   Shenhua and Dow to invest $10bn in Yulin chemicals complex. 6 November. http://www.icis.com/Articles/2009/11/06/9261371/shenhua-and-dow-to-invest-10bn-in-yulin-chemicals-complex.html (accessed 7 January 2013).

2014   China Shenhua, Dow Chemical scrap Yulin coal-chemical project. 14 May. http://www.icis.com/resources/news/2014/05/14/9780947/china-shenhua-dow-chemical-scrap-yulin-coal-chemical-project/ (accessed 3 January 2017).

JONES, Stephen
2009   *Ritual and Music of North China, Vol. 2: Shaanbei*. Farnham, Surrey, England, and Burlington, VT: Ashgate.

KENNEDY CENTER (THE JOHN F. KENNEDY CENTER FOR THE PERFORMING ARTS)
2009   National Symphony Orchestra, Iván Fischer, principal conductor, to tour China and Republic of Korea, June 2009. Press Release, 11 March. http://www.kennedy-center.org/nso/pdf/090311_nso_china_pressrelease.pdf (accessed 4 January 2013).
2012a   Americas tour – National Symphony Orchestra – The John F. Kennedy Center for the Performing Arts. http://www.kennedy-center.org/nso/americastour/ (accessed 4 January 2013).
2012b   Donors make a difference: The support of donors like The Dow Chemical Company and Whirlpool Corporation has enabled the NSO to continue its proud tradition of international touring. http://www.kennedy-center.org/support/corporate/spotlight.pdf (accessed 4 January 2013).

LAU, Frederick
2008   *Music in China: Experiencing Music, Expressing Culture*. New York and Oxford: Oxford University Press.

LI, Jing
2013   The making of ethnic Yunnan on the National Mall: Minority folk song and dance performances, provincial identity, and "the artifying of politics" (*zhengzhi yishuhua*). *Modern China* 39: 69–100.

LIU, Coco
2015   What happens in a coal boomtown as China heads toward 'peak coal'? www.eenews.net, 18 March. http://www.eenews.net/stories/1060015235 (accessed 3 January 2017).

MACKERRAS, Colin
1984   Folk songs and dances of China's minority nationalities: Policy, tradition, and professionalization. *Modern China* 10: 187–226.
2011   Tourism and musical performing arts in China in the first decade of the twenty-first century: A personal view. *CHINOPERL Papers* 30: 153–80.

MAUSS, Marcel
1966   *The Gift: Forms and Functions of Exchange in Archaic Societies*. London: Cohen & West Ltd.

MCFTA (MIDLAND CENTER FOR THE ARTS)
2008a   Celebrate China: Reflections of the Yellow River. http://www.mcfta.org/A_ABDow/ChinaSpecialEvents.htm#Dancers (accessed 18 December 2012).
2008b   Timeless warriors and relics: 1500 years of ancient China. http://www.mcfta.org/A_ABDow/ChinaHome.html (accessed 15 December 2012).

NOTAR, Beth E.
2006   *Displacing Desire: Travel and Popular Culture in China*. Honolulu: University of Hawai'i Press.

NWA (NORTHWEST AIRLINES CORP.)

2008 Northwest sponsors "A Celebration of China" cultural festival. April. http://www.nwa.com/asia/en/newsletter/apr08_2.html (accessed 18 December 2012).

OAKES, Tim

1999 Selling Guizhou: Cultural development in an era of marketisation. In *The Political Economy of China's Provinces*, Hans Hendrischke and Feng Chongyi, eds., 31–67. London and New York: Routledge.

2000 China's provincial identities: Reviving regionalism and reinventing "Chineseness." *The Journal of Asian Studies* 59: 667–92.

RAMESH, Deepti

2013 Olefin production boosts demand for coal-based methanol in China. www.chemweek.com, 6 September. http://www.chemweek.com/lab/Olefin-production-boosts-demand-for-coal-based-methanol-in-China_54949.html (accessed 9 August 2014).

REES, Helen

2012 Intangible cultural heritage in China today: Policy and practice in the early twenty-first century. In *Music as Intangible Cultural Heritage: Policy, Ideology, and Practice in the Preservation of East Asian Traditions*, ed. Keith Howard, 23–54. Burlington, VT: Ashgate.

SCHECHNER, Richard

1988 *Performance Theory*. Revised and expanded edition. New York and London: Routledge.

SHANG Airen 尚爱仁

1996 Yulin minjian yishutuan de dansheng: Cong gai tuan fu ou yanchu qude jida chenggong tanqi 榆林民间艺术团的诞生—从该团赴欧演出取得极大成功谈起 [The birth of the Yulin Folk Arts Troupe: A discussion beginning with its immensely successful European tour]. In *Shang Airen zuopin xuan* 尚爱仁作品选 [Selections of Shang Airen's works], 244–48. Xi'an: Xi'an Yinyue Xueyuan Yinshuachang.

SHEPHERD, Eric T.

2005 *Eat Shandong: From Personal Experience to a Pedagogy of a Second Culture*. Columbus, OH: The Ohio State University National East Asian Languages Resource Center.

STOKES, Martin

1994 Place, exchange and meaning: Black Sea musicians in the west of Ireland. In *Ethnicity, Identity and Music: The Musical Construction of Place*, ed. Martin Stokes, 97–115. Oxford and Providence, RI: Berg.

SUN, Nina Ying

2016 China to add 1.3 million metric tons of PE capacity in 2017. 13 December. http://www.plasticsnews.com/article/20161213/NEWS/161219958/china-to-add-1-3-million-metric-tons-of-pe-capacity-in-2017 (accessed 3 January 2017).

TURNER, Victor

1969 *The Ritual Process: Structure and Anti-Structure*. Chicago: Aldine Publishing Company.

WANG Xuqin 王旭芹

2008a Li Jinzhu shuai woshi youhao daibiaotuan yingyao fangwen Meiguo: Woshi yu Meiguo Beidun shi jiewei youhao chengshi 李金柱率我市友好代表团应邀访问美国—我市与美国贝敦市结为友好城市 [Li Jinzhu leads Yulin goodwill mission to accept invitation and visit America: Yulin and America's Baytown become sister cities]. *Yulin ribao*, 28 March. http://news.xyl.gov.cn /content/ylrb-wz/2008-3/28/20080328063819743.html (accessed 6 January 2013).

2008b Shaanbei wenhua zai Meiguo 陕北文化在美国 [Northern Shaanxi culture in America]. *Yulin ribao*, 10 April. http://news.xyl.gov.cn/content /photonews/2008-4/10/20080410094020306.html (accessed 6 January 2013).

2008c Yulin minjian yishutuan zai Mei canjia "Zhongguo yinyue wenhua jie": Li Jinzhu zai bimushi shang zhici 榆林民间艺术团在美参加"中国音乐文化节"—李金柱在闭幕式上致辞 [The Yulin Folk Arts Troupe attends the "Chinese Music and Culture Festival" in the U.S.: Li Jinzhu gives a speech at the closing ceremony]. *Yulin ribao*, 1 April. http://news.xyl.gov.cn/content /ylrb-wz/2008-4/1/200804010548087o.html (accessed 14 December 2012).

WATSON, Andrew, YANG Xueyi, and JIAO Xingguo

1999 Shaanxi: The search for comparative advantage. In *The Political Economy of China's Provinces*, Hans Hendrischke and Feng Chongyi, eds., 73–107. London and New York: Routledge.

WONG, Sue-Lin

2016 Former China boom town learns hard lessons about service economy. 22 August. http://www.reuters.com/article/us-china-economy -yulin-idUSKCN10W0ZZ (accessed 3 January 2017).

WORLD COAL ASSOCIATION

2012 World Coal Association elects new chairman. 25 May. http://www .worldcoal.org/extract/world-coal-association-elects-new-chairman-920/ (accessed 1 August 2014).

WRIGHT, Tim

2012 *The Political Economy of the Chinese Coal Industry: Black Gold and Blood-Stained Coal*. London and New York: Routledge.

XINHUA (Xinhua News Agency)

2012 "Kuwait" on northwest China's loess plateau. *Global Times*, 4 November. http://www.globaltimes.cn/content/742140.shtml (accessed 25 April 2015).

XINHUA FINANCE AGENCY

2015 Shenhua Yulin coal-chemical project moves forward. 4 March. http:// en.xfafinance.com/html/Industries/Energy/2015/60696.shtml (accessed 3 January 2017).

YANG, Mayfair

1994 *Gifts, Favors, and Banquets: The Art of Social Relationships in China*. Ithaca, NY: Cornell University Press.

ZHANG Xijian 张曦健

2010   Di er jie Shaanbei minge dasai choubei gongzuo yi kaishi 第二届陕北民歌大赛筹备工作已开始 [Preparations for the second northern Shaanxi folk song contest have begun]. 5 May. http://shaanxi.cctv.com/20100505/102773.shtml (accessed 9 August 2014).

ZHANG Xin 张鑫

2009   Meiguo guojia jiaoxiangyuetuan zai Xi'an renmin dasha jinxing fang Hua yanchu 美国国家交响乐团在西安人民大厦进行访华演出 [American National Symphony Orchestra performs at the People's Mansion in Xi'an during its visit to China]. 15 June. http://news.cnwest.com/content/2009-06/15/content_2142320.htm (accessed 6 January 2013).

ZHONGGONG SHAANXI SHENGWEI XUANCHUANBU 中共陕西省委宣传部 [Propaganda Department of the Chinese Communist Party Shaanxi Provincial Party Committee]

2009   *Shoujie shaanbei min'ge yijie quanguo xueshu yantaohui* 首届陕北民歌译介全国学术研讨会 [Inaugural national academic symposium on the translation and introduction of northern Shaanxi folk songs]. Xi'an: Xi'an Conservatory of Music.

Catherine Ingram
University of Sydney

Jiaping Wu
University of Central Queensland

Research, Cultural Heritage, and Ethnic Identity

Evaluating the Influence of Kam Big Song Research of the 1950s

Research into the songs of the Kam (in Chinese, Dong) minority people in southwestern China began in the early 1950s, bringing about the so-called "discovery" of an important group of Kam choral songs that became known in Chinese as *dage* (big song). Research into big song radically altered academic views of Chinese music, brought about the creation of a new song genre, and had a major influence on the knowledge and promotion of big song outside Kam areas. Research in the 1950s and since has also both directly and indirectly influenced big song singing within Kam communities, and is thus critical to understanding contemporary cultural performance and its implications. Through focusing on 1950s research into Kam big song, this article explores the effects of musical research and demonstrates how deeply those effects can be interconnected with issues of cultural heritage and ethnic identity.

KEYWORDS: Kam (Dong) minority—China—big song—heritage—research—Guizhou

Asian Ethnology Volume 76, Number 1 · 2017, 65–93
© Nanzan University Anthropological Institute

CHINA IS usually described as a multiethnic nation composed of fifty-five officially recognized minority groups in addition to the majority Han.* Despite
several non-Han groups having held control of the region, the ancestors of China's many non-Han peoples were previously referred to using Chinese words for
"barbarians" such as *Miao* 苗, *Man* 蛮, or *Yi* 夷. While the overt Han chauvinism
(*da Han zhuyi* 大汉主义) or ethnocentrism that was rife even into twentieth-century
China (LEIBOLD 2014, 6, 9) may not continue today, non-Han groups are still widely
considered to be culturally and economically inferior to the Han Chinese and in need
of assistance with modernization to "catch up" with the Han Chinese population
(GLADNEY 1994; MACKERRAS 2003). Such modernization is conventionally undertaken through diffusing Han culture and education to ethnic minority regions, and
by subjecting ethnic minority cultures to so-called "development" (see, for example, INGRAM et al. 2011). Thus, over the last century, China's non-Han cultures have
moved from being seen by the (largely Han) mainstream as being at the margins of
Chinese civilization to gradually becoming recognized within "Chinese culture"
(LEIBOLD 2014, 2; BARANOVITCH 2010, 89), adding a further layer to the country's historically complex relationship between cultural heritage and ethnic identity.

The new, modern recognition of minority ethnicity and culture is reflected in
the identification and utilization of Kam big song from the 1950s onwards. "Big
song" is the usual English name for a genre of choral songs originating within
certain Kam (in Chinese, Dong 侗) minority communities in southwestern China.
The songs are also known by the Chinese name *dage* 大歌 (from which the English
translation derives), and were inscribed on UNESCO's Representative List of the
Intangible Cultural Heritage of Humanity in 2009 (see *Grand Song* 2009).[1]
As detailed below, their so-called "discovery" has been described as a result of
research by Han Chinese researchers in the early 1950s, and was used as the first
evidence demonstrating that the nation's music was not solely monophonic.[2] The
documentation of big song was central in altering views of Chinese music in the
eyes of the many Europeans who once considered polyphonic or homophonic
music to be more advanced than monophony, and thus previously considered Chinese music as inferior to Western music.

The utilization of Kam big song to fill what was then perceived by some as a
deficiency within Chinese culture also demonstrated the altered status of minority
culture, and was an ironic contrast to centuries of prejudice against non-Han

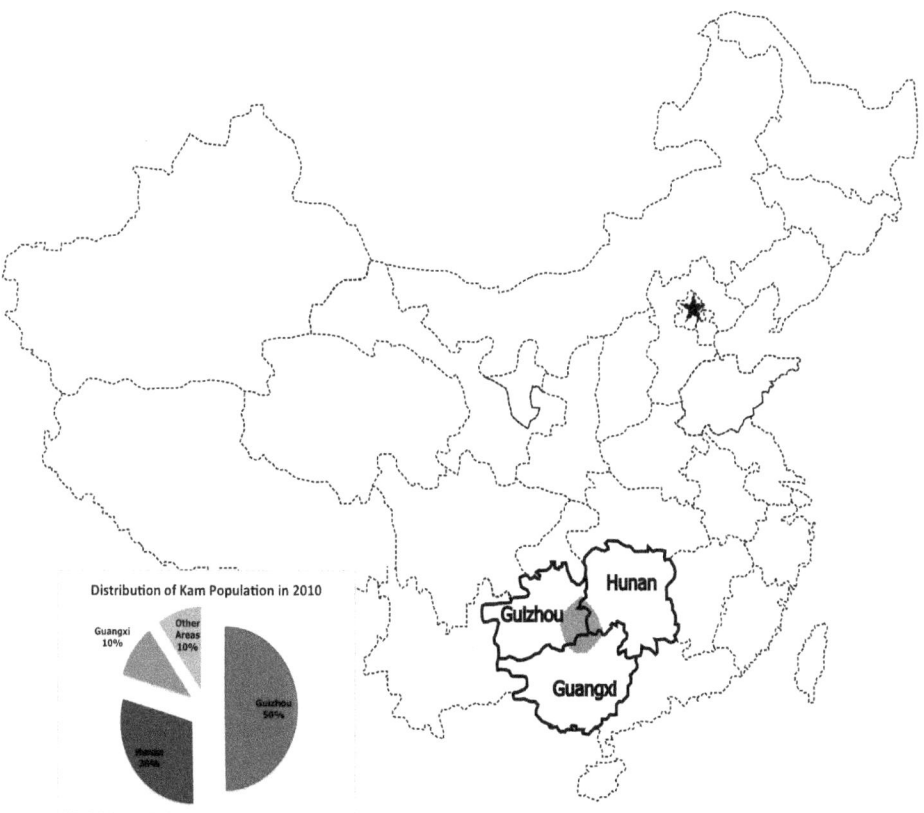

FIGURE I. Center: Map of China showing Guizhou Province, Hunan Province, and Guangxi Zhuang Autonomous Region—the three regions where most Kam people reside. The area shaded in grey indicates the precise location of Kam villages. Inset: Diagram showing the approximate distribution of the Kam population in 2010 (based upon data from GUOWUYUAN RENKOU 2012).

cultures and peoples. Research into Kam singing in the 1950s brought about the creation of a new song genre (that is, big song), and had a major influence on knowledge and promotion of big song outside Kam areas. Research undertaken and published during and following the 1950s has directly and indirectly influenced contemporary big song singing within Kam communities.

This article evaluates the influence—both within and beyond—Kam communities of the initial research into Kam big song that occurred in the 1950s, and explores how its impact is intertwined with issues concerning cultural heritage and ethnic identity. Through the case of big song we demonstrate the importance of considering the influence of previous research upon contemporary musical transmission and the performance of cultural traditions, while also foregrounding the ways that non-Han cultures are recognized and accepted to make the unified—and essentially Han-dominated—multinational state of China. Our analysis draws upon diverse disciplinary expertise and research experience. Catherine Ingram, an Australian-born ethnomusicologist based until recently in the United Kingdom,[3] has conducted more than twenty-six months of participatory ethnographic fieldwork in rural Kam areas since 2004 and draws upon various experiences of learning, rehearsing, performing, and discussing Kam music together with Kam villagers. Jiaping Wu, a Chinese-born human geographer now based in Australia, has conducted extensive research into the development of China—including the social and economic development of ethnic minority regions—and also draws upon his experience as a Kam person raised in a remote Kam village. This study thus combines multiple perspectives on the meanings of big song culture and its transmission and transformation.

KAM PEOPLE AND CULTURE

Kam people are mainly resident in eastern Guizhou, especially the southeastern part of Qiandongnan 黔东南 (or southeastern Guizhou, a joint Kam/Dong and Hmong/Miao autonomous prefecture) and the adjoining border regions of Hunan Province and Guangxi Zhuang Autonomous Region, as indicated in FIG-URE 1. According to the latest census, the Kam population was 2.88 million in 2010, accounting for 0.22% of China's total population (GUOWUYUAN RENKOU 2012). Approximately half the Kam population was distributed in Guizhou (49.7%), with the remainder in Hunan (29.7%), Guangxi (10.6%), and various other areas (10%). The first language for many of these people continues to be Kam—a tonal, Tai-Kadai family language with no widely used written form. Whether the Kam are native or migrant to their current region of residence is not clear. Analyses of Kam oral history and myths suggest that some of the ancestors of today's Kam people comprised a branch of the ancient Baiyue 百越 (Hundred Yue) people who long ago followed the rivers of the Duliu river system to reside in the area (see ZHANG 1993; 1994; SHI 1984). Large-scale migrations of Chinese from the east into today's Kam regions during the Ming and Qing periods are also documented (HERMAN 2007; GONG 1992, 907–30), and included the migration of ancestors of at least some of the people who now identify as Kam. Kam historical co-occupancy of the regions together with other ethnic minority groups also contributed to making the area culturally diverse.

Until recently Kam people relied primarily on farming, especially the farming of varieties of glutinous rice. They lived within a subsistence economy that integrated glutinous rice growing with hunting and fishing. Although rice farming remains a predominant economic activity (albeit with changes in the rice varieties grown), its importance as an income source has reduced. This has pushed many Kam people—particularly young people—to seek employment in cities. Income remittances from off-farm migrants have now become an important livelihood source for rural Kam villagers.

The migration of young people away from Kam villages for work, and sometimes also for study, has led to radical alterations in both Kam village society and the transmission of big song. Moreover, many of the migrants settle outside Kam areas: in the 2010 census, the proportion of Kam people resident in relatively developed areas on the eastern seaboard (including the provinces of Zhejiang, Guangdong, Fujian, and Jiangsu and Shanghai City) consisted of 7.2% of the total Kam population (GUOWUYUAN RENKOU 2012).

The villages in the rural regions where most Kam people live range in size from a few houses to a thousand households. The predominantly single ethnic group villages of the area are gradually increasing in ethnic diversity as more and more young Kam people travel away from their villages and marry others from an increasingly broad range of backgrounds. While previous generations of Kam established systems of local governance in later imperial periods, formal structures resembling independent nations were never developed. The tradition of Kam governance was characterized by a structure of Kam multi-village associations known in Kam and Chinese as *kuan* 款 (DENG and WU 1995; DENG 2001). The singing of songs from a range of Kam song genres—including big song, *ga sak-kun*[4] (road-blocking songs), and *ga yeh* (*yeh* circle songs)—was an integral part of the social interactions underpinning these associations, and assisted in the diffusion of Kam songs. The use of place names and the names of specific villages, regions, or multi-village associations in the names of different categories of Kam songs within these and other genres further indicates the importance of regional interrelations (see WU and ZHANG 1991; INGRAM forthcoming).

Contemporary forms of distinctive Kam cultural and spiritual/religious traditions continue to be practiced in some rural Kam areas, and many of these traditions involve singing. For example, different genres of songs are used for greeting and saying farewell to visitors, entertaining important guests during a meal, celebrating the birth of a child, building a new house, weddings and engagements, and major communal village rituals. Today, the most well known of the many Kam song genres is big song. For generations, these songs have been sung in Kam villages within one small Kam region at New Year, when they are performed in the distinctive pagoda-shaped building known as the *dare low*.[5] In this village context for big song singing, a group of male singers and a group of female singers sit opposite each other around the fire and take turns to sing big songs. The two different vocal lines of each song are sung at the same time, with each member of a singing group assigned to sing one of the lines. Since the Kam language has no widely used written form, the survival of these songs is essential for the continued transmission of much of Kam history, social structures, philosophy, and environmental knowledge (see MCLAREN et al. 2013, 59–76).

RESEARCH INTO KAM BIG SONG PRIOR TO THE 1950S

As was also the case for many other tribal peoples in southwest China, Kam people did not have an official name in Chinese history and were mentioned in various imperial records under a range of different names.[6] Partly as a consequence of this situation, there are no descriptions of Kam singing prior to the 1950s that can be directly linked to current Kam musical practices, and the origin of big song is unknown. The most widely cited historical record describing the music of residents of today's Kam areas (and which mainly describes Kam areas of Guangxi) appears in the late Ming *Chiya* 赤雅 [A Dictionary About the South] (1635) by Kuang Lu 邝露 (1604–1650):

> They do not like to kill, and are very good at music. They play the fiddle and the bamboo mouth organ. They sing long songs with their eyes closed, and bend up and down and kick their feet to perform a simple-minded dance.
>
> (KUANG 1995, 46)

Although it is sometimes suggested that Kuang's statement "long songs with their eyes closed" is an early description of big-song singing, his description of the singing is hardly one that could pertain only to big song. Moreover, it is not even clear that Kuang visited today's big-song-singing areas.

The few firsthand records of Kam areas dating from the 1940s include those produced by Inez de Beauclair. De Beauclair briefly visited many Kam big-song-singing areas in 1947, and makes mention of the *dare low* where big songs are usually sung. In one instance she draws upon her own visit and also research by CHEN Guojun (1973) to describe the *dare low* and to mention that singing took place within it, but she does not elaborate on the type of singing performed:

> A remarkable feature of the Tung-chia's [*Dongjia* 侗家, or Kam] culture is their drum tower [in Kam, *dare low*], which serves as a communal house.... In their own language the Tung-chia call the drum tower *ta lei*. Each village has to erect at least one tower on an open space within or close to the settlement.... When not accidentally destroyed by fire, the drum towers may reach a considerable age and finally collapse, as it is forbidden to tear them down. We saw such tumbled-down structures, which perhaps dated from the foundation of the village, and had been replaced by new ones.... Though the Tung-chia speak of the drum tower as an ancient institution, there is little mention of it in the records[7] ... Though the women are admitted for the joint singing, the drum tower is predominantly a men's house.   (DE BEAUCLAIR 1986, 315–17)

RESEARCH INTO KAM BIG SONG DURING THE 1950S

Research into Kam big song during the 1950s needs to be understood in its historical perspective and in the context of ethnic research agendas of the period. The People's Republic of China (PRC) had been founded in 1949, and the 1950s were focused on recuperation after decades of war. The new socialist state actively carried out land reform and other key policies, and it was a time of idealism and utopian visions.

During the 1950s, large-scale ethnic categorization was also formally established. As Thomas Mullaney persuasively argues, while "Chinese ethnologists and linguists working in the 1930s and 1940s had already committed themselves to the formation and stabilization of a highly synthetic view of non-Han peoples in China's southwest" (MULLANEY 2010, 333), the ethnic categorizations that they developed were for research rather than governance purposes. Only once groups were identified through China's ethnic classification (*minzu shibie* 民族识别) project that began in the early 1950s were these contested categorizations developed for adoption within state governance programs. Through this project, Kam people were officially recognized by the state as an ethnic group—"Dong."

In the 1950s, shortly after the establishment of the PRC, researchers and Communist Party cadres were formed into investigative groups known as "centrally-authorized ethnic visiting teams" (*Zhongyang minzu fangwen tuan* 中央民族访问团) and were sent to ethnic minority areas to commence the lengthy process of minority identification and classification. The group that visited Guizhou was led by well-known ethnographer Fei Xiaotong. Besides the group being charged with publicizing ethnic policies, they were also engaged in social and economic investigation of the areas (FEI 1951; FAN 2010). For example, they helped to unify different groups under the name Miao, and the first Miao autonomous region (the Kaili Miao Autonomous Region (*Kaili Miaozu zizhi qu* 凯里苗族自治区) was established in Qiandongnan in 1951 under their direction (GUIZHOU SHENG DIFANG-ZHI 2002, 6). However, during this period the team did not visit the Kam regions of Qiandongnan or study the Kam (LU 2011).

Similar work was conducted in Kam areas in neighboring Guangxi (QIN 2008): a multiethnic minority autonomous region (for Zhuang, Yao, and Miao as well as Kam) was established in 1951 (the Longsheng Multiethnic Autonomous Region [*Longsheng gezu zizhi qu* 龙胜各族联合自治区]) and a Kam autonomous region (the Sanjiang Kam Autonomous Region [*Sanjiang Dongzu zizhi qu* 三江侗族自治区]) was founded in 1952 (*Sanjiang Dongzu zizhixian* 2004). These two developments were made quickly in order to establish political control of these areas, particularly through the establishment of local government, the undertaking of land reform, and the elimination of bandits.

Until the first census, in 1953, ethnic identities were based largely upon people's self-claims. Following the 1953 census the techniques of ethnic observation in China were amended, with greater state intervention regarding ethnic classification leading to the national and large-scale project "Investigation of the society and history of ethnic minorities" (*Shaoshu minzu shehui lishi diaocha* 少数民族社会历史调查) that was undertaken in various locations across the country between 1954 and 1964.[8] In Kam big-song-singing areas this minority field research project was conducted in the Sheeam (Ch. Sanlong 三龙) region during October 1958 and June 1959. The resultant publication, a twenty-eight-page booklet titled "Research Materials on the Society and Economy of Sanlong Township, Liping County, Guizhou Province" (*Guizhou sheng Liping xian Sanlong xiang Dongzu shehui jingji diaocha ziliao* 贵州省黎平县三龙乡侗族社会经济调查资料), appeared in 1963 (ZHONGGUO KEXUEYUAN 1963). Although the research and publication did not focus on Kam music, the project provides a valuable firsthand description of the history, customs, economics, and daily lives of villagers in the region.

The first published account of big song singing appears in a discussion of Kam folk music in the 1953 article "A Basic Introduction to Kam Folk Music" (*Dong-jia minjian yinyue de jiandan jieshao* 侗家民间音乐的简单介绍) (XUE 1953), published in the leading Chinese music journal *People's Music* (*Renmin yinyue* 人民音乐) under the authorship of Xue Liang 薛良—a pseudonym used by Guo Kezou 郭可诹. Guo later stated that during 1950–1951 he spent a year in Kam areas: "During that period I used some of the time to learn Kam folk music" (XUE 1994, 34). Yet Mao Jiale, a researcher who subsequently worked on the first monograph about big song, describes a slightly different beginning to big song research:

[Big song research] originated in 1952 when Xiao Jiaju 萧家驹 (Nianyi 念一) and Guo Kezou 郭可诹 (Xue Liang), musicians with talented insight, went to Liping to take part in Land Reform and discovered the treasure of Kam folk music—multi-part, heterophonic big song.[9] This raised a great degree of attention. After the work of Land Reform was finished, Xiao Jiaju returned to Guiyang and took on the role of director of the Music and Dance Department of the Guizhou Province Literature and Arts Union. He suggested that a group be formed to carry out the *caifeng* [采风, collection] of big song.　　　　(MAO 2003, 33)

Regardless of whether this initial research into big song occurred in 1950–1951 or 1952, it was clearly completed during or before 1952. As the former Chairperson of the Minority Music Association FAN Zuyin writes in his major monograph on multi-part singing in China: "Soon after [the music workers had 'discovered' Kam big song], they took a Kam folk chorus to perform at the First National Folk Arts Meeting held in Beijing in 1952" (1998, 4).

It seems most likely that the "First National Folk Arts Meeting" which Fan states was held in Beijing in 1952, was actually the First National Folk Music and Dance Meeting (*Quanguo diyijie minjian yinyue wudao huiyan* 全国第一届民间音乐舞蹈会演) which, according to PU and ZHANG (2003, 6), was held in Beijing in 1953; perhaps Fan gives the date 1952 because the members of the folk chorus chosen to perform in Beijing would probably have left their villages late that year. The first known staged performances of big song within Kam areas date from even earlier, in 1951, when on at least one occasion big song was used outside the *dare low* in a staged performance to vent grievances about landlords during Land Reform.[10]

Research into Kam singing traditions, including big song, appears to have continued throughout the 1950s and perhaps also into the early 1960s—as indicated through articles published by Zheng Hanfeng (as HAN FENG 1957), FANG Jishen (1959; 1960), HONG Tao (1959), Xiao Jiaju (as NIAN YI 1960), and GU and ZHAO (2003).[11] Some early research also appears to be undocumented: for example, according to Yang Xiao:

From 1953 onwards, music scholars and experts came continuously to Xiao Huang 小黄 [a well-known big-song-singing village in Congjiang County, Guizhou] to do research with differing scope and objectives.… From 1953, Zhao Kuangren of the Central Music Institute came to do *caifeng* in Xiao Huang, and music scholars continued to come　　　　(YANG 2002, 9).

Unfortunately Yang does not list any of Zhao's publications, and none have appeared in our own extensive investigation, so it is difficult to confirm his visit.[12]

The most significant research into Kam big song during this period took place from May to August 1957. During these months, a group of five researchers (including Xiao Jiaju and Mao Jiale) undertook research in Kam big-song-singing areas. Their travels between Kam villages were entirely on foot, since at that time very few of the villages were accessible by road. With only "an accordion, a semi-tone harmonica, and a stopwatch to help them in their work" (MAO 2003, 35) they notated more than 130 big songs and visited eleven Kam villages, eventually producing the seminal monograph *Dongzu dage* 侗族大歌 [Kam Big Song] (GUIZHOU SHENG WENLIAN 1958). According to Mao,

> In April 1957 [permission was received for a group to be formed to carry out the *caifeng* of big song] … and the Music and Dance Department members Xiao Jiaju…, Long Ting'en 龙廷恩 (Beidou 北斗), and Mao Jiale (Jialuo 珈珞), with the addition of Zheng Hanfeng 郑寒风 from the Provincial Song and Dance Troupe and Qian Mingzheng 钱明正 (Qianyi 钱漪) from the Provincial Broadcasting and Television Station, formed a group … with Xiao Jiaju as leader.
>
> (MAO 2003, 33)

Because of its foundation in empirical research, depth of analysis, clarity of expression, and level of detail, the resulting monograph remains one of the most important and useful publications concerning big song. In contrast, only a small portion of the subsequent literature on Kam people is based upon actual research in Kam areas, and even reports based upon fieldwork are rarely founded on lengthy stays in Kam areas such as those of the 1957 team.

CULTURE, ETHNIC IDENTITY, AND THE SIGNIFICANCE OF THE 1950S "DISCOVERY"

Many Chinese written accounts confirm the so-called "discovery" of big song during the 1950s by describing how this "discovery" was then used to disprove Western musicologists' statements that Chinese music was entirely monophonic. These Chinese accounts refer to comments such as those of VAN AALST, who wrote of Chinese music that "the melodies being always in unison, always in the same key, always equally loud and unchangeable in movement, they cannot fail to appear wearisome and monotonous in comparison with our complicated melodies…. It is incontestable that Chinese music compares unfavorably with European music…" (1964, 84). As Fan Zuyin writes:

> Although there are some descriptions of this kind of folk art custom and activity [that is, any kind of multi-part choral singing] in a small number of historical travel writings by scholars and in a small number of old county records, only a handful of these writings include explicit records of "multi-part" performance forms…. Owing to the paucity of these records of folk arts, non-Chinese people (including professional musicians) maintained the view that "Chinese music has always been monophonic" and "Chinese folk music does not involve polyphonic music," and for a long time this view was common both within and outside China…. Finally, in the early 1950s many types of this artistic form of multi-part folk songs were discovered. Among these, the earliest to be collected, arranged, and researched was multi-part Kam folk song from the southwestern region. When music workers from the Guizhou Provincial Arts Bureau of the Masses participated in Land Reform work in Kam areas, they discovered the "Kam big song" form of choral singing.
>
> (FAN 1998, 3–4)

These early activities of the music workers and the "discovery" of big song are now mythologized and elaborated as part of Kam big song history (see, for example, LIU 2005, 4–5). The ongoing contemporary focus on the role of research into big song further indicates how radically 1950s big song research altered views of the nation's music, and highlights the contribution of non-Han minorities to current representations of China's culture. It further indicates the perceived significance of the 1950s "discovery" of the genre, and demonstrates the important influence of 1950s research in helping to shape the modern identity of Kam people and wider views of Kam cultural heritage.

Although this 1950s "discovery" was seen as leading to new understandings of "Chinese" music, the writings from the 1950s and 1960s do not give a clear picture of whether or not the music was actually perceived as "Chinese" by the researchers involved, or indeed by Kam singers of the time: at that point, how to effectively accommodate non-Han ethnicities into the new political setting of China was not entirely clear. While the changed position of the status of non-Han groups within the Chinese state was illustrated through the recognition accorded to big song, the acceptance of minority peoples as part of the Chinese nation was not a completely radical shift from earlier viewpoints.

For example, Zhao observes that before the mid 1990s most Chinese tended to present China (*Zhongguo* 中国) as "refer[ing] to no peoples other than the Han group and China proper until the 1911 revolution" (ZHAO 2006, 4). However, he demonstrates that during the preceding Qing Manchu dynasty a more expansive official definition of China was adopted. He cites the Qianlong Emperor's 1755 pronouncement that:

> There exists a view of *China* (*Zhongxia*),[13] according to which non-Han peoples cannot become *China*'s subjects and their land cannot be integrated into the territory of *China*. This does not represent our dynasty's understanding of *China*, but is instead that of the earlier Han, Tang, Song, and Ming dynasties.
>
> (ZHAO 2006, 4)

Zhao also notes the long-standing complex relationship between ethnicity and membership within the Chinese state:

> The term *Zhongguo* was first used around the tenth century BCE. Its literal meaning is "central state," but it referred to no specific ethnicity or location … because those who founded new dynasties often emerged from groups with different ethnic attributes than their predecessors, their understanding of what *China* meant varied over time.… Notably, for the non-Han people, the adoption of the concept of *China* did not lessen their sense of their own ethnic identity. For example, though the Jin and Yuan rulers[14] drew a sharp line between the Han and non-Han peoples, they clearly identified their states with *China*.
>
> (ZHAO 2006, 6–7; italics in original)

Furthermore, even ethnic categorization itself was never fixed within Chinese history, and the boundary between Han and non-Han was always variable. One example of this is the long history of the Han encouraging non-Han groups to become "cultivated" (*shu* 熟), which saw some members of those non-Han groups move from being considered "uncultivated" (*sheng* 生) people to becoming civilized, "cultivated" Han subjects, and which further complicates perceptions of non-Han within the Chinese state.[15]

The 1845 *Liping Prefecture Gazetteer*, detailing historical records of today's Liping County (the county with the highest proportion of Kam residents in the nation), provides a clear example of such a situation—with the term "Miao" used to refer primarily to the ancestors of today's Kam people:

> With the kindness and strength of our great dynasty, we successfully controlled [the "barbarians"]. Those who were stubborn and did not obey have all reformed in their ways. They have become good people. Also, charity schools were built with Confucian teachers to train and guide, and an increased quota of enrolments, to encourage those to change. Because of this more students attend school and pass examinations, and with these people there is no difference between aboriginal and Han people. *Those who were formerly known as uncultivated Miao have become cultivated Miao. Those who were formerly cultivated Miao have become today's Han people.* Furthermore, from this time on things develop daily and monthly. We can expect this place with short people with buns [that is, this backward place] can be changed into an advanced place. And the customs of singing and dancing under the moon will not be affected by these changes.
>
> (*Liping fu zhi* 1845: *juan* 5, *dili* 4, 19–20, italics added)

Many researchers now recognize the fluidity of ethnic categorization throughout Chinese history. Some point to "flexible peripheries" and "shifting ethnic boundaries" (WANG 2006a; 2006b) which permitted considerable fluidity in ethnic categorization; others, such as Stevan Harrell, describe more static conceptual categories that underwent gradual shifts over time:

> There has never been a rigid boundary around the category "Chinese." Since earliest times, the people who have called themselves Hua or Xia or Zhongguo ren (people of the countries in the middle) or, of late, Han, have held an ideology of both cultural superiority and inclusivist expansionism, conducting what I have elsewhere called a "civilizing project"... the general trend has been one of expansion of both population and geography, particularly towards the southern frontiers. And the boundary has always been a gradual rather than an abrupt one.
>
> (HARRELL 1996, 6)

Early Kam research did not focus on the cultural identity of Kam as a group aside from the researchers' clear political purpose in showing "new" (1950s) China as a unified multiethnic state. Researchers focused on identifying and recording the differences between the non-Han and Han Chinese, and highlighted individual cultural elements such as myths and music.

In the case of Kam big song, its recognition can be seen as also representing the recognition of Kam culture (and, accordingly, the cultures of all China's minorities) as part of the culture of the Chinese nation, thereby clearly indicating the status of minorities within the new Chinese state. Yet it is also significant for simply representing one particular stage in a long-standing and complex interrelation among notions of ethnicity, culture, and Chinese nationalism or identification.

THE INFLUENCE OF 1950S BIG SONG RESEARCH
ON KAM CULTURAL HERITAGE AND IDENTITY

The research on Kam song that was conducted in the 1950s drew particular attention to big song singing, and as the first published research documenting China's multi-part singing traditions, it gave big song further significance in both national and international domains. It contributed to the ensuing focus on big song above other Kam song genres, and was thus influential in big song becoming a primary cultural resource through which the state has engaged with Kam people. Moreover, the official recognition of big song has had an important role in shaping Kam people's feelings of affiliation with both their own wider Kam minority group and the entire nation, and its effects have been felt beyond the small area of big song's origins to impact on the whole Kam community.

Yet despite these processes, the exact positioning of Kam ethnic identity within the Chinese environment retains a degree of ambiguity. The use of big song in state-supported staged performances—many of which are given in the context of the unification of regional minorities or the celebration of official events related to the state or the Chinese Communist Party—has contributed greatly to a sense of Kam inclusion within the Chinese environment. It has also promoted certain aspects of Kam culture, especially among younger generations of Kam people. However, some members of the Kam community—especially those who have had limited or no experience of Chinese-language education and little exposure to modern notions of citizenship and statehood (particularly middle-aged women and older people)—do not experience such inclusion to the same degree.

The different positioning of Kam and Han people from the perspective of many rural Kam residents was particularly apparent at the time of China's nationwide celebrations for the sixtieth anniversary of the founding of the People's Republic in 2009 (further described in INGRAM 2009). Only a week or so before the 1 October anniversary, a group of Kam big song singers won a prize of 10,000 RMB (then approximately US$1,450) in one of a series of high profile singing competitions held in locations central to the establishment of the PRC. The singers involved had a clear impression about the significance accorded their singing through this award, but ideas about the significance of the competition as a whole and its relationship to national politics seemed vague. A few days later, members of the same community enjoyed watching the sixtieth anniversary National Day celebrations on television, but many rural Kam residents described the festival as being "theirs" (not "ours")—as apparent through comments such as *kay da sep* ("they [that is, Han people] are holding a festival")—indicating a sense in some parts of the Kam community of being distanced from the festivities. Yet a major Kam traditional festival held just a few days after the National Day celebrations was widely attended by and obviously significant to Kam people, despite many complaining about the difficulty of listening at length to loud, clashing performances of *gen* (Kam bamboo mouth organ; in Chinese, *lusheng* 芦笙) that formed the focus of the festival.

From the standpoint of the early twenty-first century, it appears that 1950s research into Kam big song contributed to shaping Kam and non-Kam perspectives of Kam cultural heritage in the three main areas detailed below. First, 1950s research was influential in promoting knowledge of big song outside Kam areas. Second, the research influenced subsequent increases in the cultural and symbolic capital associated with big song that were connected with the broader promotion of the genre. Finally, the new categorization of the choral genre was a clear result of this early phase of research. In addition, the social and economic transformations of the region since China's market reform that began in the 1980s have increased the ongoing impact of these early influences.

The Promotion of Big Song Outside Kam Areas

As noted above, research in the 1950s had a major role in promoting knowledge of Kam big song outside Kam areas and subsequently in radically altering understandings of Chinese music. These developments were an important foundation for the wider promotion of big song, and especially the development of staged Kam big song performances outside Kam communities. FAN Zuyin's comment regarding the direct connection between the "discovery" of big song by researchers and the immediate use of big song in staged performances (1998, 4) clearly underlines the connection between research and wider big song promotion.

The use of big song in staged performances, which began in the 1950s, followed immediately and directly from Han Chinese research into Kam musical traditions. Versions of Kam songs have now been performed in a wide variety of staged contexts ranging from village performances and county-level competitions to "Ten Thousand People Singing Big Song" (2005) and performances in major cities both within and beyond China—including in New York's Carnegie Hall (in 2009), in Australasia (in 2012), and in Washington, D.C. (at the United States White House in 2012 and the Smithsonian Folklife Festival in 2014). Today, the performance of big song literally "gives voice" to Kam people in both the national and international context, and is becoming the new symbol of Kam identity. Big song singing has since become a cultural marker that serves to unite Kam people (especially those who are outside of the original big-song-singing area), and the genre is now taken by some researchers, officials, and tourism promotors to be the core of Kam expressive culture.

Yet, at the same time, contemporary staged big song performances usually exhibit many differences from performances of big song in the village context or "village tradition." TABLE 1 outlines some of the main differences between the village and staged performance formats in terms of repertoire, lyrics, pitch, social context, and aesthetic evaluation (see also INGRAM et al. 2011; INGRAM 2012a; 2012b). Almost all the features of the big song "staged tradition" can also be found in the staging of Han folk singing—although the latter less frequently emphasizes the representation of allegedly "authentic" musical culture.[16]

Staged big song performances, now the product of more than six decades of development, have exerted a very significant influence upon Kam cultural heritage. In one sense, they have created a new, modernized expression of Kam cultural heritage which to date has been much favored outside Kam communities. Yet at the same time they have transformed elements of a dynamic singing tradition with great social significance into a static art form that is entirely divorced from

FEATURE	BIG SONG: "VILLAGE TRADITION"	BIG SONG: "STAGED TRADITION"
Repertoire	All songs selected by each group from their own local repertoire learned from a song expert in own village	Many songs are arranged versions of songs from different local repertoires, many recent performances consist of a "medley" of phrases from completely different songs
Lyrics	The most valued songs have meaningful lyrics with complex rhyming patterns, and can be up to 15 minutes in length	The most valued songs are not evaluated in relation to lyrics; those most frequently performed are melodically interesting, their lyrics often lack rhyming patterns (and sometimes also any logical meaning), and are rarely longer than 3–4 minutes
Pitch	Natural voice at a pitch suitable for each group	"Trained" voice at a high pitch
Social context	Sung as a meaningful social interaction between groups	Sung to entertain, as a symbol of authentic Kam culture, and as a source of income
Aesthetic evaluation	Singers demonstrate ability through possession of a large repertoire of high quality songs	Singers demonstrate ability through difficult vocal techniques and appealing voice quality and physical appearance

TABLE 1. A comparison of some of the most significant differences between big song performances within the village context or "village tradition" and in the staged performance format.

its original cultural context. As noted earlier in this article, the village and staged contexts for big song singing have now formed two largely distinct "traditions."

Throughout most of the twentieth century it was the village form of big song singing that provided the main musical material for the staged performances. Moreover, as relatively few Kam villagers were previously involved in performing big song on stage, staged big song singing had little direct connection with local big song singing and exerted little influence upon big song singing within Kam villages. Only a very few villagers had participated in staged performances, and there were no televisions and VCD or DVD players in Kam villages where people could hear these performances. Until the 1990s, when young people began migrating out of Kam villages (as explained below), systems of village song transmission had also remained largely intact (although most transmission did cease temporarily during the Great Leap Forward and the Cultural Revolution).

Some new musical material was introduced through the performances of *xuan-chuan dui* 宣传队 (propaganda teams). These groups operated during the collective period and were composed of local villagers who earned work points through giving staged performances rather than exclusively earning points through manual labour. The teams performed arranged or "artistically processed" (*yishu jiagong* 艺术加工) versions of big songs, especially those songs with lyrics praising the Communist Party that had become popular during the 1950s. While many of those songs are remembered fondly by older singers today, they are relatively small in number and were never considered appropriate for *dare low* performances.

However, since around the year 2000 large numbers of Kam villagers have become involved in increasingly larger-scale staged big song performances. In Kam villages, the viewing of recorded staged performances of big song on VCDs, DVDs, and now sometimes also the internet has also become common. These developments have led to many more villagers gaining familiarity with staged big song performances, and such performances becoming increasingly influential within the village context. For example, some village singers have begun to prefer singing the staged big song repertoire rather than the big song repertoire of their own region, and are frequently using the higher pitch and faster speed typical of staged big song performances when singing in the village context. While this more recent influence of staged big song singing upon village big song performances might appear to be adversely influencing local cultural heritage, the effect of the promotion of big song through staged performances within the dynamics of local cultural heritage maintenance is complex. As noted in INGRAM et al. (2011), the recent growth in the promotion of staged big song singing has largely coincided with the massive recent social changes occurring in rural Kam areas.

From our fieldwork it is clear that the majority of young Kam people aged between approximately 16 and 29 years of age (previously the key cohort of big song singers in Kam villages) have now migrated out of their communities. This migration has resulted from the gradual lifting of controls over mobility previously enforced by the *hukou* 户口 policy—a household registration system that categorized all Chinese people as either agricultural or nonagricultural residents, and controlled their movement between urban and rural areas.

In 2006, 43.7% of the 2.03 million people that comprised the total rural labor force in Qiandongnan (the largest area of Kam concentration) moved to seek employment in other places (QIANDONGNAN NIANJIAN 2009). In 2009, another survey showed that, of the young Kam people still living in Zhaoxing village, 60% preferred migration to staying in the village (XU et al. 2012, 54) (the survey apparently excluded those who had already migrated and were living outside of the village).

Many of these Kam migrants not only seek employment elsewhere but also settle outside Kam areas. The proportion of the Kam population resident in the traditional homeland of the bordering areas of Guizhou, Hunan, and Guangxi (as presented in FIGURE I) has reduced, according to census data, from 93.7% in 2000 to 89% in 2010, while those living outside the region—in particular in the coastal areas—increased during the same period (GUOWUYUAN RENKOU 2012). For example, the proportion of Kam people in Zhejiang Province increased from 0.6% in 2000 to 3.1% in 2010.

Over a similar period more than 27,700 Kam people moved to Guangdong, which increased its share of the total Kam population from 1.9% to 2.9% (GUOWUYUAN RENKOU 2012). Similar large increases in the resident Kam population also occurred in Fujian and Jiangsu provinces and Shanghai City (Guowuyuan Renkou 2012). This migration is inspired primarily by economic reasons (Wu and Wang 2012). However, the outcomes undermine the socioeconomic fabric of traditional communities. The cultural values of individuals, families, and communities and their cultural practices have been increasingly integrated with and in turn shaped by the culture of migration. Children grow up expecting to spend part of their lives outside Kam areas, and young villagers who do not migrate are seen by both the broader community and, especially, their own age group, as lacking ability. Another major change has been the development of ethnic tourism or village tourism, which is characterized by the commodification of the region's ethnic culture. This commodification is achieved through representing, packaging, and selling images of Kam culture and includes Kam singing and dancing performances (Wu 2014).

Big song performance has become a tourist brand or key "selling point" to promote the Kam tourism industry, leading to the construction of a new image of the region. Through the joint promotion of big song by both local governments and the media, big song has become more widely known and the region now appears more attractive to investors and tourists. One prominent example of the role of big song in these developments is the huge "On-Location Performance of Kam Big Song from Guizhou" (*Guizhou Dongzu dage shijing zhanyan* 贵州侗族大歌实景展演) that has been performed regularly in the evenings since March 2015 in a specially constructed three-thousand-seat outdoor performance arena near the county center of the main Kam county of Liping.[17]

In addition to the performances of big song in national and international arenas, annual big song festivals have been established in many big-song-singing villages such as Xiaohuang 小黄 in Congjiang County, and Yandong 岩洞 and Zhaoxing 肇兴 in Liping County. In Zhaoxing, for example, the tourism industry contributed 20% of the village's gross total income in 2009 (Xu et al. 2012, 57). Big song performance has accrued symbolic capital to the region and enhanced the economic participation of the villagers.

These various social changes have adversely influenced the "village tradition" of big song and many other Kam song genres, and the earlier forms of big song transmission—whereby young, mostly unmarried people learn and perform the songs—have been shattered. However, the use of big song in staged performances and the involvement of married women in performing the songs (an activity that would previously have been prohibited in most big-song-singing areas) have provided an indirect stimulus for the same group of women to relax earlier prohibitions and take up public big song singing within their own villages.

Over the last decade this new form of village transmission and performance of big song has grown in popularity and has clearly played a crucial role in sustaining the tradition. The involvement of women in new social roles has also contributed to greater gender equality within rural Kam communities (as further detailed in Ingram et al. 2011).

The Increased Cultural and Symbolic Capital of Big Song

The 1950s research into Kam big song was pivotal in attracting attention to the genre from those outside Kam communities. It thus had a major role in increasing the cultural and symbolic capital that has long been associated with Kam big song, and which can be observed in many Kam communities today. One interesting example of the recent strengthening of cultural and symbolic capital is the first staged performance of big song in 1953 mentioned above. As noted by Zhang Jing, the performances in Beijing in 1953 then led to one of the singers, Wu Peixin, being invited to perform outside China:

> In 1953 … Wu Peixin and three other young women from Liping performed big songs in Beijing for the first time. Wu Peixin was also the first Dong [that is, Kam] singer to perform outside of China, in [*sic*] Democratic People's Republic of Korea in 1953 and in the former Soviet Union in 1957.   (ZHANG 2007)

Although Zhang carefully avoids mentioning the type of Kam songs Wu Peixin sang in her performances in Korea and the former Soviet Union, local reports and anecdotes about the performance that are in circulation within and beyond Kam villages claim that Wu Peixin performed big song in her international performances.

Almost fifty years later, in 2002, a large archway commemorating Wu Peixin's overseas performances was built over the entrance to a section of one Yandong village where she had lived. Chinese characters on the archway read: "Sizhou [village], Yandong—the first Kam village to take Kam big song abroad" (*Yandong Sizhou Dongzu dage chuqu guomen diyizhai* 岩洞四洲侗族大歌出去国门第一寨; pictured in ZHONG 2007, 130). Many people (both Yandong officials and others) claim that Wu Peixin sang big song in her performances outside China, thus Yandong villagers were the first to sing big song overseas (see, for example, SHI 2003, 90; LIPING XIAN LÜYOU 2005, 34). It remains unclear whether Wu herself voluntarily made this claim or whether it was developed and promoted by state media and representatives; indeed, on a visit to Wu's natal home in 2005 a host of newspaper clippings that praised her achievement were displayed in a glass frame. Yet Kam people from other areas disputed the claim and disparaged the archway, pointing out that any claim of Wu singing big song on her solo overseas visit must be false since big song is a choral musical genre and hence cannot be sung by one person alone.

The fact that the performance of big song outside China was considered worthy of the construction of an archway, and the concern expressed by Kam villagers, clearly demonstrates the degree of capital understood to be conferred through big song performance. This is one of many examples indicating how deeply the capital associated with staged big song performance is significant within Kam villages. It also shows that any big song performances outside Kam communities—even those that are clearly within a "staged tradition"—are significant to Kam people as rare opportunities for the representation of Kam culture to a wider audience.

The New Categorization of Big Song

The third and final way in which 1950s research into Kam big song has influenced Kam cultural heritage concerns the new categorization of big song that was established through the 1950s publications. In those early writings, the Kam choral songs sung in New Year exchanges in the *dare low* first became classified as a genre known in Chinese as *dage* (and, subsequently, known in English as "big song"). *Dage* is a translation of the name of the most important category of songs sung in these exchanges—known in Kam as *ga lao*. *Ga* translates as "song," and *lao* can be variously translated as "big," "old," "main," or "important." Other categories of two-part songs were (and are) also sung in such exchanges, but each category has its own name (the names and actual categories vary among regional repertoires, but often also include *oy-hoy-ding*, *ga ma*, and *ga sor*, among others). However, 1950s researchers took *ga lao* to refer generically to all the different categories of songs with two vocal lines, not just to one of these categories.

As a result, in recent times and in certain contexts, Kam villagers now sometimes also use either the Chinese *dage* or its Kam equivalent *ga lao* to refer to all categories of choral songs sung in this context, thus revealing an altered and broader contemporary definition for the Kam name *ga lao*. However, in other instances some older villagers continue to understand the Chinese *dage* as equating only to the one particular category of choral songs that were originally known in Kam as *ga lao*. Clearly, the 1950s research in effect "created" a new genre of Kam singing that is now known as big song/*dage*, and which has influenced the way in which Kam cultural heritage is conceptualized by subsequent generations of Kam people.

While the initial categorization of big song was undertaken by Han people, it would be erroneous to view the categorization simply as the assimilation of a Kam folk genre to Han Chinese practices. The categorization made by Han Chinese was part of a trend in musical categorization that has parallels in many other countries—drawing on music research paradigms from Europe and elsewhere—and there is no indication that it was ethnically motivated. Moreover, the fact that the new big song genre is and has been recognized by many Kam and other non-Han researchers complicates viewing this categorization as being ethnically motivated.

SUBSEQUENT RESEARCH INTO KAM BIG SONG

After the research into big song conducted in the 1950s and early 1960s, the next period of empirical big song research did not occur until the late 1970s and early 1980s. As Stephen Jones notes regarding music research in the nation as a whole, "[Ethnomusicological] research was forced to cease around 1964 on the eve of the Cultural Revolution, not reviving again until around 1978" (JONES 2003, 290). Many Chinese-language publications about big song have been produced since that time, albeit rarely based on the kind of lengthy or participatory study of big song singing that forms the basis for the major works of the 1950s. While studies of recent decades cover a range of topics in relation to big song, many deal with issues of preservation of the genre and the ways in which big song might have value within cultural tourism projects (see also INGRAM et al. 2011, 75–80). For example, Fan Zuyin, in the published version of his opening remarks to the 2002 first symposium on Kam big song and the Ninth Annual Conference on Chinese Minority Music (held in Liping county, Guizhou), urges researchers to actively participate in preserving the cultures they research by providing assistance to local governments wishing to present these musical traditions on stage:

> We must earnestly practice what we preach, and actively participate in work towards the protection and transmission of minority musical cultures.... We must initiate provision of assistance to relevant local governments in their organization and development of minority musical cultures, with the aim of [developing] all kinds of musical arts activities (such as the "Drum Tower Culture and Arts Festival" occurring along with this conference).   (FAN Zuyin 2003, 5)

The promotion of big song—and especially of staged big song singing—has resulted in the production of staged forms of the tradition, in new musical arrangements of big song, and in the reinforcement of new systems of big song categorization as outlined above. Such promotion has indirectly benefited Kam musical culture by providing a useful foundation for villagers in maintaining big song singing in the face of rapid social change. Yet it presents other challenges for cultural maintenance—for example, big song promotion rarely focuses upon the aspects of the songs that form the basis of the genre (such as the themes and structure of song lyrics), or on indigenous Kam aesthetic principles (see INGRAM et al. 2011).

One recent event that has been significant to more recent research on big song has been the inscription of big song on UNESCO's Representative List of the Intangible Cultural Heritage of Humanity. The application for such inscription relied heavily on research of the 1950s as well as the continued efforts of recent scholars. Over the last decade, the research on big song and other UNESCO-inscribed folk traditions has also been utilized within a newly introduced official system purported to enhance the transmission of China's folk traditions through the identification of particular villagers as "representative transmitters" (*daibiaoxing chuanchengren*).[18]

In the context of big song singing such identification has been problematic, and the payment of individuals for their roles in this system has led to conflicts over the traditional roles of cultural custodians in a number of communities. For instance, some song experts who are not recognized by the state as "representative transmitters" have been reluctant to assume their traditional role of song teaching—thus threatening the ongoing existence of the very musical tradition that would supposedly be supported by the identification of particular villagers in this way.

CONCLUDING DISCUSSION

Early research into big song during the 1950s had a major influence on how big song has since been perceived, understood, and promoted, and consequently has both directly and indirectly influenced big song singing within Kam communities. It has also been closely connected with many important developments concerning notions of Kam cultural heritage and ethnic identity. As discussed here, in Chinese-language research, Kam singing has been used to address a perceived deficiency in "Chinese" musical styles—specifically, the lack of polyphonic music. As the unique singing style of a non-Han Chinese population was accommodated into expanded notions of national music forms within a multiethnic state, the status of Kam culture was enhanced and along with it Kam economic opportunities.

However, the initial phase of big song research had a major role in changes to the big song genre. It influenced the knowledge of big song outside Kam areas, the cultural and symbolic capital associated with big song, and the categorization of the genre. The social and economic transformations of the region since China's market reforms that began in the 1980s have further contributed to the degree to which these effects have influenced the current situation.

By identifying the ways in which 1950s research into big song has influenced big song singing today, this analysis demonstrates the importance of critical engagement with previous research in understanding current musical practice. It also shows the importance of music in understanding contemporary minority culture and cultural identity. Within Kam and other cultures that do not rely on transmission through written forms, music is particularly important in both cultural transmission and cultural representation or the creation of identity. That big song—a musical form—took on the function of signifying the status of minorities within communist China of the 1950s was not as surprising as it might seem, since musical forms have always been closely linked to ethnic identity within cultures that do not rely on languages with written forms. This was further expanded with the use of big song in staged performances that continued to promote and "fix" Kam identity.

Today, big song is not only very important in transmitting Kam culture but also in literally "giving voice" to Kam people. It creates a space for and heightened awareness of Kam people and culture within both national and international contexts, and enhances the capital associated with Kam cultural forms. As Tim Oakes notes in a study of Han communities in Guizhou, "heritage preservation and display are viewed by many Chinese scholar officials and villagers themselves as powerful tools of modernization and development" (Oakes 2013, 387). For the Kam too, modernization is achieved in a certain sense through cultural tradition. However, the coexistence of two clearly recognized Kam big song traditions—one in the village, and one on the stage (further detailed in Ingram 2012a; 2012b)—is one of the most obvious distinctions between the Kam situation and that of the Han in Guizhou as described by Oakes. The coexistence of these two Kam "traditions" indicates that no matter how Kam heritage is presented on stage, or the degree to which Kam people might seek to—or have the ability to—control that presentation, big song singing clearly retains a deep significance within Kam communities themselves.

Given the importance of big song singing within Kam communities, and its significant connections with ethnicity and heritage, research into big song must be considered as having played an important role in determining the contemporary status of the Kam people. But despite the unprecedented social transformations of recent decades, the fact that contemporary forms of big song singing continue within Kam communities demonstrates that Kam people have maintained their own cultural heritage in the face of extreme external pressures and a lack of impartial state support. The great significance of this achievement also demands recognition.

Notes

* Catherine Ingram's research for this article was supported by an Australian Postgraduate Award, an Endeavour Australia Cheung Kong Research Fellowship, a fellowship at the

International Institute of Asian Studies, a Newton International Fellowship (Royal Society and British Academy, UK) at SOAS, University of London, and a postdoctoral fellowship at the University of Sydney, as well as various grants and other support offered through PARADISEC (www.paradisec.org.au) and the University of Melbourne. The authors gratefully acknowledge the many Kam villagers without whose assistance this research could not have been conducted—in particular, Wu Meifang, Wu Pinxian, Wu Xuegui, Wu Zhicheng, and many other residents of Sheeam. Thanks also to Anne McLaren and an anonymous reviewer for helpful comments on an earlier draft of this article.

1. TAN and CHENG (2003) and HAO (2013) give the population in Kam big-song-singing areas as "less than 100,000" and "approximately 100,000" respectively. These big-song-singing areas include many parts of southern Liping County, as well as some adjacent areas of Congjiang and Rongjiang counties, and comprise approximately 4% of the total Kam population. Before big song was inscribed on UNESCO's Representative List of the Intangible Cultural Heritage of Humanity in 2009, it was among the four Kam musical genres identified in 2006 by the Chinese state as National-level Intangible Cultural Heritage (see ZHOU 2006).

2. Many Chinese musical genres may be categorized as "monophonic" or *danshengbu* 单声部 (single part/melody): of these, apart from those involving a solo musician, most are better described as heterophonic because of the widespread aesthetic preference or expectation for different performers in the group to play or sing variations of the same melody at the same time, rather than singing or performing a single melody in strict unison.

3. During the period 2013–2014, when most of the work on this article was undertaken, Ingram held a Newton International Fellowship at SOAS, University of London. She has since taken up a new position at the University of Sydney.

4. Because of the lack of data regarding the variant of the second lect of southern Kam spoken in big-song-singing areas, and because of the differences between this variant and the lect used to develop the official Kam orthography (that was promulgated in 1958 and based on the first lect of Southern Kam), Kam words in the main text of this article are transcribed using a practical phonemic orthography based on the Roman alphabet and commonly accepted (Australian) English pronunciation (see INGRAM 2010b; 2014).

5. According to Kam people, the name *dare low* is only used to refer to these tall, wooden, pagoda-like buildings and has no other meaning; it does not translate as *gulou* 鼓楼 ("drum tower/building"), as is usually used in Chinese and sometimes thence translated into English.

6. The various Qing dynasty *Bai Miao tu* (百苗图 Hundred Miao Albums) show some of that diversity in late imperial times (see, for example, YANG and PAN 2004; DEAL and HOSTETLER 2006). On the Kam and their ancestors in other historical sources, see INGRAM (2010a; 2010b).

7. It is unclear how de Beauclair comes to this conclusion. For example, the *dare low* of today may be similar to those documented in earlier written sources, including the 1845 *Liping fu zhi* [Liping Prefecture Gazetteer]: "Besides the pagodas (*ta* 塔) and multi-storeyed buildings (*lou* 楼) inside the prefecture and county center, [there are] so many [such buildings] in the countryside in all directions that they cannot all be recorded" (*Liping fu zhi* 1845, *juan* 7, *guanjian* 2, 30).

8. The connection between these 1954–1964 minority field studies and the ethnic identification project is not well understood. From the findings of the "centrally-authorized ethnic visiting teams," and from the perspective of the establishment of the ethnic autonomous regions that began in the early 1950s, the work of ethnic identification and the ethnic identification project clearly began early in the decade. The aforementioned 1954–1964 field studies, which began with a team that visited Yunnan in 1954, continued and added to the earlier work.

9. Ji Zhou (2003, 508) gives a full biography of Guo Kezou (1917–1998) and Xiao Jiaju (1909–1996); as of a meeting in 2005 Zheng was retired but still active, and details about his life appear in Yang (2003, 493–94) and Ling (2005). Mao (2003, 33) uses the Chinese term *zhisheng* 支声 (usually translated as "heterophonic") in his statement, although I have never observed Chinese language sources on multi-part singing to consider heterophony as a category of multi-part music.

10. Interview with Yang Guoren 杨国仁 on 28 November 2005. As a young People's Liberation Army soldier during the early 1950s, Yang was involved with implementing land reform in Kam villages in Liping County. Although of the Han majority, he became fluent in Kam and later had a major role in managing the first professional Liping County Kam performance troupe, then went on to research and publish extensively on Kam culture (see Yang 2003).

11. The original date of Gu and Zhao's publication is not given in the 2003 collection, but it probably dates from the 1960s. Several other short general articles for this period that make some mention of Kam music (although again not necessarily big song) include Zhu and Yang (1956), Li (1959), and Yang (1961); Kam music is also mentioned in *Guizhou Sheng Liping* (1985).

12. Zhao's research does not appear in any of the major journals of the period.

13. Italics as they appear in Zhao's translation of the *Huangchao wenxian tongkao* (see Huang 1965, 7338) in Zhao (2006, 4).

14. The Jin were Jurchen people and the Yuan were Mongolian.

15. This process of so-called cultivation can be considered to have begun with the Tang *jimi* 羁縻 ("bridle and halter" or "loose rein") policy, and was followed by various approaches in the Ming and Qing dynasties including subjugation through Confucian education, military force (including the establishment of permanent garrisons), and "using barbarians to control barbarians" 以夷制夷 (*yi yi zhi yi*), particularly through the native chieftain system (*tusi zhidu* 土司制度).

16. China's minority cultures are those most frequently exoticized or "essentialized"; see, for example, Schein (2000) and Chio (2014).

17. The performance involves Kam staged folk singing (including the performance of one big song), and is similar in conception to Zhang Yimou's "Impression Series" (*yinxiang xilie* 印象系列; see Yue [2013]).

18. *Daibiaoxing chuanchengren* 代表性传承人 has no conventional English equivalent and is translated here as "representative transmitters." In this context, *daibiaoxing* can be understood as "representative" or "typical," while *chuanchengren* is a person who does the action of "transmitting," "passing on to future generations," or "continuing a tradition."

References

Baranovitch, Nimrod
2010   Others no more: The changing representation of non-Han peoples in Chinese history textbooks, 1951–2003. *The Journal of Asian Studies* 69: 85–122. doi:10.1017/s0021911809991598

Chen Guojun 陈国钧
1973   Dongjia zhong de gulou 侗家中的鼓楼 [Kam drum towers]. In *Guizhou Miao Yi shehui yanjiu* 贵州苗夷社会研究 [Studies on the society of the Aborigines in Kweichou], ed. Chen Guojun 陈国钧, 190–94. Taipei: The Orient Cultural Service. (Originally published 1942.)

Chio, Jenny
2014   *A Landscape of Travel: The Work of Tourism in Rural Ethnic China*. Seattle and London: University of Washington Press.

DEAL, David, and Laura HOSTETLER, eds.

2006   *The Art of Ethnography: A Chinese "Miao Album."* Seattle and London: University of Washington Press.

DE BEAUCLAIR, Inez

1986   A Miao tribe of Southeast Kweichow and its cultural configuation. In *Ethnographic Studies: The Collected Papers of Inez de Beauclair*, 269–346. Taipei: Southern Materials Center, Inc. (Originally published 1960.)

DENG Minwen

2001   Dong oral poetry: *Kuant cix*. Trans. Da Hai. *Oral Tradition* 16: 436–52.

DENG Minwen 邓敏文 and WU Hao 吴浩

1995   *Meiyou guowang de wangguo* 没有国王的王国 [The kingdom without a king]. Beijing: Zhongguo Shehui Kexue Chubanshe.

FAN Liansheng 范连生

2010   Xin Zhongguo chengli chuqi goujian xinxing minzu guanxi di shijian: Yi Qiandongnan diqu weilie 新中国成立初期构建新型民族关系的实践—以黔东南地区为例 [The practice of new inter-ethnic relationships in China's early Communist era: A case study of Qiandongnan]. *Dang de wenxian* 党的文献 5: 91–95.

FAN Zuyin 樊祖荫

1998   *Zhongguo duoshengbu min'ge gailun* 中国多声部民歌概论 [An introduction to China's multi-part folk songs]. Second edition. Beijing: Renmin Yinyue Chubanshe.

2003   "Zhongguo shaoshu minzu yinyue xuehui dijiu jie nianhui ji Dongzu dage yantaohui" kaimuci "中国少数民族音乐学会第九届年会暨侗族大歌研讨会"开幕词 [Opening Remarks for "The Ninth Annual Conference on Chinese Minority Music and the Symposium on Kam Big Song"]. In *Dongzu dage yu shaoshu minzu yinyue yanjiu: Dongzu dage yantaohui ji Zhongguo shaoshu minzu yinyue xuehui di jiujie nianhui lunwenji* 侗族大歌与少数民族音乐研究—侗族大歌研讨会暨中国少数民族音乐学会第九届年会论文集 [Kam big song and research into minority music: Collected works from a symposium on Kam big song and the Ninth Annual Conference on Chinese Minority Music], Yang Xiuzhao 杨秀昭 and Wu Dingguo 吴定国, eds., 4–5. Beijing: Zhongguo Wenlian Chubanshe.

FANG Jishen 方暨申

1959   Dongzu lanluge de shouji yu yanjiu baogao 侗族拦路歌的收集与研究报告 [A report on the collection of and research into Kam road-blocking songs]. *Yinyue yanjiu* 音乐研究 4: 80–91.

1960   Dong, Zhuang, Buyi, Yao gezu minjian hechang de jiben tezheng 侗、僮、布依、瑶各族民间合唱的基本特征 [The basic characteristics of folk choral singing among the Kam, Zhuang, Buyi and Yao]. *Renmin yinyue* 人民音乐 (March): 26–28.

FEI Xiaotong 费孝通

1951   *Xiongdi minzu zai Guizhou* 兄弟民族在贵州 [Non-Han ethnic minorities in Guizhou]. Beijing: Sanlian Shudian.

GLADNEY, Dru C.

1994   Representing nationality in China: Refiguring majority/minority identities. *The Journal of Asian Studies* 53: 92–123. doi:10.2307/2059528

GONG Yin 龚荫
  1992   *Zhongguo tusi zhidu* 中国土司制度 [China's native chieftain system]. Kunming: Yunnan Minzu Chubanshe.

Grand Song (Grand Song of the Dong Ethnic Group)
  2009   UNESCO Representative List of the Intangible Cultural Heritage of Humanity. http://www.unesco.org/culture/ich/index.php?RL=00202 (accessed 14 April 2013).

GU Zongzhi 古宗智 and ZHAO Yongshan 赵咏山
  2003   Dongzu "caigetang" diaocha baogao 侗族"踩歌堂"调查报告 [An investigation and report on the Kam "circle songs"]. In ZHANG and YANG, eds., 188–98.

GUIZHOU SHENG DIFANGZHI (Guizhou sheng difangzhi bianzuan weiyuanhui 贵州省地方志编纂委员会 [Editorial Committee for Guizhou Local History]), ed.
  2002   *Guizhou shengzhi: Minzu zhi* 贵州省志·民族志 [Guizhou provincial gazetteer: Ethnic minorities]. Guiyang: Guizhou Minzu Chubanshe.

Guizhou Sheng Liping (in full: *Guizhou sheng Liping xian dimingzhi* 贵州省黎平县地名志 [Record of Placenames in Liping County, Guizhou Province]), 1985. Liping County: Liping xian renmin zhengfu.

GUIZHOU SHENG WENLIAN 贵州省文联 [Guizhou Provincial Cultural Association], ed.
  1958   *Dongzu dage (ga lao) Guizhou minjian yinyue jikan* 侗族大歌（嘎老）贵州民间音乐集刊 [Kam Big Song (Ga Lao), Guizhou folk music collected periodical]. Guiyang: Guizhou Renmin Chubanshe.

GUOWUYUAN RENKOU (Guowuyuan renkou pucha bangongshi 国务院人口普查办公室 [Population Census Office under the State Council] and Guojia tongjju renkou ye jiuye tongjisi 国家统计局人口和就业统计司编 [Department of Population and Employment Statistics, National Bureau of Statistics]), eds.
  2012   *Zhongguo 2010 nian renkou pucha ziliao* 中国2010年人口普查资料 [Tabulation on the 2010 population census of the People's Republic of China]. Beijing: Zhongguo Tongji Chubanshe.

HAN Feng 寒风 (Zheng Hanfeng 郑寒风)
  1957   Duocai de dongzu hechang yishu 多彩的侗族合唱艺术 [The colorful choral art of the Kam]. *Guizhou ribao* 贵州日报 [Guizhou daily]: 3 (10 January)

HAO Yingcan 郝迎灿
  2013   Dongzu dage, shui zai chang, shui zai ting 侗族大歌，谁在唱谁在听 [Kam big song: Who is singing and who is listening?]. *Renmin ribao* 人民日报 [The People's Daily], 17 December. http://cpc.people.com.cn/n/2013/1217/c83083-23860313.html (accessed 10 May 2017).

HARRELL, Stevan
  1996   Introduction. In *Negotiating Ethnicities in China and Taiwan*, ed. M. J. Brown, 1–18. Berkeley: Institute of East Asian Studies, University of California, Berkeley, and Center for Chinese Studies.

HERMAN, John E.
  2007   *Amid the Clouds and Mist: China's Colonization of Guizhou, 1200–1700*. Cambridge, MA, and London: Harvard University Press.

HONG Tao 洪涛
  1959   Hunan Tongdao Dongzu de minjian yinyue 湖南通道的民间音乐 [Kam folk music of Tongdao, Hunan]. *Yinyue yanjiu* [Music research] 音乐研究 4: 37–54.

HUANG Guangxue 黄光学 ed.

1965   *Huangchao wenxian tongkao* 皇朝文献统考 [A comprehensive study of the Qing imperial documents]. Taipei: Xinxing Shuju.

INGRAM, Catherine

2009   China's 60th anniversary from the margins. *New Mandala* http://asiapacific.anu.edu.au/newmandala/2009/10/24/chinas -60th-anniversary-from-the-margins/ 24 October 2009 (accessed 24 April 2015).

2010a   China's Kam minority: A short bibliographic outline of Kam-related research materials in the University of Melbourne library. *East Asian Library Resources Group of Australia Newsletter* 56 (July). http://coombs .anu.edu.au/SpecialProj/NLA/EALRGA/newsletter1007/1007_ingram .html.

2010b   *Hwun hwun jon ka* (Listen)... Kam Villagers Singing Kam Big Song in Early Twenty-first-century China. PhD dissertation, University of Melbourne.

2012a   *Ee, mang gay dor ga ey* (Hey, why don't you sing)? Imagining the future for Kam big song. In *Music as Intangible Cultural Heritage: Policy, Ideology and Practice in the Preservation of East Asian Traditions*, ed. K. Howard, 55–75. Farnham, UK, and Burlington, VT: Ashgate. doi:10.4324/9781315596723

2012b   Tradition and divergence in southwestern China: Kam big song singing in the village and on stage. *The Asia Pacific Journal of Anthropology* 13: 434–53. doi:10.1080/14442213.2012.732601

2014   Preliminary research into the influence of the process of musical transmission on the relationship between speech tone and melody in Kam singing traditions from Southwestern China. In *Jahrbuch des Phonogrammarchivs* 4, ed. J. Schöpf, 116–39. Göttingen: Cuvillier Verlag.

Forthcoming Music, environment and place in Kam big song. In *Ethnomusicology: A Contemporary Reader, Volume 2*, ed. J. Post. London: Routledge.

INGRAM, Catherine, with WU Jialing 吴家玲, WU Meifang 吴美芳, WU Meixiang 吴梅香, WU Pinxian 吴品仙 and WU Xuegui 吴学桂

2011   Taking the stage: Rural Kam women and contemporary Kam "cultural development." In *Women, Gender and Rural Development in China*, T. Jacka and S. Sargeson, eds., 71–93. Cheltenham, UK, and Northampton, MA: Edward Elgar. doi:10.4337/9780857933546.00012

JI Zhou 冀洲

2003   Cong Dongzhai gulou dao aifei'er tieta: "Dongzu dage" yiduan kuayue shikong de wenhua zhi lu 从侗寨鼓楼到艾菲尔铁塔—"侗族大歌"一段跨越时空的文化之旅 [From the Kam Village Drum Tower to the Eiffel Tower: A cultural journey of "Kam Big Song" across time and space]. In ZHANG and YANG, eds., 507–16.

JONES, Stephen

2003   Reading between the lines: Reflections on the massive *Anthology of Folk Music of the Chinese Peoples. Ethnomusicology* 47: 287–337. doi:10.2307/3113937

KUANG Lu 邝露

1995   *Chiya kaoshi* 赤雅考释 [Research into "A Dictionary About the South"], with commentary by Lan Hong'en 蓝宏恩. Nanning: Guangxi Minzu Chu-Banshe. (Originally published 1635.)

LEIBOLD, James
    2014   Xinhai remembered: From Han racial revolution to great revival of the Chinese nation. *Asian Ethnicity* 15: 1–20. doi:10.1080/14631369.2012.726138

LI Chunwang 李春旺
    1959   Cong 2,770 wan jin dao 14,000 wan jin 从 2,770 万斤到14,000 万斤 [From 13.85 million kilograms to 70 million kilograms]. *Minzu huabao* [Nationalities pictorial] 民族画报 45: 8–9.

LING Zhenxia 凌振遐
    2005   Qu bu jingren shi bu xiu: Fang zhuming zuoqujia Zheng Hanfeng 曲不惊人誓不休：访著名作曲家郑寒风 [If my compositions do not startle others, I swear not to rest: An interview with the famous composer Zheng Hanfeng]. *Fazhi shenghuo bao: Jiaotong anquan zhoukan* 法制生活报—交通安全周刊 [Legal systems and lifestyle news: Traffic safety weekly] (16 November): 6.

Liping fu zhi 黎平府志 [Liping Prefecture Gazetteer], 1845.

LIPING XIAN LÜYOU (Liping xian luüyou fazhan weiyuanhui bangongshi
    黎平县旅游发展委员会办公室 [Office of the Liping County committee for tourism development]), ed.
    2005   *Dongxiang Liping guojia zhongdian fengjing mingshengqu jianming shouce* 侗乡黎平国家重点风景名胜区简明手册 [A concise handbook to the Kam home of Liping, a national level scenic area]. Liping County: Liping Xian Yadian Zhuangshi Zhongxin [Liping County Elegant Decorations Center].

LIU Yahu 刘亚虎, ed.
    2005   *Tianlai zhi yin: Dongzu dage* 天籁之音—侗族大歌 [The sound of Heaven: Kam big song]. Ha'erbin [Harbin]: Heilongjiang Renmin Chubanshe.

LU Jingchuan 陆景川
    2011   Fei Xiaotong bu tong xunchang di Qiandongnan zhi lü 费孝通不同寻常的黔东南之旅 [Fei Xiaotong's unusual travels in Qiandongnan]. *Shaxiang wenxue* 杉乡文学 [Literature of the China Fir region]: 64–67.

MACKERRAS, Colin
    2003   *China's Ethnic Minorities and Globalization*. London and New York: RoutledgeCurzon.

MAO Jiale 毛家乐
    2003   1957 nian caiji Dongzu dage jishi 1957 年采集侗族大歌记实 [A record of actual events in the 1957 collection of Kam big song]. In ZHANG and YANG, eds., 33–35.

MCLAREN, Anne E., Alex ENGLISH, HE Xinyuan, and Catherine INGRAM
    2013   *Environmental Preservation and Cultural Heritage in China*. Champaign, IL: Common Ground Publishing.

MULLANEY, Thomas S.
    2010   *Coming to Terms with the Nation: Ethnic Classification in Modern China*. Berkeley: University of California Press.

NIAN Yi 念一 (Xiao Jiaju 萧家驹)
    1960   Dongzu minge 侗族民歌 [Kam folk songs]. *Renmin yinyue* 人民音乐 [People's music] (October): 35–37.

OAKES, Tim
2013   Heritage as improvement: Cultural display and contested governance in rural China. *Modern China* 39: 380–407. doi:10.1177/0097700412467011

PU Hong 普虹 and ZHANG Tiehong 张铁红
2003   Dongxiang yiyuan qipa: Galao (dai xu) 侗乡艺苑奇葩—嘎老（代序）[The exquisite work of art of the Kam region: Big song (additional introduction)]. In *Al Laox: Dongzu dage* 嘎老—侗族大歌 [Ga Lao: Kam big song], Guizhou sheng shaoshu minzu guji zhengli bangongshi 贵州省少数民族古籍整理办公室 [Guizhou provincial office of compiling ancient books of the minorities], ed., 4–18. Guiyang: Guizhou Minzu Chubanshe.

QIANDONGNAN NIANJIAN (Qiandongnan nianjian bianzuan weiyuanhui 黔东南年鉴编纂委员会 [Committee for Compiling and Editing the Qiandongnan Yearbook]), ed.
2009   *Qiandongnan nianjian 2008 nian* 黔东南年鉴 2008年 [Qiandongnan yearbook 2008]. Kunming: Yunnan Minzu Chubanshe.

QIN Naichang 覃乃昌
2008   Guangxi minzu xue yanjiu 50 nian fazhan huigu 广西民族学研究50年发展回顾 [A review of ethnic minority research in Guangxi over the past fifty years]. *Guangxi minzu yanjiu* 广西民族研究 [Research into Guangxi nationalities] 4: 1–10.

Sanjiang Dongzu zizhixian 三江侗族自治县 [Sanjiang Kam Autonomous County]
2004   Zhonghua renmin gonghe guo guojia minzu shiwu weiyuanhui 中华人民共和国国家民族事务委员会 [State ethnic affairs commission of the People's Republic of China]. http://www.seac.gov.cn/gjmw/zzdf/2004-07-13/1170035897111011.htm (accessed 9 April 2014).

SCHEIN, Louisa
2000   *Minority Rules: The Miao and the Feminine in China's Cultural Politics.* Durham and London: Duke University Press. doi:10.1215/9780822397311

SHI Gancheng 石干成
2003   *Hexie de mima: Dongzu dage de wenhua renleixue quanshi* 和谐的密码—侗族大歌的文化人类学诠释 [The secret code of harmony: A cultural anthropological explanation of Kam big song]. Shenzhen: Huaxia Wenhua Yishu Chubanshe.

SHI Ruoping 石若屏
1984   Qiantan Dongzu de zuyuan yu qiantu 浅谈侗族的族源与迁徙 [A brief discussion of the ancestral origins and migrations of the Kam]. *Guizhou minzu yanjiu* 贵州民族研究 4: 76–88.

TAN Yuntang 谭芸汤 and CHENG Wei 成伟
2003   Dongzu dage de "shenyi" zhi lu 侗族大歌的"申遗"之路 [The process of "Intangible Cultural Heritage application" for Kam big song]. *Xinhua wang: Guizhou pindao* 新华网—贵州频道 [Xinhua Net, Guizhou Channel], 5 August. http://gz.news.cn/ztpd/2003-08/05/content_785086.htm (accessed 10 May 2017).

VAN AALST, J.A.
1964   *Chinese Music.* Reprinted by Paragon Book Reprint Corp., New York. (Originally published 1884, Shanghai: Inspector General of Customs.)

Wang Ming-ke 王明珂

2006a What continued in history? A perspective from the history of the Qiang. In *Notions of Time in Chinese Historical Thinking*, Huang Chun-chieh and J. B. Henderson, eds., 175–201. Hong Kong: The Chinese University Press.

2006b *Yingxiong zuxian yu dixiong minzu: Genji lishi de wenben yu qingjing.* 英雄祖先与弟兄民族—根基历史的文本与情境 [Heroic ancestors and brotherly ethnic groups: Text and context of ancestors' history]. Yunchen collection n.110. Taipei: Yunchen Wenhua Shiye Gufen Youxian Gongsi.

Wu Hao 吴浩 and Zhang Zezhong 张泽忠

1991 *Dongzu geyao yanjiu* 侗族歌谣研究 [Research into Kam song]. Nanning: Guangxi Renmin Chubanshe.

Wu, Jiaping

2014 The rise of ethnicity under China's market reform. *International Journal of Urban and Regional Research* 38: 967–84.
doi:10.1111/j.1468-2427.2012.01179.x

Wu, Jiaping and Mark Y. L. Wang

2012 Ethnic migrant workers and emerging ethnic division in China's urban labor market. *Asian and Pacific Migration Journal* 21: 483–507.
doi:10.1177/011719681202100403

Xu Yan 徐燕, Wu Zaiying 吴再英, Lu Xianmei 陆仙梅, Chen Hongzhi 陈洪智, and Shi Xianchang 石贤昌

2012 Minzu cunzhai xiangcun lüyou kaifa yu minzu wenhua baohu yanjiu: Yi Qiandongnan Miaozu Dongzu zizhi zhou Zhaoxing zhai wei lie 民族村寨乡村旅游开发与民族文化保护研究—以黔东南苗族侗族自治州肇兴侗寨为例 [A study of village tourism development and the protection of ethnic culture: Taking Zhaoxing Village, Liping County, Guizhou Province, as a case study]. *Guizhou shifan daxue xuebao* 贵州师范大学学报 [Journal of Guizhou Normal University] 30: 53–58.

Xue Liang 薛良

1953 Dongjia minjian yinyue de jiandan jieshao 侗家民间音乐的简单介绍 [A basic introduction to Kam folk music]. *Renmin yinyue* 人民音乐 XII: 42–52.

1994 Dongge caifeng jianji 侗歌采风简记 [Brief records of Kam folk song collection]. *Zhongguo yinyue* 中国音乐 [Chinese music]: 32–34.

Yang Guoren 杨国仁

2003 Dongzu dage fazhan shishang de yizuo fengbei: Liping xian Dongzu minjian hechangtuan chengli qianhou de nanwang suiyue 侗族大歌发展史上的一座丰碑—黎平县侗族民间合唱团成立前后的难忘岁月 [A monument in the historical development of Kam big song: Unforgettable years preceding and following the establishment of the Liping County Kam folk chorus]. In Zhang and Yang, eds., 486–500.

Yang Quan 杨权

1961 Dongzu 侗族 [The Kam]. *Minzu huabao* 民族画报 60: 22–23.

Yang Tingshuo 杨庭硕 and Pan Shengzhi 潘盛之, eds.

2004 *Baimiao tu chaoben cibian (shang, xia)* 百苗图抄本汇编（上、下）[A compilation of handcopied hundred Miao pictures (2 volumes)]. Guiyang: Guizhou Renmin Chubanshe.

YANG Xiao 杨晓

2002 Xiao Huang geban zhong galao chuancheng xingwei de kaocha yu yanjiu 小黄歌班中嘎老传乘行为的考察与研究 [Investigation and research into the methods of Ga Lao transmission in Xiao Huang singing groups]. Masters thesis, Zhongguo Yishu Yanjiuyuan, Beijing.

YUE, Audrey

2013 New media: Large screens in China. In *The Oxford Handbook of Chinese Cinemas*, Carlos Rojas and Eileen Chow, eds., 359–76. Oxford and New York: Oxford University Press. doi:10.1093/OXFORDHB/9780199765607.013.0020

ZHANG Jing

2007 *Good Vibrations*. http://english.rednet.cn/c/2007/09/19/1324330.htm (accessed 4 January 2009).

ZHANG Min 张民

1993 Shiyi Dongzu wei tuzhu Luoyue shuo 试议侗族为土著骆越说 [A discussion of the claim that the Kam are indigenous Luoyue]. *Guizhou minzu yanjiu* 贵州民族研究 56: 127–32.

1994 Shitan Dongzu xingcheng 试探侗族形成 [An exploration of the formation of the Kam nationality]. *Guizhou minzu yanjiu* 58: 95–104.

ZHANG Zhongxiao 张中笑 and YANG Fanggang 杨方刚, eds.

2003 *Dongzu dage yanjiu wushi nian* 侗族大歌研究五十年 [Fifty years of research into Kam big song]. Guiyang: Guizhou Minzu Chubanshe.

ZHAO, Gang

2006 Reinventing China: Imperial Qing ideology and the rise of modern Chinese national identity in the early twentieth century. *Modern China* 32: 3–30. doi:10.1177/0097700405282349

ZHONG Tao 仲涛

2007 *Zhongguo Dongzu* 中国侗族 [The Kam people of China]. Guiyang: Guizhou Minzu Chubanshe.

ZHONGGUO KEXUEYUAN (Zhongguo Kexueyuan minzu yanjiusuo Guizhou shaoshu minzu shehui lishi diaochazu 中国科学院民族研究所贵州少数民族社会历史调查组 [Society and History Research Committee for Guizhou's Minorities at the Nationalities Research Institute Chinese Academy of Science] and Zhongguo Kexueyuan Guizhou fenyuan minzu yanjiusuo 中国科学院贵州分院民族研究所 [Minorities Research Institute at the Guizhou Branch of Chinese Academy of Science]), eds.

1963 Guizhou sheng Liping xian Sanlong xiang Dongzu shehui jingji diaocha ziliao 贵州省黎平县三龙乡侗族社会经济调查资料 [Research materials on the society and economy of Sanlong Township, Liping County, Guizhou Province]. *Guizhou shaoshu minzu shehui lishi diaocha ziliao* 贵州少数民族社会历史调查资料之十二 [Research materials on the society and history of Guizhou's minority groups], vol. 12.

ZHOU Heping 周和平, ed.

2006 *Diyipi guojiaji feiwuzhi wenhua yichan minglu tudian (shang, xia)* 第一批国家及非物质文化遗产名录图典（上、下）[An illustrated register of the first series of national-level intangible cultural heritage, 2 vols.]. Beijing: Wenhua Yishu Chubanshe.

ZHU Kangle 朱康乐 and YANG Guoren 杨国仁

1956 Dongzu yi cunzhai 侗族一村寨 [A Kam village]. *Minzu huabao* 民族画报 5: 6–7.

MARGARET CHAN
Singapore Management University

The Sinophone Roots of Javanese Nini Towong

This article proposes that Nini Towong, a Javanese game involving a possessed doll, is an involution of fifth-century Chinese spirit-basket divination.
The investigation is less concerned with originist theories than it is a discussion of the Chinese in Indonesia. The Chinese have been in Southeast Asia
from at least as early as the Ming era, yet Chinese contributions to Indonesian
culture is an understudied area. The problem begins with the asymmetrical
privileging of Indic over Sinic influences in early European scholarship, a situation which in turn reveals the prejudices that the Europeans brought to
bear in their dealings with the Chinese of Southeast Asia in the seventeenth
to nineteenth century. Europeans introduced the Chinese-Jew analogy to the
region. Their disdain contributed to indigenous hostility toward the Chinese.
Racialism is a sensitive topic but a reminder of past injustices provides a timely
warning in this moment of tense world geopolitics.

KEYWORDS: Nini Towong—*jelangkung*—spirit-basket divination—
Sinophone—Sinophobia

Asian Ethnology Volume 76, Number 1 · 2017, 95–115
© Nanzan University Anthropological Institute

Nini Towong is a Javanese rain ritual that involves a female effigy made with a coconut-shell ladle head mounted upon a basket body.* The soul of a dead person possesses the doll when it self-animates to answer questions put to it by rapping, nodding, and pointing. There is a second Indonesian spirit-basket game, *jelangkung*, from the Chinese *cai lan gong* (菜篮公), meaning "vegetable basket deity." Two people hold onto a basket which moves to write using a pen stuck into its reeds. *Jelangkung* is the more popular of the two divinatory games. It is played all over Indonesia at temple séances and for amusement. *Jelangkung* has even featured in Indonesian horror movies.[1]

Jelangkung baskets are not anthropomorphized like Nini Towong but it is necessary to drape a shirt over the basket as a condition for spirit possession. However, in the Dr. Adhyatma Health Museum on Jalan Indrapura in Surabaya, there is a unique *jelangkung* made in the image of a Chinese man, with slanted eyes and moustache. The male Chinese *jelangkung* is set next to a Nini Towong effigy which is clearly female (FIGURES 1a and 1b). The word "Nini" means "grandmother," but it is also an affectionate term for addressing girls (ROBSON and WIBISONO 2002, 512). This explains the feminized Nini Towong, but why was the Surabaya *jelangkung* made male? We can only guess at an answer; for although there are studies on Nini Towong, research on *jelangkung* is in its nascent stages.[2]

This article proposes that Javanese Nini Towong is a cultural involution of Chinese spirit-basket divination. GEERTZ (1963, 81–82) describes involution as "a sort of technical hairsplitting." Cultural artefacts are often embellished upon over time: a mask is made more ornate; a dance develops an increasingly complicated choreography. The changes may be elaborate but the original idea remains intact. This investigation into the Sinophone roots of Nini Towong adds to the knowledge of Chinese contributions to Indonesian culture, and highlights in the process the silence of early European scholarship on the subject. Indeed, the asymmetrical privileging of Indic influences to the almost total exclusion of the Chinese voice recalls early European Sinophobia. The Europeans of the seventeenth to nineteenth centuries compared the Chinese disparagingly with the Jews, and this analogy contributed to indigene resentment of Chinese communities. In the present time when anti-Semitic conspiracy theories have revived in the Muslim world, and the situation in the South China Sea grows increasingly tense, a reminder of the unfortunate persistence of racialism might not go amiss.

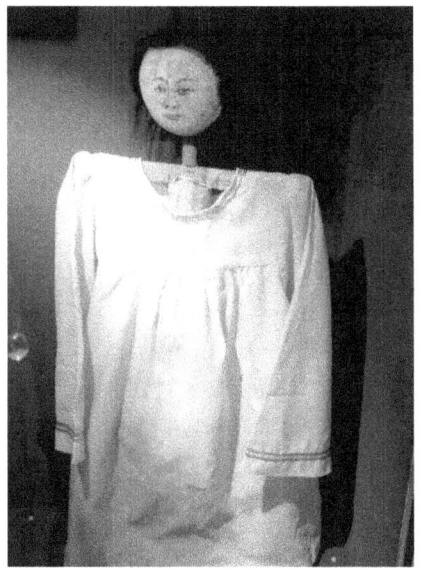

FIGURES 1a and 1b. The Nini Towong and *jelangkung* effigies displayed at the Dr. Adhyatma Health Museum. Photos used with the kind permission of Frenavit Kusman Setia Putra. See frenavit.com (accessed November 1).

NINI TOWONG, THE DOLL THAT DANCES

Nini Towong is a basket effigy moved by a female spirit. RASSERS (1982, 36) and WESSING (1999, 664 note 38) propose that it is the female Javanese ancestral spirit, while KARTOMI (1973, 180) suggests Dewi Sri, the rice goddess, as the possessing deity. Many dictionaries define Nini Towong with specific reference to a coconut-shell head (STEVENS and SCHMIDGALL-TELLINGS 2004, 665; ATMOSU-MARTO 2004, 371). Another suggestion is that *towong* alludes to the pallor of the coconut-shell face that is usually colored white with chalk with features drawn in lampblack (SITOWATI and MIKSIC 2006, 135). The celebrated Javanese dancer, Didik Nini Thowok, said that *towong* derives from *wong*, the Javanese word meaning "person," so that Nini Towong means a doll which can move like a human.[3]

Nini Towong is performed as a rainmaking ritual (HAZEU 1901, 55, in WESSING 1999, 662, note 35; KARTOMI 1973, 180), or it is a divinatory game where the doll is asked to predict the coming harvest, to name a future mate, or to point to where medicinal herbs or lost objects might be found (SCHELTEMA 1912, 73–74; SUDIARNO 2002). Children, imitating adults, made Nini Towong child's play (HUGRONJE 1906, 206; RASSERS 1982, 29–44; JORDAAN 1984, 102; PURWANING-SIH 2006). Since the 1980s, Nini Towong has been commodified as a cultural performance featuring a beautifully dressed doll, a chorus of singers, and gamelan musicians. I went in search of the touristy Nini Towong, the latest incarnation in the process of cultural involution. I collected primary evidence for this study on field trips to Semarang in July–August 2008; Singkawang, West Kalimantan, February 2008 and June–July 2009; Yogyakarta in June 2009; Jakarta in July and October 2009; and Kebumen and Cirebon in July 2010.

CULTURAL COMMODIFICATION OF NINI TOWONG

SCHECHNER (1990, 26) describes the process that can turn a village performance into a cultural treasure. It begins when curators decide that a folkloric practice constitutes an intangible heritage culture that must be conserved. The village performance, inherently improvisational, then becomes "museumified." A "normative expectation" is authorized with "proper" choreography and music. Fancy props and attractive costumes are added to make a suitably polished showpiece that becomes a standard against which all future performances are evaluated. Nini Towong has evolved along this line.

First came the impetus for conservation: SUJARNO (2002) names Nini Towong as an ancestral game. PURWANINGSIH (2006, 45–46) proposes that the ancestral game should be taught to children at home. Then, Gadjah Mada University collaborated with the Dinas Pariwisata, Yogyakarta [the Yogyakarta Tourist Office] to stage Nini Towong as a traditional farmer's folk performance (*Harian Jogja*, 4 May 2009). Now Nini Towong is a standard in the Yogyakarta cultural tourism repertoire.

In the evolution of Nini Towong from village ritual into cultural artefact, the performance by the Sabdo Budoyo troupe of Bantul sets out the "normative expectation." When I asked around in Yogyakarta about Nini Towong, only one name, Sabdo Budoyo, was ever mentioned, signalling the preeminence of this group. Three important leads were a recommendation by the dancer Didik Nini Thowok;[4] an Internet video clip of a Nini Towong performance posted by the Tembi House of Culture (https://www.youtube.com/watch?v=MdLPHcw2Ud4 [accessed 13 April 2017]); and an article in the *Jakarta Post* (SUDIARNO 2002). All these sources referred to the Sabdo Budoyo troupe. Thus on the night of 27 June 2009, I went to the village of Grudo Panjangrejo in Pundong, Bantul, where I met sixty-eight-year-old Pak Suwardi, leader of Sabdo Budoyo. Pak Suwardi presented me with a long list of Sabdo Budoyo performances starting from 1983. This testified to regular appearances at official celebrations and at educational institutions. In 2002, the troupe performed at Jakarta's TMII (Taman Mini Indonesia Indah, Beautiful Indonesia Miniature Park), which constitutes a cultural imprimatur as TMII is a showcase for indigenous Indonesian culture.

Pak Suwardi also presented me with notes stating that the troupe's Nini Towong performance was created in 1938 by Pak Suwardi's ancestors—Udisedo, Marto Jumar, and Paerah. Nini Towong was often performed in the village until 1942, when the Japanese occupation put a stop to the shows. Sabdo Budoyo resumed their Nini Towong performances in 1960 only to falter again in the economic and political turmoil of that time. In the 1980s, the Yogyakarta cultural authorities began to curate a traditional culture inventory, following through with government sponsorship and institutional patronage. Sabdo Budoyo, rising to the occasion, created a show featuring a beautiful Nini Towong doll and village performers self-consciously uniformed in Javanese costumes.

The involution of Nini Towong from village performance to cultural artefact included the modification of the doll. When once, Pak Suwardi told me, this doll was fashioned out of a basket fish trap, the doll that the troupe now employs is a

FIGURE 2. The Nini Towong doll of Sabdo
Budoyo being dressed. Photograph by author.

more durable and handy prop that was made in 1980. A spare was made in 1983.
The new design features foam and straw firmly wrapped around four bamboo
rods. A padded bra has been added to give Nini Towong an alluring feminine
silhouette. The cultural commodification of Nini Towong in the Sabdo Budoyo
performance is a process of involution, for despite the costumed performers and
decoratively embellished doll, the performance retains the essential mysticism of a
spirit-possession ritual.

NINI TOWONG AS PERFORMED BY SABDO BUDOYO

Famous dancer Didik Nini Thowok accompanied me on my date with
Nini Towong in the village of Grudo Panjangrejo. We arrived before 5 p.m. so that I

could see Nini Towong being dressed. The doll stood upon the floor of the veranda of Pak Suwardi's home, a one-storey village house. It measured about 1.5 meters tall upon its bamboo stilts. The face, made out of half a coconut shell, was painted with the features of a woman. There was no basket in the structure. The doll had long straw arms complete with five straw fingers for each hand (FIGURE 2). A woman expertly dressed the doll in Javanese costume; a green *kebaya* (blouse) over a batik sarong, with a yellow-colored sash about the waist, and a long red shawl upon its shoulders. The head was decorated with flowers and leaves (FIGURE 2).

By 6 p.m., many other villagers had gathered at Pak Suwardi's house, including Pak Paeran, a stern-looking man, aged seventy-three. He was the *pawang* (magician) and his costume, a green high-collared tunic worn over a sarong completed by a traditional Yogyakarta turban, marked him as out of the ordinary.

I was invited to dine with the village elders. We sat on the floor in a circle and ate boiled groundnuts, boiled taro, boiled banana, fried tempeh (fermented soya bean wafers), catfish curry and a stew made with beef skin crackers. We also drank lots of hot, very sweet tea. Around 6:45 p.m., after it became dark, Pak Paeran stood up and we followed him out of the house.

In the courtyard we joined a group of eleven women who were flanked by boys carrying lit bamboo torches. The women were uniformed in burgundy-colored *kebaya*s over sarongs. One bore the Nini Towong doll, resting upon her shoulder, and another carried a tray of offerings—two large combs of bananas, betel leaves, tobacco, and a few sticks of incense. Pak Paeran led the way as we walked, perhaps a kilometer through the village, to a cemetery. Along the way, the women sang *sotto voce* the song *Padha mbuwang bocah bajang, rambute arang abang* (see below). When we reached the cemetery, we had to remove our shoes before crossing the threshold, even though this meant that we had to walk barefoot upon the earth.

It was pitch black in the cemetery. Pak Paeran scanned the surroundings using a battery-powered torch. He shone the light into a tall tree. It seemed to me like a scene from a horror movie; a group of people gathered in silence, the flickering light of bamboo torches revealing shadowy glimpses of faces and tombstones. Despite myself, I found that I was afraid to follow the beam of Pak Paeran's torch into the branches and leaves of the giant tree looming overhead.

Pak Paeran crouched under the tree to burn incense to invoke the spirit of the dead to possess the doll. After about twenty minutes, he put a *kanthil* (*Michelia champaca L.*) bud into the bosom of the doll. The deed was done. Pak Paeran told me that the doll had been possessed by the spirit of a dead woman named Nyi Roro Wardia Sih, a woman not personally known to anyone in the party. We left the cemetery and walked back to Pak Suwardi's home. On the return journey, the women sang *Padha mupu bocah bajang, rambute arang abang* to the same tune as the song they sang on their outward journey.

In the meantime, a gamelan orchestra had been set up in the courtyard of Pak Suwardi's house. A space of about four meters square had been laid out with straw mats. The musicians—ten men dressed in uniform burgundy, some wearing the distinctive Yogyakarta turban—were lined along one side of the performing space. When our party came into view, they struck up the tune that the women were

FIGURE 3. The Sabdo Budoyo performance, Grudo Panjangrejo village, in Pundong, Bantul, 27 June 2009. In the foreground in the green tunic is Pak Paeran, the *pawang*. Photograph by author.

singing, but an up-tempo version. The women sat down in a second line. My party of five formed the audience on a third side, while a small crowd of about fifteen villagers watched from the fourth side.

Four women came forward to form a cluster at the center. They sat upon their heels holding the Nini Towong doll high over their heads. They began to bounce the doll vigorously. The other women sang, while clapping their hands to a rousing rendition of the children's song *Ilir-Ilir*, and, as if touched by the rhythm, the doll moved faster and faster, its arms and shawl swinging left and right (FIGURE 3).

We were invited to take turns holding the doll. Three women continued to hold on to the bamboo handles while the fourth ceded her place to the guest who came forward when his or her name was read out by Pak Paeran. When it was my turn, I took hold of one bamboo handle in one hand as instructed. Perhaps this made the doll seem unusually heavy to me. The swinging and bouncing caused the bamboo handle to cut into the flesh of my palm, and I gave up after less than five minutes.

The men in my party fared better for they said they went with the momentum. One described the experience as akin to Chinese dragon dancing when a cloth-and-bamboo dragon is held aloft and swung by a troupe to make it seem as if the beast is writhing in the air. Another reported that he was able to affect the trajectory of the swing of the Nini Towong doll by varying his hold on the handle. Whether people manipulated the doll, or whether it moved on its own accord, Nini Towong began to swing low and in a wide arc so that people holding onto it were forced to bend forward to prevent their heads from being hit by the doll (FIGURE 4). This elicited much laughter from the audience which had by now swelled to perhaps thirty adults and children. When the doll continued to swing

FIGURE 4. Nini Towong swings low and wide. Photograph by author.

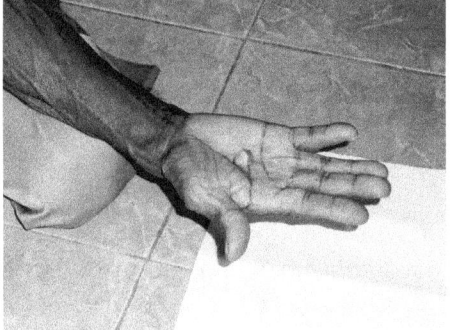

FIGURE 5. Pak Paeran fanning Nini Towong when she was hot from dancing. Photograph by author.

FIGURE 6. Pak Paeran's magic agate stone held in his palm. Photograph by author.

in this way, Pak Paeran told it off for being naughty. The doll, behaving like a little girl, snuggled her head upon Pak Paeran's bosom. He acted the father figure, chiding and cajoling Nini Towong, fanning her when she was hot from dancing (FIGURE 5). He also held up a mirror to the doll.

HUGRONJE (1906, 206) had written that the mirror was the vehicle through which the spirit entered and animated the Nini Towong doll, a suggestion that has since been repeated in other texts, but Pak Paeran told me that the mirror is only for the doll to admire itself. The power to invoke a spirit into the doll came not from the mirror, he said, but a magic, creamy-brown, oval agate stone which he kept wrapped in paper in his pocket (FIGURE 6). In Indonesia, it is popularly believed that agate stones can serve as repositories for possessing spirits.

The performance lasted about an hour-and-a half with the women and orchestra performing a list of seventeen songs that included popular numbers such as *Gambang Semarang* and one entitled *Pariwisata Njajah Desa*, a song welcoming tourists to the village. Midway through the show there was an interval for food and drinks when the doll also took a break from dancing. Finally, the *pawang* took hold of the doll to calm it down. He plucked the *kanthil* bud from its bosom and threw this away. The doll fell back, lifeless.

MYSTICISM DESPITE CULTURAL COMMODIFICATION

It was clear that I had seen Nini Towong as cultural commodity performed for the consumption of tourists. The costumed chorus and musicians, the beautiful doll and its endearing childlike behavior were embellishments that mitigated dark notions of spirit possession.

Pak Paeran told me how the Sabdo Budoyo Nini Towong developed from ritual to cultural showpiece. When he first became a Nini Towong *pawang* in 1963, Paeran performed to divine cures for illnesses, but he stopped this practice four years later. People were ungrateful, he explained, and he had to bear the brunt of the anger of the spirits who felt that they had not been sufficiently repaid for the boons they granted. Pak Paeran said Nini Towong used to be performed as a cleansing ceremony at the close of the harvest whenever a Sunday coincided with *Pon* of the five-day Javanese week.[5] He said the last time the Nini Towong was staged as a cleansing ritual at Grudo Panjangrejo village was in 1995.

But although Nini Towong had been commodified, its roots in mysticism were not deeply buried away. There was the trip to the cemetery to invite the spirit of a dead person to possess the doll, and there were the songs "Padha mbuwang bocah bajang, rambute arang abang," which translates as "To abandon the child with sparse red hair," and "Padha mupu bocah bajang, rambute arang abang," which is "To adopt the child with sparse red hair." The first action suggests the abandoning, even the murder, of a *bocah bajang*, a deformed newborn. The second song is about recalling the spirit of a dead child (a fuller discussion follows). The song sets out the popular belief that Nini Towong is possessed by a *bocah bajang*. Despite this reference to dark magic, the lyrics of the *Mupu bocah bajang* song sung that night in Bantul included a homily urging listeners to work hard and not just sit around "shaking their legs" (a popular phrase meaning idling). It reminded people to think of God and to become pillars of society by observing the principles of Pancasila.[6] The politically correct reference to the state ideology in a song named for the *bocah bajang* spirit showed the reach of curatorial and custodial power even to a magical ritual performed in a rural village.

THE BOCAH BAJANG

The mystical idea of the *bocah bajang* is of a deformed child, despised and abandoned, even murdered.[7] A *bocah bajang* has been described as "a stunted child; a child whose hair has never been cut" (ROBSON and WIBISONO 2002, 65). Another suggestion is a "spirit malignant to pregnant women and to infants" (STEVENS and SCHMIDGALL-TELLINGS, eds. 2004, 78 and 146). Usually a baby has its first hair shaved off in a naming ceremony when it is about five days old, thus the spirit of a dead unshaven child is one who has not lived long enough to be recognized as a human soul. The stunted *bocah bajang* spirit is magically powerful, like the retinue of dwarves and albinos kept by Javanese kings as a source of the ruler's kingly power (ANDERSON 1990, 27; RICKLEFS 1998, 223).

Nini Towong is also a *bocah bajang* in her personification as Dewi Sri, the rice goddess. The myth tells of a murdered bride-to-be. Rice plants and food crops sprouted from her corpse. Denied marriage and the fruitfulness of her womb, Dewi Sri offered her body to be eaten thus transferring her fertility to food for the people. Reflecting this notion of life reborn after death, harvest rituals in the sub-district of Kerek, near Tuban, are annual communal enactments that take place on the graves of the ancestors at the start of a new agricultural cycle (HERINGA 1997, 370). This perhaps explains why the spirit that possesses the Nini Towong doll has to be invited at a cemetery.

THE IDENTITY OF NINI TOWONG

Rassers noted that Nini Towong is the name of a female servant character accorded only passing mention in two shadow puppet dramas, "Pandu-papa" and "Sudamala." In the latter play she is married to Semar, the Javanese ancestral deity, so that RASSERS proposed Nini Towong as the female ancestor of the Javanese people (1982, 36). Hazeu offered two suggestions: he proposes Nini Towong as a *widadari* (celestial nymph), an invited spirit of Indian origin (HAZEU 1901 in RASSERS 1982, 35), and then posits Nini Towong as a character in Malayo-Polynesian spiritualism (34–35). JORDAAN proposed Nini Towong as Nyai Lara Kidul, the Javanese goddess of the sea, on the basis of the water elements in the performance—Nini Towong's head is a water scoop, and she is often made with a basket fish trap (1984, 104). Jordaan further notes that Lara Kidul is the chthonian Malayo-Polynesian deity of agriculture, equivalent to the Hindu Dewi Sri (JORDAAN 1984, 110 and 113, note 10). The many possible identities for Nini Towong remind us that any attempt to ascribe origins of folkloric figures can at best be speculative.

Zigu chinese spirit-basket divination

It is with this warning fully in mind that I link Nini Towong to the goddess Zigu of Chinese spirit-basket divination through the common element of the *bocah bajang* (the frustrated spirit). Zigu (紫姑; Purple Lady) is the Chinese goddess of the latrine, where "Zi" is a genteel homonym for toilet, *ce* (厕). Zigu legends tell of a secondary wife who was murdered in the privy by the jealous first wife. In ancient times latrines were built over pig pens from which night soil and dung could be collected for essential fertilizers (ZHANG 2001, 78; LIN 2008, 5). The economic aspect of the latrine is signalled in the Chinese character for toilet 厕 which includes the radicals for "factory" 厂 (*chang*) and "shell money" 贝 (*bei*). Thus, the death of Zigu relates how a murdered young bride transfers the potential fruitfulness of her womb to the agricultural crop. The Heavenly Emperor, having taken pity upon the murdered Zigu, had made her the goddess of the latrine (CHAO 1942, 26). Zigu has been invoked in spirit-basket divination from as early as the fifth century (CHAO 1942; JORDAN and OVERMYER, 1986; QIN 2010).

Originally, only women took part in Zigu divination, but by Song times the literati, including male scholars, would invite the goddess to move their writing and painting brushes. By then not only Zigu but also other spirits, even the ghosts of dead men, began to possess the basket. Importantly, what had been a woman's game began to be played by men (CHAO 1942, 20–21). A nineteenth-century account of an encounter by Europeans of Chinese spirit-basket divination reported in *Chambers's Journal*, a popular weekly out of Edinburgh, and later London, might provide us with an answer to the question, "Why female Javanese Nini Towong and male Chinese *jelangkung*?" The séance described in *Chambers's* involved a male medium with boys supporting the basket. The *Chambers's* report also observed how the practice of spirit-basket divination had invaded Ningbo (a seaport in Zhejiang province) like "an epidemic: there was scarcely a house in which it was not practiced for a season almost daily" (CHAMBERS and CHAMBERS 1854). Perhaps *jelangkung* is this latter-day vulgar game played by men for amusement, introduced by nineteenth-century Chinese immigrants into the urban centers of Indonesia, whereas Nini Towong is a cultural involution of Zigu spirit-basket divination that had come to Indonesia at an earlier time.

Similarities between zigu
spirit-basket divination and nini towong

The striking similarities between Zigu spirit-basket divination and Nini Towong performances make a compelling argument for a connection between both practices. In Zigu spirit-basket divination, the spirit of Zigu is invited into an effigy usually made with a ladle for the head and a winnowing basket for the body (CHAO 1942, 15–18). A favorite time to play Chinese spirit-basket divination is during the night of a full moon when the *yin* energy (the sun represents *yang* energy) is at its fullest. The best time to summon Nini Towong is also when there is a *bulan purnama* (full moon) (RASSERS 1982, 37). In the Nini Towong possession, game old women make the doll and invite the spirit to enter the doll (RASSERS

FIGURE 7. The Nini Towong doll at Indonesia's National Museum is clearly a basket effigy. Photograph used with the kind permission of Bambang Areongbinang. See the website Areongbinang Travelog. (This entry is no longer available although in a more recent posting Areongbinang notes that there used to be a Nini Thowok doll in the Museum Nasional Jakarta.)

1982, 31–32), or the *siwur* coconut-shell bailer that makes the head of the doll must be stolen from an old maid (KARTOMI 1973, 180). Matrons, not young girls, take Nini Towong to the cemetery (HUGRONJE 1906, 206), and this was how it was with the Sabdo Budoyo performance I observed. In Zigu spirit-basket divination, the basket has been described as draped with an old woman's dress (ELLIOTT 1990, 146). Then there is the crucial shared element of the basket body. Several texts describe the Nini Towong doll's body as being fashioned out of basketry, including a winnowing sieve, bamboo rice steamer, or fishing creel (HUGRONJE 1906, 206; KARTOMI 1973, 1980; RASSERS 1982, 31; Pak Suwardi interview quoted above). There is a nineteenth-century Nini Towong doll in the ethnography collection of the Museum Nasional Republik Indonesia (National Museum of Indonesia, popularly known as Museum Nasional Jakarta, also known as Museum Gajah) in Jakarta (SITOWATI and MIKSIC 2006, 135) where the basket is clearly visible (FIGURE 7). More recently, KARTOMI (1973, 179–89) described a *Tjowongan*, a rainmaking ritual that she witnessed on 14 January 1970 in Desa Ajam Alas in the Banjumas area of the district of Kroja, near the central southern Javanese coast. Her account includes a photograph of the ceremony, which involved a Nini Towong doll made with a plaited bamboo rice-streamer body (KARTOMI 1973, 181).

IGNORING SINIC INFLUENCES UPON INDONESIAN CULTURE

Edward B. TYLOR (1879) proposed that when games of a complex nature are found in different geographical locations, the evidence makes the anthropological argument for cultural diffusion having taken place, since the complexity of games argues against their having "sprung up independently" at later locations. The thesis that Nini Towong is derived from Chinese spirit-basket divination has merit, but the point of this article is not to argue the origin of Nini Towong. This writer's view follows the arguments made by VAN BINSBERGEN that cultural invo-lution can endow a borrowed item so completely with the recipient symbolism and cosmology that the resultant product cannot be other than uniquely local-ized (1996–1997, 239). Besides, sieve divination has also been reported in Europe and India (CHAO 1942, 21), an observation that in itself does not negate the Chi-nese origin of basket/sieve divination; for example, BODDE ascribes China as the source for games played worldwide, including card games, dominoes, and kite-flying (2002–2013). Rather than belabor the point of origin, the arguments for a Nini Towong Chinese spirit-basket connection made here seeks to foreground the dearth of attention given to Sinic contributions in Western scholarship on Indone-sian cultural heritage (see also the arguments in DRAKELEY 2005, 14).

For example, HURGRONJE asserts that South India is the birthplace of much of Malay and Achehnese literature even though he admits that he is "unable even to fix the portion of South-India where the threads meet which unite that coun-try with the mental life of the Indonesians" (1906, 122). BRAKEL-PAPENHUYZEN connects the Javanese *Jaka Tarub* fable with the fourteenth-century tale of Rajput Pabuji Dhandhal Rathaur (2006, 75–76). But the tale of a hero who steals the gar-ments of one of seven divine nymphs he spies bathing is more persuasively argued as a rendition of the Chinese "Cowherd and the Weaver Maid" legend, which dates back three thousand years. This is the acknowledged originary myth of the Tanabata festival in Japan and the Chilseok celebrations of Korea.[8] The love of the "Cowherd and the Weaver Maid" is celebrated by the Qixi (七夕) "Festival of the Double Seven" on the seventh day of the seventh moon, the most portentous day for Chinese spirit-basket divination (CHAO 1944, 5).

Historian SOMERS HEIDHUES discusses the contradiction of the definite pres-ence of the Chinese in Indonesia and the absence of presence in the social narra-tives of Indonesian culture. She attributes the situation to indigenous anti-Chinese sentiments and early European fascination with Indonesian archaeology (2010, 10).[9] To this list we can add Western Sinophobia.

EXCLUDING THE CHINESE VOICE
IN SOUTHEAST ASIAN CULTURAL NARRATIVES

Western Sinophobia was born out of Sinophilia. ZHANG (2008) writes how rapturous reports from Jesuit missionaries in sixteenth-century China ignited the imagination of Enlightenment thinkers, but produced a backlash. Rising Euro-pean imperialism in the eighteenth century needed justification, and European dynamism in trade and the sciences was reified against a Chinese model where the longevity of Chinese historiography, admired by Voltaire, was turned on its head and made to become an attribute of stagnation.

This philosophical about-turn found a more prosaic iteration among the Europeans who came out to Southeast Asia in the seventeenth to nineteenth centuries. They were merchants, and it was the "pariah capitalism" of the Chinese minority communities that caught the colonizer's eye (CHUN 1989). The Europeans disparagingly compared the Chinese to the Jews (REID 2010, 375–77). European anti-Semitic anti-Sinicism provided King Vajiravudh (Rama VI, 1910–1925) reason for the repudiation of the Chinese. He defined the Thai national identity against the ethnic Other of the Chinese who were the "The Jews of the Orient" (VELLA and VELLA 1978, 194; RENARD 2006, 308–12). In 1938, Luang Wichitwathakan, Thailand's Director General of the Department of Fine Arts,[10] proposed that Siam should emulate Nazi policies in dealing with the country's "own Jews" (BARMÉ 1993, 129).

Nineteenth-century American and European anti-Chinese sentiments took on a racist bent in Yellow Peril anxieties, fetishized in offensive cartoon caricatures in the popular press, a medium that had great influence upon public opinion. Reductionist cultural stereotypes continued into the twentieth century with Fu Manchu, Charlie Chan, and Mickey Rooney's yellow face portrayal (complete with taped eyelids, over-sized spectacles, buck teeth, and sibilant accent) in the 1961 movie *Breakfast at Tiffany's*. More recently we have Bowring's Lee Kuan Yew obituary for *The Guardian* in which he described Lee as "a 'banana'—yellow on the outside, white inside … with all the intolerance of a Chinese emperor." Lee, BOWRING pronounced, "did not create modern Singapore's prosperity. The city state thrived naturally in a region of economic growth and rapid development of world trade" (22 March 2015). In a 2008 interview, Rooney said that it broke his heart to learn that many Asian Americans had found his *Breakfast* turn as Mr. Yunioshi offensive, and that he would not have played the part if he had known. He said that the director Blake Edwards hired him for the role, "and we had fun doing it" (MAGAGNINI, 7 September 2008).

This is an important point. We might self-reflexively ask if an insidious Sinophobia comes into the phrasing of our language; for example, in academic writing we have REID (2009), CHUN (1996), and YAO's description of the Chinese diaspora as the Chinese race "without the shackles of China" (2009, 258). SHIH (2011) is less compelling in her need to justify the repudiation of China. Her arguments for an alternative discourse that can account for Chineseness outside the boundaries of a national China are more persuasive in her earlier, more straightforward discussion of Nobel Laureate Gao Xingjian as "a writer who happens to write in Chinese and [who] may live anywhere in the world" (SHIH 2004, 26). It may all be mere rhetoric, but the tense situation in the South China Sea asks for more circumspection than the comparison by former president of the Philippines Benigno Aquino of China with Nazi Germany in a *New York Times* interview (BRADSHER 2014), and in a speech he delivered at the Upper House of the Japanese parliament in June 2015 (TAKENAKA 2015).

In his naming of Jews and Chinese as "essential outsiders" who are the targets of xenophobia, CHIROT grimly noted that while Jewish genocide might have blunted European anti-Semitism, the situation of the Chinese in Southeast Asia

FIGURE 8. Muslim high school girls performing in a Chinese temple procession. Jakarta, 17 October 2009. Photograph by author.

remains precarious (1997, 3–4). REID's (2009, 293) catalogue of anti-Chinese riots in Indonesia in modern times—1945, 1947, 1959–1960, 1963, 1965–1967, 1973, 1980, 1994, and 1996–1998—supports this view. More recently, in November and December 2016, the protests against the ethnic Chinese Basuki Tjahaja Purnama (Ahok) governor of Jakarta for alleged blasphemy has taken racialist overtones. We also note REID's (2010) investigation into the possibility that the Chinese of Southeast Asia might be targets for anti-Semitic hostility. We note his concluding advice that racism should never be taken lightly.

Against these dark closing thoughts, we look for hope in the unselfconscious side-by-side arrangement of Javanese Nini Towong next to Chinese *jelangkung* in the Surabaya museum. The display is as artless as the way the lion dance is performed, even outside the Chinese New Year festive season, by Javanese youths going shop-to-shop in Jakarta's Glodok Chinatown. It is as unselfconscious as the performance of Chinese dragon dance by soldiers from the Yon Armed-11 Kostrad, a land artillery battalion of the Indonesian Army's Strategic Reserve that I saw in a Jakarta Chinese temple procession in 2009. The men, in their army uniforms, participated alongside two Muslim high school marching bands and a contingent of girls wearing headscarfs who twirled large flags (see FIGURE 8).

No one seemed to find it remarkable that Muslims were taking part in a Chinese temple procession. It was straightforward; the soldiers, students, and lion dance troupes were performing for a fee. It was not a matter of religion, and everything was in order in the quotidian.

NOTES

* This research was supported by the Singapore Ministry of Education (MOE) Academic Research Fund (AcRF) Tier 1 grant. I am grateful to many people without whom I could not have done this research: Ardian Cangianto, my friend and guide, Pui Khian Fung, Susi Wu,

Liu Sa Min, Lio Kuniarwan, Amien Nusantio Setiadi, Chin Miau Fuk for showing me Sing-kawang, and Didik Nini Thowok and Linda Harsini for opening Yogyakarta to me. I thank my steadfast friends to whom I could always turn to check facts and share ideas with: Mary Somers Heidhues, Rudi Dustika Teja, Victor Yue, Jave Wu, Timothy Pwee, Raymond Goh, Hoon Chang Yau, and my son Jonathan Chan who assisted me on my research trips. I extend my gratitude to Anne McLaren and Carol Chia of the University of Melbourne, and to the anonymous reviewers for their guidance and advice with regard to the writing and publishing of this article.

1. MANTOVANI and POERNOMO's *Jelangkung* (2001) was the top box office hit of its year, drawing the highest sales record in Indonesian history at that time.

2. An examination of spirit-basket divination is included in a discussion of the sociopoliti-cal performance practices of the Chinese of Singkawang, West Kalimantan (CHAN 2012).

3. Personal interview with Didik Nini Thowok in English, at Yogyakarta on 27 June 2009. Didik Nini Thowok is a moniker; the dancer is Didik Hadiprayitno.

4. Email correspondence with Didik Nini Thowok, 9–24 June 2009.

5. The Javanese *pasaran* uses a five-day week. The five days are *Legi, Pahing, Pon, Wagé,* and *Kliwon.*

6. See also RASSERS (1982).The song that I had heard in Bantul in June 2009 must have been a later version for Pancasila was promulgated only in 1945.

7. For example, in the 1975 film *Penghuni Bangunan Tua* [Spirit of the old building; SHARIEFFUNDIN 1975], the spirit of a murdered boy possesses an effigy to haunt the youths who had summoned it. The story of the vengeful spirit of a murdered boy also featured in the film *Jelangkung* (MANTOVANI and POERNOMO 2001).

8. The story of Nui Lang 牛郎, the Cowherd, and Zhi Nu 织女, the Weaver Maid, is refer-enced in the Qin Jian 秦简 bamboo-strip books found in the Shui Hu Di 睡虎地 excavation in Hubei province, China, in 1975. In the *Ri Shu* 日书 *Day Book*, a divination diary, Jia Zhong Di Yi Wu Wu Jian 甲种第一五五简, bamboo slip number 155, the following is written: 戊申、己酉日牵牛迎取(娶)织女、不果、三弃 [On the day of *wu shen* and *ji you*, Qian Niu and Zhi Nu's wedding ceremony cannot be sealed. If people marry on this day, the husband will abandon the wife within three years]. This suggests that the story of the "Cowherd and the Weaver Maid" probably preceded Qin. In the *Shijing* 诗经, dating to as early as 1000 BCE, the star Aquila, west of the Milky Way, was already named the Cowherd, and Vega, east of the Milky Way, was named the Weaver Maid (LI 2006, 97–98).

9. MIKSIC (2000) also reports on the bias in Southeast Asian archaeology for monumental orthogenetic sites. The evidence of small items such as money and ceramic shards at hetero-genetic sites such as trade settlements where the Chinese congregated proved less compelling.

10. Wichitwathakan became Minister of Foreign Affairs from 1942–1943 under the fascist government of Plaek Phibunsongkhram (1938–1944).

REFERENCES

ANDERSON, Benedict
    1990   *Language and Power: Exploring Political Cultures in Indonesia.* Ithaca, NY, and London: Cornell University Press.

AREONGBINANG, Bambang
    2017   Museum Nasional Jakarta, The Areongbinang Travelog. Updated 30 January. https://www.thearoengbinangproject.com/museum-nasional -jakarta/ (accessed 14 March 2017).

ATMOSUMARTO, Sutanto
    2004   *A Learner's Comprehensive Dictionary of Indonesia.* Harrow, Middlesex: Atma Stanton.

BAMBANG, Areongbinang
n.d.   *The Areongbinang Travelog*. www.http://thearoengbinangproject
        .com/ (accessed November 1, 2012).

BARMÉ, Scot
1993   *Luang Wichit Wathakan and the Creation of a Thai Identity*. Singapore:
        Institute of Southeast Asian Studies.

BODDE, Derk
2002–2013 China's gifts to the West. *China: A Teaching Workbook*. Asia for Edu-
        cators, Columbia University 2002–2013. (Originally published 1942.)
        http://afe.easia.columbia.edu/song/readings/inventions_gifts.htm#intro
        (accessed 29 April 2015).

BOWRING, Phillip
2015   Lee Kuan Yew obituary. *The Guardian* (22 March). http://www.the
        guardian.com/world/2015/mar/22/lee-kuan-yew (accessed 30 April
        2015).

BRADSHER, Keith
2014   Philippine Leader Sounds Alarm on China. *The New York Times*, Febru-
        ary 4. http://mobile.nytimes.com/2014/02/05/world/asia/philippine
        -leader-urges-international-help-in-resisting-chinas-sea-claims.html
        (accessed 9 March 2016).

BRAKEL-PAPENHUYZEN, Clara
2006   Jaka Tarub, a Javanese culture hero? *Indonesia and the Malay World* 34
        (March): 75–90.

CHAMBERS, William, and Robert CHAMBERS
1854   Table-turning in China. *Chambers's Journal of Popular Literature, Sci-
        ence and Arts* 35. 2 September, 151–53. London: W. & R. Chambers. Dig-
        itized 5 Jul 2007.
        http://books.google.com.sg/books?id=ol8EAAAAYAAJ&p-
        g=RA2-PA152&lpg=RA2-PA152&dq=the+rod+always+raps+the+table&-
        source=web&ots=b5RyawIGkG&sig=3eu_NgHdsVQJGNo-
        SI2StSS_tjEU&hl=en&sa=X&oi=book_result&resnum=1&ct=re-
        sult#PRA2-PA151,MI (accessed 14 March 2017).

CHAN, Margaret
2012   The spirit-mediums of Singkawang: Performing peoplehood. In *Chinese
        Indonesians Reassessed: History, Religion and Belonging*, Siew Min Sai and
        Hoon Chang-Yau, eds., 138–58. London and New York: Routledge.

CHAO, Weipang
1942   The origin and growth of the Fu Chi. *Folklore Studies* 1: 9–27.
        doi: 10.2307/318292d

1944   Games at the mid-autumn festival in Kuangtung. *Folklore Studies* 3: 1–16.
        doi: 10.2307/3182894

CHIROT, Daniel
1997   Conflicting identities and the dangers of communalism. In *Essential Out-
        siders: Chinese and Jews in the Modern Transformation of Southeast Asia and
        Central Europe*, Daniel Chirot and Anthony Reid, eds., 3–32. Seattle: Uni-
        versity of Washington Press.

CHUN, Allen J.
1989   Pariah capitalism and the overseas Chinese of Southeast-Asia: Problems in the definition of the problem. *Ethnic and Racial Studies* (April) 12: 233–56.
1996   Fuck Chineseness: On the ambiguities of ethnicity as culture as identity. *Boundary* 2, 23: 111–38. doi:10.2307/303809

DRAKELEY, Steven
2005   *The History of Indonesia*. Westport, CT: Greenwood Press.

EDWARDS, Blake, dir.
1961   *Breakfast at Tiffany's*. Los Angeles, CA: Jurow-Shepherd Production.

ELLIOTT, Alan J. A.
1990   *Chinese Spirit-Medium Cults in Singapore*. London and Atlantic Highlands, NJ: The Athlone Press. (Originally published 1955.)

FRENAVIT KUSMAN SETIA PUTRA
2008   Ilmu kedokteran dengan ilmu gaib [Medical sciences and magic]. *frenavit .com*, 17 November. http://frenavit.com/ilmu-kedokteran-dan-ilmu-gaib .html (accessed 1 November 2012).

GEERTZ, Clifford
1963   *Agricultural Involution: The Process of Ecological Change in Indonesia*. Berkeley and Los Angeles, CA: University of California Press.

Harian Jogja [Jogja Daily]
2009   Gelar lagi tradisi usir batara kala [Performing again: The tradition of chasing away Batara Kala]. May 4. http://www.harianjogja.com/web2 /beritas/detailberita/5171/gelar-lagi-tradisi-usir-batara-kalaview.html (accessed 27 October 2012).

HAZEU, G. A. J.
1901   Nini-Towong. *Tijdschrift voor Indische Taal-, Land- en Volkenkunde* 43: 36–107.

HERINGA, Rens
1997   Dewi Sri in village garb: Fertility, myth, and ritual in Northeast Java. *Asian Folklore Studies* 56: 355–77.

HURGRONJE, C. Snouck
1906   *The Achehnese*. Volume 2. A. W. S. O'Sullivan, trans. Leiden: E. J. Brill. http://www.archive.org/details/achehnese02hurg (accessed 26 October 2011).

JORDAAN, Roy E.
1984   The mystery of Nyai Lara Kidul, goddess of the southern ocean. *Archipel, Année* 28: 99–116.

JORDAN, David K., and Daniel L. OVERMYER
1986   *The Flying Phoenix: Aspects of Chinese Sectarianism in Taiwan*. Princeton, NJ: Princeton University Press.

KARTOMI, Margaret J.
1973   Music and trance in central Java. *Ethnomusicology* 17 (May): 163–208. doi: 10.2307/849881

LI Ying 李莹
2006   Qi Xi Jie Kao Shu 七夕节考述 [The origin of the Qixi Festival]. *Heilongjiang Jiao Yu Xue Yuan Xue Bao* 黑龙江教育学院学报 [Journal of Heilongjiang Institute of Education] 25 (November): 97–99.

LIN Jifu 林继富
    2008   Zigu Xin Yang Liu Bian Yan Jiu 紫姑信仰流变研究 [On changes in Zigu beliefs]. *Changjiang Da Xue Xue Bao (She Hui Ke Xue Ban* 长 江大学学报 (社会科学版) [Journal of Yangtze University (Social Sciences)] 31 (February): 5–11.

MAGAGNINI, Stephen
    2008   Rooney is stunned to hear film offended: Actor, 87, insists he never meant to insult Asians in "Tiffany's" role. *Sacramento Bee*, 25 August 2008, p. BI.

MANTOVANI, Rizal, and Jose POERNOMO, dirs.
    2001   *Jelangkung.* Jakarta: Rexinema.

MIKSIC, John N.
    2000   Heterogenetic cities in premodern Southeast Asia. *World Archaeology* 32, Archaeology in Southeast Asia: 106–20.

PURWANINGSIH, Ernawati
    2006   Permainan tradisional anak: Salah satu khasanah budaya yang perlu dilestarikan [Traditional children's games: A cultural treasure that must be preserved]. *Jantra, Jurnal Sejarah dan Budaya* [Jantra, Journal of History and Culture] 1 (June): 40–46. http://www.scribd.com/doc/50213392/7/Permainan-tradisional-anak-salah-satu-khasanah-budaya-yang-perlu-dilestarikan. Yogyakarta: Balai Pelestarian Sejarah dan Nilai Tradisional [Center for the Preservation of History and Traditional Values] (accessed 23 October 2011).

QIN Ying
    2010   The Purple Lady and blessings of fertility. Paper presented at the American Association for Chinese Studies (AACS) 52nd Conference. 16 October. Wake Forest University in Winston-Salem, North Carolina

RASSERS, W. H.
    1982   On the meaning of Javanese drama. (Originally published in Dutch in 1925). In *Panji, The Culture Hero: A Structural Study of Religion in Java.* Second edition, 3–61. The Hague: Martinus Nijhoff. (First English edition published in 1959).

REID, Anthony
    2009   Escaping the burdens of Chineseness. *Asian Ethnicity* 10: 285–96.
    2010   Jewish-conspiracy theories in Southeast Asia. *Indonesia and the Malay World* 38: 373–85.

RENARD, Ronald D.
    2006   Creating the other requires defining thainess against which the other can exist: Early-twentieth century definitions. *Southeast Asian Studies* 44: 295–320.

RICKLEFS, M. C.
    1998   *The Seen and the Unseen Worlds in Java, 1726–1749: History, Literature, and Islam in the Court of Pakubuwana II.* St. Leonards, NSW, and Honolulu: Allen & Unwin and University of Hawai'i Press.

ROBSON, Stuart, and Singgih WIBISONO
    2002   *Javanese English Dictionary.* Hong Kong: Periplus.

SHARIEFFUDIN, M. A., dir.
    1975   *Penghuni bangunan tua* [Spirit of the old building]. Medan: P.T. Surya Indonesia Medan.

SCHECHNER, Richard
    1990   Wayang kulit in the colonial margin. *TDR* 34 (Summer): 25–61.

SCHELTEMA, J. F.
    1912   *Java: Peeps at Many Lands.* London: Adam & Charles Black.
            http://www.archive.org/stream/peepsatmanylands025441mbp
            /peepsatmanylands025441mbp_djvu.txt (accessed 26 October 2012).

SHIH, Shu-mei
    2004   Global literature and the technologies of recognition. *PMLA* 119, Special
            Topic: Literatures at Large (January): 16–30.
    2011   The concept of the Sinophone. *PMLA* 126: 709–18.

SITOWATI, Retno Sulistianingsih, and John N. MIKSIC
    2006   *Icons of Art: National Museum Jakarta.* Jakarta: BAB Publishing.

SOMERS HEIDHUES, Mary
    2010   *Chinese Presence in Malay-Indonesian Narratives: Founders and Heroes or
            Merchants and Wife-Givers?* Hamburger Südostasienstudien Band 4, Ham-
            burg: University of Hamburg.

STEVENS, Alan M., and A. SCHMIDGALL-TELLINGS, eds.
    2004   *A Comprehensive Indonesian-English Dictionary.* Athens, Ohio: Ohio Uni-
            versity Press.

SUDIARNO, Tarko
    2002   Ninithowong, a Javanese that can tell the future. *The Jakarta Post,* 25
            March, https://article.wn.com/view/2002/03/25/Ninithowong_a
            _Javanese_that_can_tell_the_future/ (accessed 30 May 2017).

SUJARNO
    2002   Permainan tradisional Nini Towong, fungsi dan nilainya bagi masyara-
            ket [The traditional game of Nini Towong, its function and value for the
            community]. In *Patra-Widya,* September 3. *Kementerian Pendidikan dan
            Kebudayaan. Direktorat Jenderal Kebudayaan* [Ministry of Education and
            Culture, Directorate General of Culture], 19 August 2014. http://keb
            udayaan.kemdikbud.go.id/bpnbyogyakarta/2014/08/19/permainan
            -tradisional-nini-thowong-fungsi-dan-nilainya-bagi-masyarakat/ (accessed
            14 March 2017).
    n.d.   Tembi Rumah Budaya (Tembi House of Culture). *Nini Thowong.* Youtube
            https://www.youtube.com/watch?v=MdLPHcw2Ud4 (accessed 14 March
            2017).

TAKENAKA, Kiyoshi
    2015   Philippine's Aquino revives comparison between China and Nazi Germany.
            Reuters, 3 June. http://www.reuters.com/article/us-japan-philippines
            -idUSKBN0OJ0OY20150603 (accessed 9 March 2016).

Tembi rumah budaya [Tembi House of Culture]
    2002   YouTube film of a Sabdo Budoyo performance of Nini Towong in the
            district of Bantul Yogjakarta. http://utopianvision.co.uk/bollywood
            /videos/?v=MdLPHcw2Ud4 (accessed 31 October 2012).

TU, Wei-ming
    1991   Cultural China: The periphery as the center. *Daedalus* 120 (Spring): 1–32.
    1994   *The Living Tree: The Changing Meaning of Being Chinese Today.* Stanford:
            Stanford University Press.

TYLOR, Edward B.
  1879   Geographical distribution of games. *Fortnightly Review* 25: 23–30. http://healthy.uwaterloo.ca/museum/Archives/Tylor/ (accessed 15 June 2017).

VAN BINSBERGEN, Wim M. J.
  1996–1997   Rethinking Africa's contribution to global cultural history: Lessons from a comparative historical analysis of mankala board-games and geomantic divination. *Talanta* 1996–1997, 28/29: 219–51. Leiden University Repository. http://www.ascleiden.nl/publications/rethinking-africas-contribution-global-cultural-history-lessons-comparative-historical (accessed 25 October 2012).

VELLA, Walter F., and Dorothy B. VELLA
  1978   *Chaiyo! King Vajiravudh and the Development of Thai Nationalism.* Honolulu: University of Hawai'i Press.

WESSING, Robert
  1999   A dance of life: The Seblang of Banyuwangi, Indonesia. *Bijdragen tot de Taal-, Land- en Volkenkunde* 155: 644–82.

YAO, Souchou
  2009   Being essentially Chinese. *Asian Ethnicity* 10: 251–62.

ZHANG, Chunjie
  2008   From Sinophilia to Sinophobia: China, history, and recognition. *Colloquia Germanica* 2: 97–110.

ZHANG, Xiaoshu 张晓舒
  2001   Ying Zigu Yi Su Qi Yuan Xin Lun 迎紫姑习俗起源新论 [A new study into the origin of the custom of welcoming Zigu]. *Zhong Nan Shi Zu Xue Yuan Xue Bao (Ren Wen Du Hui Ke Xue Ban)* 中南是族学院学报 (人文杜会科学版) [Journal of South Central University for Nationalities (Humanities and Social Sciences)] (July) 21: 78–81.

CAROLINE CHIA
University of Melbourne

"Negotiation" Between a
Religious Art Form and the Secular State

Chinese Puppet Theater in
Singapore and the Case Study of Sin Hoe Ping

Traditional art forms often face rapid decline if they are not able to keep pace with a changing society. This article will examine puppet theater as performed by Chinese descent groups in temples and public spaces in Singapore as a case study of the adaptation of particular ethnic traditions at a time of an intense process of modernization. The island state of Singapore comprises various ethnic groups from different religious backgrounds living together in an advanced economy. On the one hand, the government ensures that the ethno-religious framework is protected through policies and laws. On the other, it seeks to maintain social cohesion by not favoring any religious group and by downplaying religious and ethnic divides. As discussed here, notions of "Chineseness" need to be accommodated within state policies based on the "harmonization" of racial and religious differences. The traditional art form investigated here, Chinese puppet theater, is characteristically linked to ethnicity and religion. How, then, does this ritual art form "negotiate" with a state that emphasizes secularism and seeks to elide multiracial and multi-religious differences? This study proposes a distinction between the "state-regulated realm" and the "state-tolerated realm" to suggest how Chinese puppet theater has engaged in negotiation with the Singaporean state to enable it to survive and even flourish. The focus will be on the Sin Hoe Ping Puppet Troupe, which has demonstrated considerable flexibility in adapting to secularized Singapore.

KEYWORDS: religion—ethnicity—Chinese puppet theater—state-regulated—state-tolerated—Singapore

Asian Ethnology Volume 76, Number 1 · 2017, 117–144
© Nanzan University Anthropological Institute

I N THE early twenty-first century Singapore has become an advanced economy while still retaining the framework of a multiethnic and multi-religious society.* Nonetheless, the public expression of religious and ethnic difference is treated with caution by a state intent on managing social cohesion. One of the lesser known ritual arts in modern-day Singapore is a type of puppet theater (木偶戲; *pok giao hi* in Henghua) commonly performed in temples.

For Chinese descent groups, the puppet show performed at their local temple is an important expression of ethnic and religious identity. For this reason, it has survived the vicissitudes of state formation in postwar Singapore to the present day, although it faces many challenges in transmitting this heritage into the future. In the Chinese tradition, temples would stage spectacular shows in order to "please the gods," to entertain devotees, and to effectively communicate the prayers and concerns of the congregation to temple deities. In popular Chinese understanding, it is the visualization of religious activities in staged performances that is fundamental to the efficacy of the temple deity (RUIZENDAAL 2006, 181). This study will focus on the Sin Hoe Ping 新和平 Puppet Troupe, which has exhibited a remarkable adaptability in retaining its relevance in modern times. The Sin Hoe Ping troupe offers a valuable case study of a Sinophone cultural form that is not Mandarin speaking and hence in danger of marginalization within Mandarin-dominant Singapore. As discussed here, it survives by accommodating both Mandarin dominance and state secularization policies. This ethnographic study is based on eleven months of observation of Singaporean puppet performances from 2010 to 2011 and interviews carried out in a mixture of Mandarin, Hokkien, and Henghua with puppeteers, musicians, and ritual specialists.[1]

CELEBRATION OF THE BIRTHDAY OF THE CITY GOD AT LI JIANG TEMPLE

It was the birthday of the City God 城隍爺 on the eighteenth day of the fifth moon in the year 2010 and the celebration was held at Li Jiang temple 鯉江廟. The temple was one of the many that belonged to the Henghua 興化 group in Singapore.[2] Everyone involved, from the ritual specialists and temple helpers, to puppeteers and musicians, was busy making preparations for the event. The usually quiet Li Jiang temple was suddenly filled with life. The Taoist priest 道士 in charge set up the altar, presented offerings to the gods, and chanted prayers.[3] Temple helpers

118 | *Asian Ethnology* Volume 76, Number 1 · 2017

FIGURE I. Interlude of "Getting a Promotion and an Increase in Salary."

assisted in the preparation of incense paper and the display of food offerings. Members of the Sin Hoe Ping, the puppet troupe engaged in this performance, had set up a makeshift stage near the temple shortly before the performance. Mr. Yeo, the troupe leader, pulled up in a large truck and hauled down a number of metal boxes containing the puppets. It was his task to erect and dismantle the temporary stage. The musicians, mostly male, helped him set up the musical instruments on stage. Throughout the celebration of the deity's birthday, there were feasts comprising various Henghua delicacies where everyone involved would be treated to a meal.[4]

By 8:00 p.m., the event was ready to commence. As night approached, the illuminated stage, which was riddled with fluorescent bulbs, suddenly lit up and the sounds of cymbals and *suona* (Chinese shawm) filled the neighborhood. As usual, the performance was divided into a ritual section followed by the performance proper.[5] The ritual prelude included the set pieces, the "Eight Immortals" play 八仙戲 and "Getting a Promotion and an Increase in Salary" 加官進祿. In the case of the "Eight Immortals" play, the puppets acting as the Eight Immortals were seen as manifestations of deities whose duty was to "communicate" with the City God.[6] When the puppets representing the Eight Immortals had appeared on stage, the puppeteer would then recite:

Li: Inviting all deities!

Crowd: Invitation has been done!

Li: There is an event today.

Crowd: What event is it?

> Li: The event is held at Li Jiang Miao to celebrate the City God's birthday. We are here to express our birthday wishes.
>
> Crowd: Let's proceed!

The puppets then "knelt and bowed" to the City God on stage. Following this, four members of the Sin Hoe Ping troupe, including Mr. Yeo, carried the eight puppets from the stage to the temple. Stopping at the altar of the City God, the eight puppets carried out the "kneel and pray" pose and in this way sent their birthday regards to the God. The puppets were then placed backstage. Another puppet dressed in an official robe appeared on the stage for about thirty seconds before proceeding backstage. When it reappeared, the official was holding a red strip of paper with the Chinese characters "Getting a Promotion and an Increase in Salary" written on it (FIGURE 1).[7] The puppeteer appeared from behind the stage and took the official puppet "holding" the red strip of paper to the statue of the City God, where it was made to "bow" to this deity.

This brief ritual playlet is known as "Getting a Promotion and an Increase in Salary." When this solemn obeisance to the City God was concluded around 8:15 p.m., the puppeteers exclaimed "Prosper ah!" before proceeding back behind the stage.[8] The red strip of paper was placed on the temple altar and the priest then conveyed the message to the City God that the temple keeper had staged a performance to celebrate this festive occasion.

The ritual playlet concluded, it was time for the performance proper to begin. According to sources about Henghua puppet performances and in line with my observations, the play proper is usually a story set in imperial China. The performance of "Chen Wenlong" 陳文龍 was no exception. It is a story about a poor scholar studying hard for the imperial examinations, as this was his only chance to break away from poverty. The ending of this type of story is usually auspicious in nature—the scholar achieves top results in the examinations, he marries the lady he loves, and is reunited happily with his family (RUIZENDAAL 2006, 351).[9]

The performance for the birthday celebration of the City God performed in the fifth lunar month of 2010 was typical of the genre. The play, "Chen Wenlong," was staged to entertain the City God. The puppeteers used a written script, about thirty pages long, as *aide-mémoire* during the performance. "Chen Wenlong" was depicted as a budding scholar who was reduced to poverty after his father passed away. Forced by circumstances, he decided to visit his future father-in-law's family to ask for help. However, the latter looked down upon Chen because of his poverty and even suggested giving him some money to call off the marriage arrangement. The unfortunate Chen was beaten and almost lost his life in his struggle against the father-in-law. However, his mother-in-law and betrothed kindly gave him some money, and he was later rescued by a stranger who saved his life. With the little money in his possession, Chen was able to set off for the capital where he sat for the imperial examinations. He eventually emerged as the top scholar 狀元 and was able to win back his beloved's hand in marriage. Chen forgave the father-in-law for what he had done in the past and the story ended with a happy reunion. This performance of "Chen Wenlong" was mainly based on the script, although puppeteers occasionally extemporized on the text.[10] The performance lasted for about two hours. Around 10:00 p.m., the entire event was brought to a close when the Taoist priest sent off the gods, a ritual farewell known as *song shen* 送神.

The above account is a typical scene of Henghua puppet theater in contemporary Singapore. Although Singaporean puppet theater has been performed in temples for almost a hundred years, it has been relatively little studied and its role in Singaporean society is not well understood.[11] There are four types of Chinese puppet theater that still exist in Singapore today. They can be categorized according to the regional speech used and puppet type, specifically Hokkien glove puppet 福建/閩南布袋戲, Henghua string puppet[12] 興化提線木偶, Hainanese rod puppet[13] 海南杖頭木偶, and Teochew iron stick puppet 潮州鐵枝木偶.

Scholarship on Singaporean puppet theater often covers the ritualistic or exorcistic aspects but tends to neglect the broader function of puppet theater within the framework of a secular state. Here I will adopt Lily Kong's idea of a process of "negotiation" that goes on between religious practices and the officially secular state of Singapore, in all its multicultural and multi-religious dimensions (KONG 2008). I will also draw upon Edwin Lee's notion of "selectivity" by the state in managing the ethnic dynamics of Singapore (LEE 2008, 534).[14]

This notion of the "selective" use of ideology is important as it applies to other policies adopted by the state to maintain a stable ethno-religious framework. This selectivity, or rather, oversimplification, conceals the diversity of cultures related to ethnicity and religion. This may partly explain why there has been little focus on how particular art forms, intrinsically linked to ethnicity and religion, may find themselves in conflict or engage in negotiation with the state policy of maintaining social cohesion. I will argue here that a contrasting modality—tradition and modernity, religious and secular, state-regulated and state-tolerated—is important in understanding how seemingly opposing forces can engage in a complex process of "negotiation" that serves to reinforce social cohesion.

The ritual nature of Chinese puppet theater

Numerous studies on traditional theater in China have demonstrated that a symbolic relationship exists between religious ritual and theater, which includes opera and puppet performance (SCHIPPER 1993; RUIZENDAAL 2006; CHEN 2007).[15] One of the most explicit examples to illustrate this relationship is the location where the performance is staged. A temporary stage is usually positioned directly opposite or a short distance away from the temple. The location is important, as it is believed that only a temple-based site will allow for direct "communication" with the gods. In addition, various types of "rituals" are conducted during a typical puppet theater performance. In the case of the Henghua puppet performance described above, the ritual segment was the "Eight Immortals" play and "Getting a Promotion and an Increase in Salary."[16] In the former example, puppets representing the Eight Immortals of traditional mythology came on stage (Han Zhongli, Tieguai Li, Zhang Guo Lao, He Xiangu, Lan Caihe, Lü Dongbin, Han Xiangzi, and Cao Guojiu). These are all figures well known in Chinese mythology or Taoist culture. This ritual plays an important role in the invocation of the gods

which, in this case, is the City God. According to Taoist Priest Dai Wen Rong 戴
文榮 who was in charge of this event, the "Getting a Promotion and an Increase
in Salary" playlet is performed by a puppet representing the prime minister (*zaix-
iang* 宰相). In traditional Chinese society, the prime minister is the highest ranking
official in the imperial court. The enactment of this playlet can be understood as
a wish to be promoted to the rank of prime minister.[17] In contemporary times,
long after the conclusion of the imperial examination system, the continuation of
this ritual playlet can be interpreted as a symbol of the people's wish for success
in their careers and a belief that the gods have the means to grant their requests.

Although the duration of the ritual takes up a small proportion of time
compared to the performance proper, which usually lasts for two to three
hours, the ritual playlet is considered the core of the whole performance. This
is because it is regarded as highly efficient in transmitting the wishes of the
organizers and devotees to the gods. This religious belief explains why puppet performances continue to exist even though there is hardly any audience
in contemporary Singapore.[18] The "ritual" in theatrical performances is only
a part of a larger set of ritual practices to ensure that the wishes of organizers
and devotees are conveyed properly to the gods. It is believed that the increase
in the number of rituals being performed will reassure organizers and devotees that their wishes are properly communicated (RUIZENDAAL 2006, 184).

Even though the performance proper is regarded as "entertainment" that
includes live singing and musical accompaniment, it is staged primarily for the
gods and secondarily for the human audience (CHAN 2006, 133, 135; RUIZENDAAL
2006, 3). Puppet performance is not the only means of communication between
gods and mortals but the dramatic effect of theatrical performance does allow for
the visualization of religion and communication between gods and mortals (RUI-
ZENDAAL 2006, 181). In the case of the celebration of the birthday of the City
God, the deity is invited to "watch" the performance.

The nature of the play proper is also important. In Henghua puppet theater, the
repertoire is usually auspicious in nature. For example, the story chosen for the birthday of the City God, "Chen Wenlong," is regarded as an "auspicious play" (*cai xi*
彩戲). The term "auspicious play" is related to the Chinese belief in "good omens"
(*hao cai tou* 好彩頭) and is an expression of the people's wish for happiness and
prosperity. In imperial China, the literati class hoped that a family member would
emerge as a successful scholar in the imperial examinations, while the common people wished for prosperity and good luck for their family, and so on. Even in a modern society like Singapore, the traditional wish for a good omen still continues.[19]

The story of "Chen Wenlong" is closely related to auspicious meanings such as
"emerging as the top scholar" (*Zhong zhuang yuan, jin bang ti ming* 中狀元, 金榜題
名). An "auspicious play" tends not to include scenes like death, murder, or other
events deemed "inauspicious" (YE 2004, 141–42).[20] "Auspicious plays" are typically directed at deities, in this case the City God, to please him with celebrations.[21]
Through this performance, the community hopes that the City God will reciprocate by giving them blessings and protecting them from calamity and illnesses.

The celebration of a god's birthday (*shen dan* 神誕) can be quite elaborate and involves a significant amount of resources and manpower. Temple helpers prepare the food and incense offerings, Taoist priests are employed to conduct rituals, and a theatrical troupe is invited to perform. The cost of inviting a troupe can range from several hundred to a few thousand dollars. This is paid for by the temple, which in turn may be sponsored by donations from devotees and successful businessmen of the Henghua group. The willingness to sponsor stems from the belief that the gods will be able to grant the wishes of the people for good health, prosperity, and success. Successful businessmen may contribute more donations when their business prospers as an expression of gratitude to the gods.[22] As there is little or no human audience watching the performance, Chinese puppet theater staged in religious institutions in contemporary Singapore is different from a ticketed performance where the audience pays to watch. In other words, if the puppet troupe has no other means of earning a living outside religious celebrations, it will have to depend on the celebration of religious festivals, such as the celebration of a deity's birthday, to make a living.

THE CHALLENGES OF MODERNIZATION

The live performance by Sin Hoe Ping at Li Jiang temple as described above is one of the many puppet shows staged throughout the year. There will be performances whenever there is a birthday celebration of a deity and during the Hungry Ghosts' Festival, which is held during the seventh lunar month.[23] However, these lively performances form a small and often neglected part of the life of contemporary Singapore today. Such performances can easily go unnoticed by the public. Although I grew up in Singapore during the 1980s, my first encounter with a Chinese puppet show was as late as 2007. Most people, particularly the young, have never seen a puppet performance in their lives. For those who have, it is regarded as something from a bygone era.[24] Performances are usually staged in temples located away from the bustling city. Even when performances are staged in housing estates where most Singaporeans reside, there is a limited audience aside from a few curious onlookers who may occasionally stop by for a glimpse. This lack of interest can be attributed to a number of factors. First, performances are staged in Chinese regional vernaculars which are generally incomprehensible to the public, particularly the younger Chinese who speak mainly English and Mandarin. According to the Population Census of 2010, only 5.7% of Chinese aged 34 and below speak one or more non-Mandarin Chinese languages.[25]

This lack of proficiency in regional speech forms is due to the language policy implemented by the state from the late 1970s. When Singapore gained independence in 1965, the newly-established government chose to adopt English as the lingua franca, as it was believed that a workforce competent in English was needed to keep up with the global economy (CHONG 2011, 460). However, decades later, this emphasis on English resulted in too much exposure to Western ideas among the younger generation, to the extent that they have little regard for their traditions, and so the government decided to rectify the situation.

In 1979, the Speak Mandarin Campaign (SMC) was launched. One of its objectives was to counter Western "decadence," which was believed to be adversely affecting young Singaporeans. While Mandarin was emphasized in this campaign, it was done at the expense of eradicating the other regional vernaculars, which were regarded as hampering the bilingual learning of English and Mandarin in schools. The then Prime Minister, Lee Kuan Yew, made this announcement on the importance of learning English and Mandarin during the launch of SMC in 1979:

> Children at home speak dialect; in school they learn English and Mandarin. After twenty years of bilingual schooling, we know that very few children can cope with two languages plus one dialect, certainly not much more than the 12% that make it to junior college. The majority have ended up speaking English and dialect.
> (TEO and LIM 2002, 3–4)

The effects of the campaign were far-reaching. The use of Mandarin in the homes of Primary One Chinese students rose from 25.9% in 1980 to 54.1% in 1999 whereas the use of non-Mandarin Chinese languages (dialects) dropped drastically, from 64.4% in 1980 to 2.5% in 1999 (TEO and LIM 2002, 5). The SMC resulted in a dramatic decline in the use of non-Mandarin Chinese vernaculars among the younger generation. Scholars and opera practitioners have expressed concern about the impact on traditional Chinese art forms like puppet theater, which uses regional speech as the performance medium. Some believed that the decreasing audience base could be attributed to a lack of understanding of the regional tongue by the younger generation, who now speak mainly English and Mandarin (CHONG 2011, 461).[26] According to one observer of puppet performances:

> Chinese puppet shows here are performed by the travelling troupes in dialect … They are for religious festivals and their stories of romantic classics do not appeal to the young.[27]

Apart from language difficulties, the explicitly religious nature of puppet performance and the repertoire of traditional stories set during the imperial era are seen as unappealing to a contemporary audience. Language proficiency largely determines one's choice of entertainment. Television programs in non-Mandarin Chinese regional languages were phased out by the end of 1981. This eradication of regional speech in the media meant that opera- and puppet-related programs lost much of their audience. The older generation tend to watch Mandarin television programs while the younger generation watch programs in English and Mandarin, rather than traditional art forms that are performed in dialects that they can hardly comprehend. In this way, puppet shows that had flourished in Singapore for a hundred years have come to play a minimal role in the lives of most Singaporeans. The difficulty of appealing to contemporary audiences has been captured in these comments by puppeteers:

> Even if we were performing just outside their flats, they would prefer to stay in and watch television or video shows.[28]

> When I was a child, kids of my age were fascinated with puppet shows. We would stand for hours on end watching the puppets. I suppose nowadays children are more interested in television shows.[29]

The lack of understanding and interest in Chinese puppet theater has made it harder for youths to consider performance as a career. It is viewed as an industry that will be gone with the older performers. Even parents who are performers themselves do not encourage their children to perform.

> The problem with puppetry is that it cannot help one to earn a living. That is why no one bothers to learn it.[30]

> I wouldn't want my children to follow in my footsteps, it's a hard life.[31]

> The younger people are not keen to learn it.… I feel that after our generation has passed away, puppet shows may vanish altogether.[32]

The same goes for Mr. Yeo Lye Hoe 楊來好, troupe leader of Sin Hoe Ping, who used to have his sisters helping him in the business until they got married. Now in his sixties, he is still looking for someone to take over his business.

While the decline of puppet theater in Singapore may be largely attributed to its lack of appeal to a modern audience, the state's attitude towards the art form has a role to play as well. Even though ethnic Chinese comprise more than 70% of the population, there are other ethnic groups such as Malays and Indians.[33] This context of Singapore as a multicultural, cosmopolitan city and secular state is important in understanding the impact of the social and political climate on the development of Chinese puppet theater today. Policies and laws have been established to protect the ethno-religious framework of this secular state and to foster art activities that support the state agenda. This objective was established not long after Singapore gained her independence. Wee Tong Boon, then Acting Minister of Culture, stated in a speech in 1969:

> The development of art and crafts is one of the means by which the multiracial aspect of our national life can be made tangible.[34]

The same applies for traditional art forms like Chinese opera and puppet theater. For example, the Traditional Theater Festival in 1987 was regarded as a "social defence project" that promoted harmony among Singaporeans of all races and religions. This was echoed by Miss Valerie Lim, assistant director of Cultural Programmes from the Ministry of Community Development, who stated that the festival was "a means for imbibing (inculcating) awareness, understanding, and appreciation of the three main ethnic groups' heritage, across racial boundaries."[35]

The state's attitude towards the arts was that it should serve to "perform multi-racialism" and hence any state-endorsed arts will have to conform to this ideology (CHONG 2011, 26). This means that in the interests of racial harmony, the Singaporean state does not encourage strong expressions of religious difference.

In the case of Chinese ethnic expression, the state endorses performing arts that are Mandarin-speaking rather than non-Mandarin speaking, that attract broad multiracial audiences, and that are secular rather than religious. In other words, it promotes a version of "Chinese" ethnicity that elides non-Mandarin, regional, and religious expression. This investigation of a Singaporean puppet theater troupe explores the impact of state notions of "Chineseness" on the strategies adopted in the case of this Henghua-speaking ritual art form.

"Negotiating" the divergence
between chinese puppet theater and the state

Given the emphasis placed by the state on secularization, multicultural-ism, and multiracialism, how can a performance form such as Chinese puppet the-ater, that is characteristically ethnic and religious in nature, "negotiate" with the state? (Kong 2008).[36] The analysis of Chua Beng Huat is pertinent here. Chua has proposed the idea of a "private" realm where the government places itself in a neu-tral space so that it does not privilege any ethnic or religious group. In this way, "racial cultural activities are then relegated to the realm of private and voluntaris-tic, individual or collective, practices…. While racial tolerance was given constitu-tional recognition, promotion of racial differences is carefully restricted to largely privatized celebration of festivals" (Chua 1997, 106–107). However, the notion of a "private" realm may give the impression that these activities are conducted in a private home or institution to which the public has no access. In the case of Chinese temples and/or a temporary installation where puppet performances are staged, members of the public are free to visit these places. Nonetheless, the like-lihood of participating in related religious celebrations is low due to ethnic and religious differences.

Instead of the concept of a "private" realm, I would like to propose the idea of a "state-tolerated" realm. By this I mean that the state tolerates religious and racial activities as long as these are confined to a defined domain, such as a tem-ple. Within the defined domain the activity does not need to conform to the state requirement to "perform multiculturalism and multiracialism." In other words, it does not need to explicitly promote racial or cultural harmony among Singa-poreans of all races and religions. Arguably this is the situation for puppet per-formances staged in temples. Of course, there remain civic restrictions for certain sorts of activities. In densely populated Singapore, most people live in public hous-ing and under the Ethnic Integration Policy (EIP), such housing will have a mixed proportion of residents from different ethnic backgrounds in order to better pro-mote racial integration and harmony.[37] Due to this ethnic mix in residential hous-ing, religious activities have to conform to regulations concerning public order even though they are tolerated by the state. For example, the noise level is regu-lated. In the past, when most people lived in shop houses or low-rise houses, the duration of opera and puppet performances used to be longer, some lasting till midnight. Performances today must stop by 10:30 p.m.[38] As religious activities in Chinese temples usually involve the burning of joss sticks and incense paper, reg-ulations have also been put in place limiting their use.[39] Temples and temporary installations are sometimes located near residential housing. Sound production in the form of live performances and music as well as incense burning that produces smoke may be regarded as intrusive by those who are not involved in the events and hence subject to regulation (Lee 1999, 89). The puppet performance by Sin Hoe Ping in Li Jiang temple described earlier is an example of a performance in such a "state-tolerated realm."

In contrast to the "state-tolerated realm," I will also propose the idea of "state-regulated realm." In the "state-regulated" realm, the arts or cultural activities have to conform more specifically to state regulations and be seen to promote racial harmony. As previously discussed, the state of Singapore sees the arts as a way of "civilizing" society and advocating multiracialism and multiculturalism (CHONG 2011, 26).[40] The "civilizing" effect of the arts hence justifies the regulation of the arts in order to make it accessible to the public within "state-regulated" realms, such as public theaters, museums, and schools. The same goes for state-encouraged arts which may take the form of arts festivals, arts programs, and museum exhibits or performances. In order to maintain religious harmony, religious elements have to be downplayed or omitted. Examples of state-endorsed Chinese puppet group activities include the event known as "Traditional Drama," performed during Heritage Week in 1988, and the "Traditional Theater Festival" of 1989.[41] Puppet performances in the "state-regulated" realm are not staged in temples or religious grounds, but in "secular" grounds such as public theaters and museums. They are often staged alongside art forms belonging to other ethnic groups like Malay *wayang kulit* (shadow puppet) and Indian *therukoothu* (folk dance).[42]

Another difference between the "state-regulated" and "state-tolerated" realms is the medium of performance. Chinese puppet performance in the "state-tolerated" realm is staged in non-Mandarin regional vernaculars. While some Chinese puppet performances in regional languages are allowed in the state-regulated realm, English is seen as the medium of "bridging cultures" and allowing the different ethnic groups to "enjoy each other's rich theatrical heritage." For this reason, within the state-regulated realm, English translations will usually be projected on stage or included in detailed brochures.[43] A good example of a puppet troupe which has flourished within the "state-regulated realm" is the Sin Hoe Ping Puppet Troupe.

THE SIN HOE PING PUPPET TROUPE

The Sin Hoe Ping Puppet Troupe has managed to maintain its vitality in contemporary Singapore by constantly modifying and adapting to shifting conditions. Sin Hoe Ping performs in both the state-regulated and state-tolerated realms and thus provides an illuminating study of how a traditional art form can creatively adapt within a dominant context of secularization and modernization.

To demonstrate the nature of this accommodation to state norms, I will turn now to an event, "Life, on a string" (FIGURE 2), held on 16 and 17 February 2012, that was part of a three-part arts and culture initiative called "Regenerating Communities." This event, a joint initiative of the Asian Civilisations Museum and the Arts House, drew upon Singapore's rich cultural heritage to revitalize Empress Place, a venue overlooking the iconic Singapore River. A temporary stage was set up on the grass plot outside the Asian Civilisations Museum and benches were provided for the audience. A television screen displaying a synopsis in both English and Chinese was placed next to the stage, together with a poster stand that stated "a puppet show not to be missed." Besides the traditional string puppets that were hung backstage, there were modern puppets shaped like monkey dolls and glove puppets displayed in front of the stage. The troupe leader of Sin Hoe Ping, Mr.

FIGURE 2. Performance by Mr. Yeo, troupe leader of Sin Hoe Ping, at Empress Place. (Photo courtesy of Mr. Ng Cheng-Kiang.)

Yeo, and other performers, including puppeteers and musicians, were already there before the show commenced. They were dressed in Chinese dress suits and wearing lanyards stating their identities as artists. The shows were set to commence at 6:00 p.m., 7:00 p.m., and 8:00 p.m.—three shows lasting one hour each. By 6:00 p.m., there was a crowd seated at the benches provided. Seeing that most people had settled themselves comfortably, the host of the event made a brief introduction in English on the performance history of Sin Hoe Ping.

The first show that commenced at 6:00 p.m. was "Journey to the West." This story is very popular among both adults and children, and characters like the Monkey King, Pigsy, and Tripitaka were well known to many. Glove puppets in the form of the Monkey King, Pigsy, Tripitaka, and Sandy were placed on the front side of the stage to serve as an illustration of the performance story. The sounds of cymbals, *suona*, and flute soon filled the air as the show commenced. It was performed in Henghua but as there were English and Chinese synopses available on the television screen, and especially because the show was a popular story known to many, the audience had a general idea of what was being performed. The spectators included a fair mix of adults and children, Chinese and non-Chinese. They were drawn to the bright colored lights that lit up the stage and the colorful costumes that Mr. Yeo had specially chosen for the event. The Monkey King, known for his magical skills, fought various enemies that tried to obstruct the pilgrims' journey to the West. Somersaults and flying kicks were among the highlights that caught the attention of the audience. The show ended with a big round of applause. During the brief intermission before "The Monkey's Wedding," due to commence at 7:00 p.m., the host explained to the audience that the show and the puppets were created by Mr. Yeo himself. The part battery-operated, part hand-manipulated puppets consisted of monkey-like dolls, one pair dressed in Chinese dress suits, and the other pair in Western suit and dress. Their cuddly and adorable appearances drew the younger members of the crowd and a few children went near the stage to have a closer look. The show was a hilarious story about monkeys who still lived in the forest but tried to imitate humans by reenacting a marriage ceremony. Laughter and applause filled the air as the comedy unfolded.

The last show, staged at 8:00 p.m., was "Wu Song Fights the Tiger," another well-known Chinese classic where the main protagonist, Wu Song, triumphs over the ferocious tiger that had claimed many innocent lives.[44] Under the manipulation of the skilled puppeteer, the tiger puppet looked as if it had come to life. The battle was accompanied by the banging of cymbals and exclamations by the puppeteers, adding vivacity to the performance. Other than the vibrantly-colored puppets, there was also a brightly-lit prop to represent the battle of Wu Song fighting the tiger in a mountainous area. When the shows ended, there was a question-and-answer session with the audience and a demonstration of the puppets by Mr. Yeo. While Mr. Yeo spoke in Mandarin, the host translated in English for the non-Chinese audience. After the sessions, audience members were free to go backstage to interact with the performers, and before the event ended, members of the Sin Hoe Ping troupe posed for some photographs.

The above performance at Empress Place is an example of how Sin Hoe Ping has participated in the "state-regulated" realm. In this realm, Sin Hoe Ping took on a distinctly different role from its performances in Chinese temples. One could regard the Empress Place performance as an example of "negotiating" with and conforming to the state ideology of multiracialism and secularization. First, the venue outside the Asian Civilisations Museum in Empress Place could be regarded as a "state-regulated" realm because it was open to the public and supported by state-related arts organizations such as the Arts House, Asian Civilisations Museum, and the National Arts Council. This was in contrast to the performance in the "state-tolerated" realm which was sponsored by the temple committee and had no association with state-related arts organizations. The venue itself was closely related to the history of the Singaporean state. Empress Place is located near Singapore River. In colonial times it served as a Court House that was home to many government departments before being renamed Empress Place in 1907 to commemorate Queen Victoria's visit to Singapore.[45] This event could be said to "perform multiculturalism" in that it was part of the initiative "Regenerating Communities" featuring Asian contemporary and heritage dance together with the Maya Dance Theater and ContempCo, and a Malay Bangsawan performance by Sri Anggerik Bangsawan.[46] The multiracial nature of this cultural event also aimed to promote racial harmony by featuring arts and heritage from the various ethnic groups of Singapore.

The notion of using the arts to "perform multiculturalism" was also reflected in the attempt to attract a multiethnic audience, including both adults and children. This could be seen in the use of English and Mandarin synopses, a poster display written in English, and the host speaking to the audience in English. The medium used during the event was a mixture of Mandarin, English, and Henghua.

Mr. Yeo's creation of modern puppets could also be seen as a way of attracting a younger crowd. His cute battery-operated puppets stood in marked contrast to traditional puppet performances, which are now commonly seen as an art form of a bygone era, or as something that only older people would appreciate. From my own observations, Sin Hoe Ping is the first traditional Chinese puppet troupe in Singapore to have invented modern puppets and used them in public performances.

As previously mentioned, religious elements are characteristically downplayed or omitted in the "state-regulated" realm. The audience in this realm was not the gods but human beings. There was no ritual conducted or ritual specialists involved in the event. Although shows like "Journey to the West" and "Wu Song Fights the Tiger" are set in imperial China, as one finds also with stories performed in the "state-tolerated realm," these tales were drawn from popular classics known to broad audiences in Singapore. I also noticed that although Sin Hoe Ping customarily uses scripts in its temple performances, this was not the case in their performances in public spaces in the "state-regulated realm." In the latter, plays were improvised according to the reaction of the audience and performers were not confined to follow a set script. The use of a variety of puppets, such as string puppets, glove puppets, and modern puppets, was also an attempt by Sin Hoe Ping to demonstrate the variety of Chinese puppetry to the audience. Traditional Henghua puppet performances usually use only string puppets. In the state-tolerated realm of temple performances, the string puppet, seen as a god itself, is believed to be the most sacred of religious dramas. String puppet performances are believed to be meant for the Heavenly Emperor (CHAN 2006, 136). Marshal Tian (*Tian du yuan shuai* 田都元帥), the God of Theater, usually takes the form of a string puppet while engaging in exorcism. However, in a state-regulated realm such as the performance in Empress Place, all of these religious elements were removed. The audience saw the string puppets simply as objects of entertainment. Under the clever manipulation of the puppeteers, they could perform stunts and bring good cheer to their multiracial audiences.

THE VITALITY OF THE SIN HOE PING TROUPE IN CONTEMPORARY SOCIETY

In Singapore, where traditional puppet theater has become a neglected part of life, Sin Hoe Ping has displayed vitality in continuing to prove its relevance in contemporary society. This has been illustrated in the two accounts provided above. According to my observations, since 2009, Sin Hoe Ping has been one of the most active troupes in Singapore with monthly performances staged throughout the year. In this study, a distinction has been made between the "state-regulated realm" and the "state-tolerated realm" in order to explain how a traditional art form like Chinese puppet theater "negotiated" with a secular state that placed emphasis on multiracialism and multiculturalism. It is clear that in the contemporary period, Sin Hoe Ping performs in both realms. Although most of the troupe's performances are still staged in the Henghua vernacular, Sin Hoe Ping has increased the frequency of its performances by performing in religious institutions outside its own

FIGURE 3. Mr. Yeo performing as a puppeteer. Photo by author, 24 June 2010.

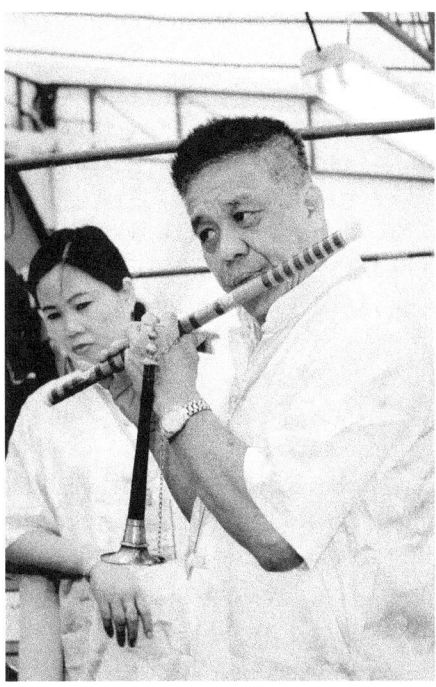

FIGURE 4. Mr. Yeo playing the *suona* (Chinese shawn)
and flute. Photos courtesy of Mr. Ng Cheng-Kiang.

regional speech group. Other than the typical scene of performing at Li Jiang temple, Sin Hoe Ping established a Hokkien troupe under the same name. By performing in both Henghua and other Chinese vernacular religious institutions, as well as in public venues that come under the aegis of the "state-regulated realm," Sin Hoe Ping has considerably increased its influence in the Singapore cultural domain.

The kind of adaptability demonstrated by Sin Hoe Ping is hardly seen in other puppet troupes in Singapore. The success of Sin Hoe Ping is due largely to the competitive strategy adopted by troupe leader, Mr. Yeo Lye Hoe (1950–). The troupe name "Sin Hoe Ping" (meaning "New Peace" in Mandarin) was registered as a Henghua puppet troupe during the 1980s by Mr. Yeo. However, the existence of Sin Hoe Ping (under a different name) can be traced back to the 1950s.[47] Even though the Henghua speech group made up less than 1% of the Chinese population in Singapore, there were at least four or five troupes in existence when Henghua puppet theater thrived from the 1950s to the 1970s. There was intense rivalry among troupes in competing for audiences. The competition between Sin Hoe Ping and Xin De Yue 新得月, from the 1950s to the 1970s, was particularly fierce. Troupes had to compete among themselves for survival in the market for temple performances. Sin Hoe Ping was more adaptable than its rivals and was able to maintain its relevance in contemporary society.

To understand the adaptability of Sin Hoe Ping, it is informative to explore the professional choices made by its current troupe leader. Mr. Yeo started out as a drummer and *gong* (percussion instrument in the shape of a flat, circular disc) musician at the age of seven. He stopped for a short period but has continued to perform until the present. Starting out as a musician, Yeo learned the art of puppetry at eighteen from his grandfather's friends.[48] At many puppet performances that I have observed, the versatile Mr. Yeo would sometimes switch between his roles as musician and puppeteer (FIGURES 3 and 4), especially when there was a lack of manpower.

Mr. Yeo is also familiar with the various types of plays performed in Henghua puppet theater. In contrast to the "state-regulated" realm that has to downplay or omit religious elements in a typical puppet performance, Mr. Yeo must make sure he can meet the various demands required of a Henghua puppet troupe in the "state-tolerated" realm. In addition to "auspicious plays," he conducts "ritual plays" (*yi shi ju* 儀式劇). There are two main types of Henghua ritual plays still performed today: the Mulian play (*Mulian xi* 目連戲) and the Northern Dipper play (*Beidou xi* 北斗戲). The Mulian play is usually performed during the Seventh Lunar Month, better known as the Hungry Ghosts' Festival. The puppeteer, usually Mr. Yeo as he was more familiar with the ritual, would chant and call upon the souls of the dead to "watch" the Mulian play and "participate" in the purification ritual conducted later. This requires the skills of a religious specialist in order for the ritual to be carried out effectively. The other type of ritual play, the Northern Dipper play, is less frequently performed and only staged upon request. Typically this is a play of thanksgiving to the deities for protecting a sick child. As these plays were less frequently performed, other puppeteers and musicians would have to be led by Mr. Yeo, who was familiar with the ritual and story. Hence, in the "state-tolerated" realm, a skilled performer like Mr. Yeo has to make sure he is well-versed in the traits of "Henghua-ness" to meet the requirements of temple sponsors. This involves the ability to master the repertoire, to play musical instruments, and to carry out religious and ritual customs. In this way he will be able to sustain himself and his troupe in the Henghua puppet theater industry.[49]

Another reason for the success of Sin Hoe Ping was the way that the troupe, under the direction of Mr. Yeo, established an extensive network both in Singapore and internationally.[50] As noted by Dean and Zheng, who have conducted research on Putian, theater and puppet troupes have helped to maintain networks linking Putian to Southeast Asia (DEAN and ZHENG 2010, 248). In the context of Singapore, Mr. Yeo's troupes, both Hokkien and Henghua, have created a name for themselves within the Chinese community. Sin Hoe Ping is frequently invited by both Henghua and Hokkien temples to perform. Considering that there are a number of Hokkien puppet troupes in Singapore, Sin Hoe Ping can be regarded as having maintained its competitive status with these troupes in order to continue its strong presence in the puppet scene. In addition to its connections within Singapore, Sin Hoe Ping has also established links in Malaysia, where it participates in Henghua temple and ritual celebrations (ZHENG 2008, 60; YUNG 1994). Mr. Yeo's reputation has also spread to his ancestral hometown, Putian, in Fujian Province. According to Mr. Yeo, he has not needed to recruit puppeteers and musicians as there had often been requests from Putian to join his troupe.[51]

The recruitment strategy of Sin Hoe Ping has been particularly important in ensuring the ongoing resilience of this puppet troupe in contemporary Singapore. Today most of the puppeteers and musicians of Sin Hoe Ping are from Putian. As mentioned earlier, many puppet troupes feared extinction because there was no local interest in continuing with the art. In a way, the use of employees from China solves the problem of the lack of local manpower. As these puppeteers and musicians are also experienced in the opera or puppet theater in Putian, there is little or no need to provide intensive training when they arrive in Singapore, which in turn saves time and money. In addition, these foreign puppeteers have full-time jobs and do not rely on performing as a means for survival.

Sin Hoe Ping has also been innovative with regard to musical accompaniment. The troupe has mostly employed conventional musical instruments such as the *suona*, cymbals, drum, and octagonal lute (*ba jiao qin* 八角琴); however, the electronic keyboard has also been added, and this has helped to modernize the performances. It also means that fewer musicians can be employed, which saves expenses. Further, the keyboard is able to produce certain sounds that may be unattainable for Chinese musical instruments, thus enlivening the musical repertoire.[52]

Conclusion

The ongoing survival of Chinese puppet theater is mostly invisible to those Singaporeans who believe that this art form belongs to a bygone era and only remains popular among the older generation. However, while modernization has been the main factor influencing the general decline of Chinese puppet theater in Singapore, state policy has also played a dominant role. The eradication of regional vernaculars in order to promote English and Mandarin as the shared medium for education and daily use is one example of the impact of state policy. Younger Singaporeans who lack proficiency in their ancestral Chinese vernacular form will not find puppet theater appealing, because it is performed in a language which is hardly comprehensible to them. Despite the conflict between this traditional art form and the modern state, this does not mean that Chinese puppet theater is on the verge of extinction. Quite the contrary, one of the most active troupes in Singapore, Sin Hoe Ping, has demonstrated vitality both in the temple puppet scene and state-sponsored public performance spaces in contemporary society. The case study of Sin Hoe Ping and the profile of its troupe leader, Mr. Yeo Lye Hoe, can serve as an illustration of a traditional art form that can still "negotiate" with the state for survival. In this study, I have put forward the notion of a "state-tolerated realm" and a "state-regulated realm" to explain how the Sin Hoe Ping troupe has made this "negotiation" possible by successfully performing in both realms. Notions of Chinese ethnicity are also central to the type of accommodation the Sin Hoe Ping troupe has made in order to survive in multiracial, secular Singapore. In this case, the troupe has expanded its repertoire to include a cosmopolitan Mandarin-speaking public expression of pan-Chinese identity, while at the same time preserving an old ritual art form that continues to shower blessings on Singapore's Henghua-speaking community.

NOTES

* I would like to thank all my interviewees, particularly Dai Wen Rong and Yeo Lye Hoe, for providing me with useful information on Henghua tradition and puppet theater. I am grateful to my Master's degree supervisor, Crossland-Guo Shuyun, for her patience in guiding me through my research on Sin Hoe Ping from 2009 to 2011. Special thanks to my PhD supervisor Anne McLaren for her kind patience in guiding me through the writing of this article. I would also like to thank Ng Cheng-Kiang for his generosity in sharing his photos that are used in this article.

1. I have been observing the Sin Hoe Ping Puppet Troupe and the Henghua community since 2009, and I conducted the observation at Li Jiang temple from 30 June 2010 to 20 June 2011. I continued further verification with informants, including puppeteers, musicians, and ritual specialists, until early 2013. All interviews were conducted in Mandarin but at times I asked for the pronunciation of basic terms related to puppet theater in the Henghua language. The local-born Henghua Chinese also spoke Hokkien, which I was able to comprehend.

2. The "Henghua group" here refers to Singapore-born Chinese descendants whose forefathers migrated from Putian (Southeast China) and also, in more recent cases, the new wave of immigrants born in Putian. These people speak *Puxian hua* (莆仙話) or *Puxian fangyan* (莆仙方言). The term "Puxian" refers to "Putian" (莆田) and "Xianyou" (仙游), the former being a city in southeast Fujian and the latter a county. Speakers of Puxian are also known as Xinghua (興化), which is spelled "Henghua" in the Southeast Asian context. As the term "Henghua" is commonly used in official Singapore statistics, I shall adopt this term throughout the article. Even though the term "dialect" has been commonly used in the Singapore context, I will choose to use terms like "regional vernacular," "regional speech," and "regional variant" interchangeably and the use of "dialect" will be minimized in this article. The Chinese term, *fangyan* (方言), is quite different from the Western notion of dialect as the latter usually refers to mutually intelligible varieties of a single language. On the contrary, the Hen-

ghua speech is a Min (閩) language but the speech forms of the different groups of the Min language group are in fact mutually unintelligible. The English term "dialect" is misleading in this context. Until the mid-twentieth century, Chinese speaking different regional speeches (*fangyan*) resided in different parts of Singapore. However, this phenomenon is less visible in contemporary Singapore.

3. According to Taoist Priest Dai Wen Rong, there are different ritual texts for different occasions. For example, there will be a ritual text meant for congratulating the deity on his birthday. However, because there are many occasions of celebrating the god's birthday, he does not need to rely on the ritual text for his chanting. The "spiritual petition" (*shu wen* 疏文) will still have to be written in order to convey the message to the deities. Dai Wen Rong, personal interview, 21 March 2013.

4. In the course of my observations I came to know the community quite well and was often invited to have a meal with them.

5. The ritual playlet consists of the "Eight Immortals" play and "Getting a Promotion and an Increase in Salary." In daytime performances, the ritual playlet is staged after the performance proper because the Taoist priests require some time to invoke the gods. During the night performance, the ritual playlet is staged after the performance proper because the gods have already been invoked in the day (Dai Wen Rong, personal interview, 21 March 2013). I was also told that there is no specific time for staging the ritual playlet but it should start only when the deities have "arrived" upon invitation. In the Li Jiang temple, I have not observed the presence of spirit mediums (*shen tong* 神童) but in other Henghua temples, disciples go into a trance on the arrival of the deities. This would signal to the troupe it was time to start the ritual playlet. (Observation made at Ling Ci Xing Gong 靈慈行宮, 1 May 2013.)

6. Dai Wen Rong explained to me that the seniority of the City God is such that it is appropriate that the Eight Immortals send birthday regards to him. In the case of a deity with a lower seniority like the Earth God (Tudigong 土地公), the "Eight Immortals" play would not be performed. Instead, a ritual known as "Ushering Wealth and Prosperity" (*zhao cai jin bao* 招財進寶) is performed instead (Dai Wen Rong, personal interview, 9 May 2011).

7. I revisited and again witnessed the celebration of the City God's birthday at Li Jiang Miao on 20 June 2011.

8. The exclamation "Prosper ah!" was also observed by the Hokkien community in Singapore. There is likelihood that the Henghua borrowed this custom from the Hokkien. However, it is not known when this custom began. In Putian where I conducted my fieldwork in 2013, they do not utter this exclamation.

9. Ruizendaal noted that the scholar, the highest graduate of the imperial examinations, is the most important character in frequently performed plays. Since the Song Dynasty (960–1279), the scholar has been one of the most auspicious symbols in Chinese culture (RUIZENDAAL 2006).

10. Even though Sin Hoe Ping uses a script, the performance may vary according to the context and the required duration. If the performers realize that the performance is coming to an end and the two-hour target is not met, they may think of ways to extend the performance time by decreasing the speed of singing or speaking. Also, improvisation may affect the actual time of a performance.

11. To date there is no record of the earliest existence of Chinese puppet theater in Singapore. According to the information I gathered from interview records of the National Archives of Singapore, one of the earliest puppet troupes that existed in Singapore could be a Teochew iron stick puppet troupe known as San Zheng Xing (三正興). According to the interviewee, Mr. Tay Lee Huat (1940–), it was established between the late nineteenth century and early twentieth century. However, Mr. Tay was unsure of the exact date. Another troupe was Chye Sin Hong or Cai Xin Feng (彩新鳳) believed to be derived from Zhongzhou (中州), Henan, in China. It arrived in Singapore in 1926. This troupe comprised Hakka speakers and sang the Waijiang (外江) tune, a melody believed to derive from the ancient Zhongzhou tune in Henan (OU 1988).

12. Tanaka Issei (2008) and Yung Sai-Shing (1997) have examined the ritual aspects of Henghua puppet theater in Singapore; see also the update by Zheng (2008).

13. For Hainanese rod puppet theater, see Wang Zhenchun (2000); Lin Jia (2009); Teh Seh Hwee (2004).

14. An example of the notion of "selectivity" is the decision by the state to adopt Confucian ideology. See Lee (2008, 534).

15. Chinese opera and puppet theater are similar in that both are theatrical art forms that require music accompaniment and singing. Dai Wen Rong has commented that compared to Chinese opera, puppet theater is the "bigger show." He relates this to a common belief among the Henghua folk that he heard as a child. The high status of puppet theater was related to Emperor Liang Wudi (AD 464–549) who was a vegetarian. His family followed his vegetarian habits but his mother, the Empress Dowager, was reluctant to do so. The vexed Emperor Liang Wudi was unsure of what to do but he was approached by a scholar who invited the emperor and his family to watch the show titled "Mulian Saves his Mother" (目連救母). The Empress Dowager was shocked to see how people who feasted on meat would suffer in the underworld and decided from then on to become a vegetarian. The emperor was overjoyed by the outcome and ordered that all temple celebrations in the country should engage puppet shows on the first day followed by opera performed by humans. Dai Wen Rong, personal interview, 21 March 2013.

16. Other ritual plays include "Ushering in Wealth and Prosperity" and "Playing the Big Gods" (*nong da xian* 弄大仙). According to Dai Wen Rong, "Ushering in Wealth and Prosperity" is meant for gods of a "lower" rank like the Earth God (土地公). "Playing the Big Gods" is a play of a longer duration, lasting about one and a half hours. It is performed for gods of "higher" rank such as Mazu (媽祖), God of Mystic Heaven (Xuan tian shang di 玄天上帝), and the Heavenly Emperor (Yu huang da di 玉皇大帝). However, these plays are rarely performed today. Dai Wen Rong, personal interview, 13 March and 21 March 2013. See note 21 for the explanation of gods of high and low ranks.

17. Dai Wen Rong, personal interview, 20 June 2011.

18. A similar observation has been made by Ruizendaal in his study of marionette theater in Quanzhou, China (Ruizendaal 2006, 184).

19. As Ruizendaal has noted, this is also the case for Quanzhou in China. New Year prints illustrating successful imperial graduates still symbolize status (*gong ming* 功名) and wealth (*fu gui* 富貴) in Quanzhou today (Ruizendaal 2006, 103).

20. Ye Mingsheng classified the "auspicious play" under the category of *san xi* (散戲), also known as *qing xi* (清戲), which is distinguished from ritual or liturgical play (*yi shi ju* 儀式劇) (Ye 2004, 61–62; 141–42). Regardless of the name given, these plays are of an auspicious nature and are contrasted to ritual plays like the Mulian play and Northern Dipper play. I have also verified the term "auspicious play" with Ms. Li and Dai Wen Rong (Ms. Li, personal interview, 6 October 2010; Dai Wen Rong, personal interview, 9 May 2011).

21. Margaret Chan observes that Chinese marionette theater is mainly designed to attract the attention of the deity and spirit guests, whereas opera is performed mainly to entertain the spirits (Chan 2006, 135, 137). In the Taoist religious system, gods (神) and spirits (鬼) may be categorized as spiritual beings but it is sometimes hard to make a clear distinction. Dai Wen Rong, who has trained as a Henghua Taoist priest for more than two decades, states that it is a case of "human when alive, a god when dead" (*sheng wei ren, si wei shen* 生為人，死為神). This implies that both gods and ghosts are people who have died but who are now regarded as spiritual or supernatural beings. However, the gods rarely descend to the mortal world to take charge of human affairs and instead call on ghosts to undertake these tasks. Ghosts are spiritual beings who committed good deeds when they were alive. They are "assigned" by gods to help out with human affairs, including the receiving of temple offerings. They also report back to Heaven which temple has engaged in celebrations meant for the gods. Ghosts who do the bidding of the gods are set apart from another category of ghosts who bring harm to humans. Offerings are made to appease the latter. Feuchtwang has also made a dis-

tinction between gods and ghosts in terms of how offerings are made. For example, offerings made to the former are usually placed on an altar inside the temple, whereas offerings made to the latter are often placed on the ground outside the temple. The ranking of gods may differ as well, depending on whether they received honorary titles from imperial emperors (FEUCHTWANG 1974, 109–11). Dai Wen Rong used the example of Mazu and mentioned that she was bestowed the title of "Water Celestial" (水上神仙) by the Jade Emperor (玉皇大帝). She was "promoted" to the rank of "Goddess of Heaven" (Tian shang sheng mu 天上聖母) by reigning emperors for her good deeds. This means that gods that had received honorary titles from reigning emperors may be promoted to a higher rank than gods who did not receive such titles. In this way one can distinguish between "big gods" (大神) and "small gods" (小神) (Dai Wen Rong, personal interview, 21 March 2013).

22. I observed a celebration where a businessman invited Sin Hoe Ping to perform in celebration of Zhanggong Shengjun's birthday. The performance was held at an industrial estate at 31 Defu Lane 10, Singapore.

23. During the seventh month, Sin Hoe Ping is invited to the main Henghua temple, Hin Ann Thain Hiaw Keng (興安天后宮), to engage in universal salvation for the purgatory (*pu du* 普度). In this event, the Mulian show (目連戲) is staged.

24. In 2013, I conducted an online survey with 32 Singaporeans aged 20 to 35 about their experience with puppet shows. In response to the question whether they had ever seen a Chinese puppet performance before, about 70% (22 out of 32) of the participants said they had never seen one. Further questions explored how they perceived puppet performances, even if they had no previous experience of watching them. The general impression is that Chinese puppet performance is an outdated art form meant mostly for old people. Even for those who had seen one, the perception was also that such performances were old-fashioned and outdated. See the results of the survey at https://www.surveymonkey.com/results/SM-F2L239YD/ (accessed 31 May 2015).

25. Even though statistics from the census indicate the number of Chinese who claim to speak non-Mandarin regional languages, the level of actual proficiency is unknown. This is important because understanding the performance requires at least an intermediate level of proficiency in a regional language. The percentage of fluent speakers of Chinese regional languages may be even lower than the census figures indicate. See Singapore Department of Statistics Table 49, Census of Population 2010, https://www.singstat.gov.sg/docs/default-source/default-document-library/publications/publications_and_papers/cop2010/census_2010_release1/cop2010sr1.pdf (accessed 13 June 2017).

26. The author also conducted brief research on Cantonese opera in Singapore from 2009 to 2011. Cantonese opera practitioners like Chee Kin Foon, Joanna Wong, and Lynn Ng Mui Leng have expressed concern about the impact of the lack of understanding of regional speech in Cantonese opera (CHIA 2013). Chee also added that since non-Mandarin regional languages could not be used in schools, it had become a challenge to promote Cantonese opera to students (Chee Kin Foon, personal interview, 15 June 2009; Joanna Wong, personal interview, 7 August 2009; Lynn Ng, personal interviews, 24 July 2009 and 27 August 2009).

27. Interview with Chow Pak Hong, *The Straits Times*, 4 December 1985, 3, NL15286.

28. Interview with Madam Huang Yamei of the Bai Hua Chun Fujian Glove Puppet Troupe, "Playing for the Gods," *The Straits Times*, 23 August 1984.

29. Interview with Madam Ooi Kooi Geok of the Beng Geow Hong Hokkien Puppet Show troupe, "Playing for the Gods," *The Straits Times*, 23 August 1984.

30. Interview with Lui Choo Guan of the disbanded Chye Sin Hong (still performing during the time of the interview in 1990), "Puppet Passion," *The Straits Times*, 11 September 1990, 5.

31. Interview with Madam Ooi Kooi Geok, "Madam puppeteer," *The Straits Times*, 14 December 1979, 10, NL10401.

32. Interview with Madam Huang, "Playing for the Gods," *The Straits Times*, 23 August 1984.

33. Singapore Department of Statistics Population Census 2010, http://www.singstat.gov
.sg/docs/default-source/default-document-library/publications/publications_and_papers
/cop2010/census_2010_release1/cop2010sr1.pdf (accessed 7 August 2015).

34. Speech by Acting Minister for Culture at the Opening of the Art and Crafts Exhibition, held in conjunction with the Singapore Youth Festival, Victoria Memorial Hall, 9 July 1969 (CHONG 2011, 26).

35. "Room for festival to grow," *The Straits Times*, 23 October 1989, 1, NL16796.

36. In her discussion on the religious processions of Thaipusam (a Hindu festival) in Singapore, Kong explored the kinds of conflicts that have to be negotiated in the continued performance of religious practice. This question is explored using the multicultural, multireligious case of Singapore, a modern city and officially secular state (KONG 2008).

37. Housing Development Board (HDB) InfoWeb, http://www.hdb.gov.sg/fi10/fi10321p
.nsf/w/BuyResaleFlatEthnicIntegrationPolicy_EIP (accessed 15 February 2013).

38. National Environmental Agency, "Noise Pollution," http://www.nea.gov.sg/anti
-pollution-radiation-protection/noise-pollution-control (accessed 7 August 2015).

39. According to the National Environmental Agency (NEA) of Singapore, the government introduced control measures on 1 March 1998 to minimize problems when burning joss paper, candles, and so on: "Joss sticks shall not exceed 2 metres in length and 75 mm in diameter. For large joss sticks up to 2 metres in length and 75 mm in diameter, no more than six may be burnt at any one time. Candles shall not exceed 600 mm in length. For large candles up to 600 mm in length, no more than two may be burnt at any one time. The burning of large joss sticks and candles shall not be within 30 metres from any building." See http://statutes.agc.gov.sg/aol/search/display/view.w3p;page=0;query
=CompId%3Ac10459fd-7d86-4488-96f7-8828d6fe6eb1%20
ValidTime%3A20160103000000%20TransactionTime%3A99991231000000;rec=0 (accessed 17 June 2017).

The Ministry of Environment and Water Resources has introduced specially designed joss burners for use at wayang (theatrical performance) sites, which will be loaned to organizers who will ensure that there is no indiscriminate burning that will dirty or damage common property. See http://www.nas.gov.sg/archivesonline/data/pdfdoc/MEWR20010816001
.pdf (accessed 7 August 2015).

40. Chong quoted Acting Minister of Culture Wee Toon Boon's speech in 1969: "The development of art and crafts is one of the means by which the multiracial aspect of our national life can be made tangible."

41. The Traditional Theater Festival started out as a project financed by the Singapore Tourist Promotion Board and was supported by the then Ministry of Culture. This festival has also been singled out as a social defence project in which "social defence" refers to "Singaporeans of all races and religions living and working together in harmony." See "Room for festival to grow," *The Straits Times*, 23 October 1989, NL16796, 1; "Capture traditional art forms on video," *The Straits Times*, 8 September 1988, NL16248, 22. For the definition given by the Ministry of Education (Singapore) of "Social Defence," see: https://www.mindef.gov
.sg/imindef/mindef_websites/topics/totaldefence/about_us/5_Pillars.html (accessed 8 May 2016).

42. "Room for festival to grow," *The Straits Times*, 23 October 1989, 1.

43. "Room for festival to grow," *The Straits Times*, 23 October 1989, 1.

44. The stories of the Monkey King ("Journey to the West" and "Wu Song Fights the Tiger") are classic pieces in Chinese glove puppet theater. The latter is often performed as a classic in Zhangzhou puppet theater and has received international acclaim.

45. See http://www.singaporeflyer.com/visitor-guide/views-from-the-top/empress
-place-2/ (accessed 18 February 2013).

46. See https://www.facebook.com/RegeneratingCommunities/info.

47. There are two accounts offered by scholars on the establishment of "Sin Hoe Ping" and the names of its previous troupe leaders. Zheng Li mentioned that the predecessor of "Sin Hoe Ping" was "He Ping." The name was changed when its previous troupe leader, Huang Ah Fa, sold the troupe to Yeo Lye Hoe in 1981 (ZHENG 2008, 60). On the other hand, Jennifer Chen believes that "Sin Hoe Ping" had kept this troupe name since its establishment (CHEN 1995, 8). Its previous troupe leader, Chen Jin Chang, sold the troupe to Mr. Yeo.

48. Yeo Lye Hoe, personal interview, 7 January 2010.

49. Mr. Yeo demonstrated the "eight-trigram dance" (*cai ba gua*) to me. This exorcistic dance is conducted by the God of Theater, Chief Marshal Tian (*Tiandu yuanshuai*), to engage in the expiatory purification of the souls of the dead.

50. For a list of activities participated in by Sin Hoe Ping both locally and internationally, see the Appendix.

51. Yeo Lye Hoe, personal interview, 7 January 2010.

52. The author has witnessed the use of keyboard during one of Sin Hoe Ping's performances. The musical instruments used during the performance included the keyboard, drum and cymbals. In a way, the keyboard was seen as a replacement of the *suona* and octagonal lute. However, the keyboard is only occasionally used in most of Sin Hoe Ping's performances in Henghua temples. Personal fieldwork, 20 April 2011, Singapore.

REFERENCES

ASIA ON THE EDGE
  https://www.facebook.com/RegeneratingCommunities/info

CHAN, Margaret
  2006   *Ritual is Theater, Theater is Ritual: Tang-ki, Chinese Spirit Medium Worship*. Singapore: SNP Reference.

CHEN, Fan-Pen Li
  2007   *The Chinese Shadow Theater: History, Popular Religion, and Women Warriors*. Montréal: McGill-Queen's University Press.

CHEN Ling Ling 陳玲玲
  1995   Xinjiapo putian juben yanjiu 新加坡莆田劇本研究 [The study of Putian scripts in Singapore]. Honours thesis. National University of Singapore.

CHIA, Caroline Boon Han 謝汶亨
  2011   Yi koutou taoyu lilun fenxi Xinjiapo Xinghua mu'ou xi ban de biaoyan wen ben 以口頭一套語理論分析新加坡興化木偶戲班的表演文本 [The oral formulaic theory applied to Henghwa puppet theater performing texts in Singapore]. Masters thesis, Nanyang Technological University.
  2013   *The Development of Cantonese Opera in Singapore*. Singapore: The Chinese Opera Institute.

CHONG, Terence
  2011   *Theater and the State in Singapore*. New York: Routledge.
         doi:10.4324/9780203837283

CHUA, Beng Huat
  1997   *Communitarian Ideology and Democracy in Singapore*. London: Routledge.
         doi:10.4324/9780203033722

DEAN, Kenneth, and Zhenman ZHENG
  2010   *Ritual Alliances of the Putian Plain. Volume 1: Historical Introduction to the Return of the Gods*. Leiden and Boston: Brill.
         doi:10.1163/ej.9789004176027.i-437

FEUCHTWANG, Stephan
1974   Domestic and communal worship in Taiwan. In *Religion and Ritual in Chinese Society*, Emily Martin and Arthur P. Wolf, eds., 105–30. Stanford: Stanford University Press. doi:10.2307/2053283

KONG, Lily
2008   Religious processions: Urban politics and poetics. In *Religious Diversity in Singapore*, ed. Lai Ah Eng, 298–317. Singapore: Institute of Southeast Asian Studies jointly with Institute of Policy Studies.

LEE, Edwin
2008   *Singapore: The Unexpected Nation*. Singapore: ISEAS Publishing.

LEE, Tong Soon
2009   *Chinese Street Opera in Singapore*. Urbana: University of Illinois Press.
1999   Technology and the production of Islamic space: The call to prayer in Singapore. *Ethnomusicology* 43: 86–100.

LIN Jia 林嘉
2009   Xinjiapo kuilei xi de xianzai yu weilai: Qiong yin mu'ou tuan zhangtou mu'ou he neng wen sen zhangzhong ban budai xi ge'an yanjiu 新加坡傀儡戲的現在與未來—瓊音木偶團杖頭木偶和能文森掌中班布袋戲個案研究 [The present and future of puppet theater in Singapore: Case studies of Hainanese rod puppet and "Neng Wen Sen" glove puppet]. In *Huazu xiqu de biange yu chuangxin: Yantao hui lunwen ji* 華族戲曲的變革與創新—研討會論文集 [Change and innovation in Chinese opera: A post-conference publication], ed. Chua Soo Pong, 134–43. Singapore: National Heritage Board and Dominic Press Pty Ltd. Housing Development Board (HDB).

MINISTRY OF EDUCATION (Singapore)
2012   https://www.mindef.gov.sg/imindef/mindef_websites/topics /totaldefence/about_us/5_Pillars.html (accessed 8 May 2016).

MINISTRY OF THE WATER ENVIRONMENT RESOURCES (Singapore)
2015   http://www.nas.gov.sg/archivesonline/data/pdfdoc /MEWR20010816001.pdf (accessed 7 August 2015).

NATIONAL ENVIRONMENTAL AGENCY
2012   http://statutes.agc.gov.sg/aol/search/display/view.w3p;ident=c10459fd -7d86-4488-96f7-8828d6fe6eb1;page=0;query=DocId%3Ad6dff5c7-4d6e -44a7-a3d2-996864f386a0%20Depth%3A0%20Status%3Ainforce;rec=0 (accessed 8 May 2016).
2015   http://www.nea.gov.sg/anti-pollution-radiation-protection /noise-pollution-control (accessed 7 August 2015).

OU Rubo 区如柏
1988   *Su shuo chuantong wenhua jin zai zhangzhong* 诉说传统文化尽在掌中 [Telling a tale of traditional culture through the hands]. *Lianhe Zaobao*, 21 August, 52.

RUIZENDAAL, Robin
2006   *Marionette Theater in Quanzhou*. Leiden and Boston: Brill.

SCHIPPER, Kristofer
1993   *The Taoist Body*. Trans. Karen C. Duval. Berkeley: University of California Press.

SINGAPORE DEPARTMENT OF STATISTICS
> http://www.singstat.gov.sg/docs/default-source/default-document-library
> /publications/publications_and_papers/cop2010/census_2010_release1
> /cop2010sr1.pdf (accessed 7 August 2015).

TANAKA Issei 田仲一成
> 2008 *Zhongguo jisi xiju yanjiu* 中國祭祀戲劇研究 [The study of ritualistic plays in China]. Chinese trans. Bu He 布和. Beijing: Beijing Daxue Chubanshe.

TEH Seh Hwee 鄭詩慧
> 2004 Xinjiapo Hainan Zhangtou mu'ou: "San Chun Long mu'ou ban" ge'an yanjiu" 新加坡海南杖頭木偶班—"三春隆木偶班"個案研究." Honours thesis, National University of Singapore.

TEO, Thompson, and Vivien LIM
> 2002 *Language Planning and Social Transformation Strategies to Promote Speak Mandarin Campaign in Singapore.* Singapore: Faculty of Business Administration, National University of Singapore.

The Straits Times
> 1970 Devan warns against imitating the "ugly Westerner." 13 September, NL6609, 8.
> 1971 How to resist evil lure of West. 6 August, NL6777, 20.
> 1979 Madam puppeteer. 14 December, NL10401, 10.
> 1984 Playing for the Gods. 23 August, NL14496, 1.
> 1985 Age-old art form gets new lease of life. 4 December, NL15826, 3.
> 1988 Capture traditional art forms on video. 8 September, NL16248, 22.
> 1989 Room for festival to grow. 23 October, NL16796, 1.
> 1990 Puppet passion 11 September, NL17104, 5.

WANG Zhenchun 王振春
> 2000 *Liyuan hua dang nian* 梨園話當年 [The yesteryears of dialogue on opera]. Xinjiapo: Lingzi Dazhong Chuanbo Gongsi.

YANG Rong 楊榕
> 2002 Putian kuilei xi yu Lu xi, beidou xi zhi tantao" [A discussion of puppet theater, the Smallpox play, and the Northern Dipper play in Putian]. *Minsu quyi* 136: 41-112.

YE Mingsheng 葉明生
> 2004 *Fujian kuileixi shilun* 福建傀儡戏史论 [A history of puppet plays in Fujian]. Zhongguo Xiju Chubanshe.

YUNG Sai-shing 容世誠
> 1994 Nanyang Xinghua de Mulianxi yu chaodu yishi 南洋興化目連戲與超度儀式 [The Xinghua Mulian play and exorcistic rituals in Nanyang]. *Minsu quyi* 92: 819–52.
> 1997 *Xiqu renlei xue chu tan: Yishi, juchang yu she qun* 戲曲人類學初探—儀式、劇場與社群 [Anthropology of Chinese drama: Ritual, theater, and community]. Maitian Chuban Gufen Youxian Gongsi.

ZHENG Li 鄭莉
> 2008 Xinjiapo Xinghua ren de mu'ou xi yu yishi chuantong 新加坡興化人的木偶戲與儀式傳統 [The puppet theater and ritual tradition of the Henghua people in Singapore]. *Journal of South Seas Society* 南洋學報 62: 51–72.

Appendix

List of activities of Sin Hoe Ping, 2010–2015 *

*Those marked with "ST" denote performances in the "state-tolerated" realm and "SR" for the "state-regulated" realm. All events were held in Singapore unless otherwise stated.

2010

6 February: Sin Hoe Ping (Henghua) performance at Kiew Lee Tong (ST)

14 February: Sin Hoe Ping (Henghua) performance at An Ren Gong (ST)

17 February: Sin Hoe Ping (Henghua) performance at Hao Pu She (濠浦社) (ST)

8–10 March: Sin Hoe Ping (Henghua) performance in celebration of Monkey God/Qi Tian Da Sheng (齊天大聖)'s feast day at Tian Xing Gong (天性宮) (ST)

31 March: Sin Hoe Ping (Hokkien) performance at Po Chiak Keng (保赤宮) (ST)

15 April: Sin Hoe Ping (Henghua) performance at Hokkien celebration of Xuan Tian Shang Di (玄天上帝)'s feast day (ST)

15 April: Sin Hoe Ping (Henghua) performance at Chong Fu temple (崇福堂) (ST)

28 April: Sin Hoe Ping (Henghua) performance at Xian Gong temple (ST)

23–24 June: Sin Hoe Ping (Henghua) all-male performance at Hokkien celebration for the feast day of Zhang Tian Shi (張天師) (ST)

30 June: Sin Hoe Ping (Henghua) performance at Li Jiang temple (ST)

21 July: "In the main hall of Cao Family's Residence," 8:00–8.30 p.m., 9:00–9.30 p.m., Central's River Promenade, in conjunction with "Singapore Food Festival 2010," held from 16 to 25 July (SR)

28 August: Mulian performance by Sin Hoe Ping at Hin Ann Thain Hiaw Keng (ST)

5 September: Sin Hoe Ping (Henghua) performance at Futsing Association (ST)

6 November: Beidou/Northern Dipper play by Sin Hoe Ping at Xian Ying Gong (顯應宮) (ST)

16 November: Sin Hoe Ping (Henghua) performance at Zhao Ling temple (昭靈廟) (ST)

2–5 December: Sin Hoe Ping (Henghua) performance at secret meditation event held at An Ren Gong (ST)

2011

8 January: "Journey to the West," Bukit Merah Community Library (SR)

16 January: Sin Hoe Ping (Hokkien) performance in celebration of Dua Ya Pek (大爺伯)'s birthday at private residence (ST)

18–19 January: Sin Hoe Ping (Henghua) performance at Hin Ann Thain Hiaw Keng (ST)

20 April: Sin Hoe Ping (Henghua) performance at industrial site, 31 Defu Lane 10 (ST)

27 October: "Puppetry in Chinese Opera," 2–4 p.m., Sun Yat Sen Memorial Hall (SR)

29 October: "Puppetry in Chinese Opera," 10 a.m.-12 p.m., Sun Yat Sen Memorial Hall (SR)

2012

February (exact date unknown): Mr. Yeo Lye Hoe's TV appearance, OKTO channel (SR)

16–17 February: "A puppet show not to be missed," Asian Civilisations Museum (SR)

24 February "Young President Organiser": Presentation of "Journey to the West" & "Wu Song Fights the Tiger," Sunday, Marina Bay Sands, Event Plaza (SR)

2013

13 March: Sin Hoe Ping (Henghua) performance at Hin Ann Thain Hiaw Keng (ST)

7 April: Sin Hoe Ping (Henghua) performance at Tian Xing Gong (天性宫) (ST)

10 April: Sin Hoe Ping (Henghua) performance at Chong Fu temple (崇福堂) (ST)

16 June: Sin Hoe Ping (Henghua) performance at Hin Ann Thain Hiaw Keng (興安天后宮) (ST)

26 June: Sin Hoe Ping (Henghua) performance at Li Jiang temple (鯉江廟) (ST)

15 July: Puppet performance and demonstration at River Valley High (Secondary and High school institution) (SR)

19–20 July: Sin Hoe Ping (Henghua) performance at Zhao Ling Miao (昭靈廟) (ST)

2014

15–16, 22–23 March: "Reliving Haw Par Villa," organized by the Singapore Tourism Board (STB) in conjunction with Tourism. (SR) The Haw Par Villa (虎豹別墅), originally called Tiger Balm Gardens, was established in 1937 by the famous Aw brothers, Aw Boon Haw and Aw Boon Par. The name "Haw Par" was derived from the names of the Aw brothers. It is now regarded as a heritage building symbolizing Chinese culture in Singapore.

24 October: Heng Ann Association Melaka (马六甲兴安会馆), Malaysia.

http://mykampung.sinchew.com.my/node/325465 (accessed 23 March 2015).

2015

25 January: Invitation by Nick Shen of Tok Tok Chiang (SR)

7 February Performance in conjunction with SG50 (SR)

20 February: (second day of first lunar month): Sin Hoe Ping (Hokkien) performance at Xian Zu Gong (仙祖宫) (ST)

22 February: (Fourth day of first lunar month): Sin Hoe Ping (Henghua) performance at Kiew Lee Tong (ST)

27 February: (Ninth day of first lunar month): Sin Hoe Ping (Hokkien) performance at Jin Shan Si (金山寺) (ST)

2 March: (Twelfth day of first lunar month): Sin Hoe Ping (Henghua) performance at An Ren Gong (安仁宫) (ST)

5 March: (fifteenth day of first lunar month): Sin Hoe Ping (Henghua) performance at Kiew Lee Tong (九鯉洞) (ST)

21 March: (second day of second lunar month): Sin Hoe Ping (Hokkien) Tua Pek Kong (大伯公) birthday celebration at Amoy Street (ST)

22 March: Sin Hoe Ping (Hokkien) at Gor Cho Tua Pek Kong temple (梧槽大伯公廟) at Balestier Road (ST)

21–22 April: (Third and fourth day of third lunar month): Sin Hoe Ping (Hokkien) performance at Rong Fu Tang (榮福堂) (ST)

26 April: (Eighth day of the third lunar month): Sin Hoe Ping (Henghua) performance at Xian Gong Tang (仙宮堂) (ST)

9 May: Performance for elderly folks in conjunction with SG50 (50th anniversary of Singapore) (SR)

11–12 May (Twenty-third and twenty-fourth day of third lunar month): Sin Hoe Ping (Hokkien) performance at Ping An Tang (平安堂) (ST)

16–17 May (Twenty-eighth and twenty-ninth day of third lunar month): Sin Hoe Ping (Hokkien) at Wu Feng Miao (五風廟), Geylang Lorong 34 (ST)

FILMS

Jeff Roy, Director, *Mohammed to Maya*
Bangkok, Jeff Roy Productions, 2012. 74 minutes. Color. No
price. http://mohammedtomaya.com/

THE 2012 FILM *Mohammed to Maya* documents the experience of the actress, dancer,
and homeopathic medical practitioner Maya Jafer as she undergoes sexual reassign-
ment surgery in Thailand and returns to her life in Los Angeles. An earlier short film
version, *Rites of Passage* (19 minutes), premiered at the Los Angeles Transgender Film
Festival in 2011, where it earned the Audience Choice Award for Best Film. *Rites of
Passage* and *Mohammed to Maya* have since been screened at over fifty film festivals,
universities, and community centers and have garnered another five awards on the
film festival circuit. The title of the shorter film invites the viewer to interpret Maya's
journey through Van Gennep's well-known framework whereby "all rites of passage
or 'transition' are marked by three phases: separation, margin (or *limen*, signifying
'threshold' in Latin), and aggregation" (TURNER 1969, 94). The title of the longer
version similarly suggests Maya's journey to be as much spiritual as it is physical.

With good humor and frequent use of crude language, Maya is an articulate and
affecting protagonist. Born Mohammed Gulam Hussain in the South Indian city of
Madurai, Tamil Nadu, Maya was raised in a conservative Muslim family within the
Memoni community, a group that traces its roots to Sindh and Gujarat on both sides
of the present-day border of Pakistan and India. Punctuated with video montages of
street scenes in Thailand, the film begins with Maya in transit three days before her
surgery. Some of the most revealing moments in the documentary are in large part
possible due to her comfort in front of the camera, especially when Maya seems to
be evaluating herself as she is being observed. Early in the film, for example, during
a discussion in a taxi, Maya appears interested in learning from a new acquaint-
ance whether he knew that she was a preoperative transgender woman. Not satisfied
with his answer ("Not by the look, but by the manners, yes"), she reinterprets his
response so that it is more in keeping with her own self-perception ("I think my

mannerisms are also feminine, it's my voice mainly, probably. But … thank you for the honesty").

Early in the film, we observe as Roy teaches Maya how to operate a handheld video recorder so as to keep a video journal. Roy's interest in incorporating participatory and reflexive camerawork is part of his broader efforts (see for example Roy's *Dancing Queens: It's All About Family* [2016]) to apply queer theory through documentary filmmaking. By deftly joining footage of Maya framed by Roy's camera in long shot with Maya's own close-up footage of herself, sharp divisions between observer and observed or viewer and participant become confused—indeed, I would suggest, felicitously so. Roy's role, too, seems to shift throughout the film from filmmaker to friend and supporter. Maya's self-consciousness is accentuated by the ironic—that is to say, distanced—commentary on her appearance and plans for life after the operation. Her use of English gives the viewer the sense that her medium of self-expression is often, as BARTHES famously argued in his analysis of the phrase "I love you" (1977, 147–49), highly intertextual and stylized. This "camp talk" draws upon "a stock of language features that are invested with cultural (and stereotypical) values in order to achieve the *effect* of a specific communal identity" (HARVEY 1998, 298), and perhaps even takes on a special urgency in these moments of transformation:

> Maya: After I get my vagina, I am going to have men all over me, wanting me, desiring me. Okay, maybe I should stop now. That's enough of diva-ishness. It's a little too much. It's kind of disgusting…
> Jeff Roy: Put the camera straight.
> Maya: Put the camera straight. Jeff says "put the camera straight."

This dissociative quality is most acute when Maya goes through an album of photographs taken before emigrating to the United States in 2000. When examining photos from India in which she appears with a mustache and in male-gendered clothing, she remarks:

> I was just doing what I had to do, during my days when I was trying to make it in [the] entertainment industry in India…. This is the total opposite of who I am, especially this one. This is the total opposite of who I am. The complete opposite. It's just insane.

Despite her self-consciously performative affect, Maya's honesty is raw and, at times, even unsettling. In obvious pain while convalescing after the operation, she is curt with the hospital staff. In teaching this film as part of a course on gender in South Asia, my students observed that Maya's tone, while perhaps not out of place in some South Asian contexts, would nevertheless be unfamiliar and even shocking to middle- and working-class American students who had not grown up in households with domestic employees. In other scenes, however, she appears very concerned with how they perceive her and even flirtatiously inquires after a handsome male member of the staff.

Maya's participation as both object and agent in the creation of this documentary has the effect of attenuating the voyeurism that would otherwise be inherent in capturing Maya at such a vulnerable time and in so intimate a manner. Maya clearly struggles with the immense social cost of her transition, particularly the strain it has placed on the relationship with her family. It is apparent, especially upon her return to Los Angeles in the last third of the film, that it has also taken a toll on her health and financial stability. Whether in scenes in which she undergoes hair removal through electrolysis or reads aloud emails from family members, one is quickly disabused of any lingering suspicions of Maya having entered lightly into this process.

Maya's extended soliloquies on her faith and depictions of devotional practices make this film a useful component of courses on religion and contemporary Islam. While this documentary could be paired with some recent memoirs in English translation by members of the South Asian *hijra* community (for example, RĒVATHI [2010] and VIDYA [2007]), Maya is very clear (in personal communication, April 2016) that she does not wish to claim a *hijra* identity (on the problem of employing Western gender and sexuality terminology within South Asian contexts see DUTTA and ROY [2014]). In this regard, the film is more appropriately categorized within Asian American studies. The production quality is generally excellent, and Roy is to be commended for including subtitles for the few scenes in which the audio is not fully clear. A version of the film that is entirely subtitled in English is also available for international audiences.

REFERENCES

BARTHES, Roland
   1977   *A Lover's Discourse: Fragments*. New York: Hill and Wang.
DUTTA, Aniruddha, and Raina ROY
   2014   Decolonizing Transgender in India: Some reflections. *TSQ: Transgender Studies Quarterly* 1: 320–37.
HARVEY, Keith
   1998   Translating camp talk: Gay identities and cultural transfer. *The Translator* 4: 295–320.
RĒVATHI, A.
   2010   *The Truth About Me: A Hijra Life Story*. New Delhi: Penguin Books.
TURNER, Victor
   1969   *The Ritual Process: Structure and Anti-Structure*. Ithaca: Cornell University Press.
VIDYA, Living Smile
   2007   *I Am Vidya*. Chennai: Oxygen Books.

Walter Hakala
State University of New York, Buffalo

Susan Østigaard and Beathe Hofseth, Directors,
Light Fly, Fly High

Norway/India, 2013. 80 minutes, color. $89.00 (K-12, public libraries, and select groups); $350 (universities, colleges, and institutions). https://www.wmm.com.

THIS FILM opens with an attractive yet boyish woman taking a shower, over which is dubbed the voice of the defiant, bathing woman speaking in Tamil about how being Adi Dravidar ("original Dravidian" = Dalit in North India) and a woman demands "obedience." However, she quickly states, "this is my life." Her name is Thulasi. At the age of twenty-four, she has now been boxing for a decade in the "light fly" category

(48 kg). She ran away from home at the tender age of fourteen because her father wanted her to marry an elderly man. Recounting this, she says in broken English, "married life is jailed life!" Boxing liberates her from the commitment to be the stereotypical woman who submits to becoming a stay-at-home housewife.

Another Adi Dravidar family, who initially supported her alternative vision of life, adopted Thulasi, but now she has only one year remaining to prove herself competent to make the national team that would go to the Olympics. Her chances look good, since she ranked third in the country during the previous year, having even defeated the reigning champion of India on several occasions. Her adopted family thus goes out on a limb and secures a loan to cover her costs, most of which get lost in a corrupt sporting system in which government funds are purloined for personal gain by coaches, sponsors, and so on.

Under pressure to perform well, the film then follows her female team traveling by train to the competition, where she will fight in her light fly class. She loses the match, due to a sore shoulder. Angered and frustrated, she gets in an argument on the return journey and is expelled from her fight club. Thulasi is determined to turn around her bad luck, so gets a "boxer" tattoo on her shoulder. Only one last chance remains to make the nationals before turning twenty-five, but her stepfather is trying to convince her to settle down and get married, due to her loss. She stubbornly refuses, despite a doctor's prognosis that her bad shoulder has a 50/50 chance of failing her again in the next round. To everyone's surprise, she wins her qualifying match, but is refused a place on the national team for refusing the sexual advances of Sir Karuna of the selection committee.

Her boxing career ends at the age of twenty-five, but not the story, since she files harassment charges against Sir Karuna, who is arrested, but later let out on bail. Meanwhile, Rajesh seeks permission to marry her. We see the festive preparations for the wedding taking place. On the wedding day, however, we spy a forlorn Thulasi dreading the nuptials. She refuses to consummate the marriage with her husband, so he punishes her by banning her use of a mobile phone. In addition, he will not allow her to leave their humble dwelling, where she sleeps uncomfortably on the floor. She is also forbidden to work, wear jeans, or use Facebook. "My life is boring," she opines in English. Meanwhile Sir Karuna makes several attempts to bribe her to drop the lawsuit, but she refuses, then leaves her husband and moves back in with her adopted family.

Just when Thulasi's luck seems to have run out, she suddenly gets a phone call from an international fitness club (Gold's Gym) and gets offered a job as a personal trainer. This allows her to finally achieve economic independence, so she divorces her husband, buys a motorcycle, then moves into her own flat, where she dreams of one day starting her own gym. As we witness her riding off into the sunset, the credits begin scrolling, and we learn that her court case has still not been settled, and unlikely to be adjudicated in the near future, despite the fact that governmental forces closed her former boxing club.

Thulasi's narrative was filmed over a three-year period, so we benefit from seeing her life evolve. It shatters many of the stereotypes people have of both women and so-called "untouchables" in India as being disempowered beings totally subjected by a harsh, paternalistic, and stratified social system crying out for reform. By ending on an ambiguous note that simultaneously suggests life is what you make it but is also fraught with injustice, the film leaves the viewer wondering if caste issues will ever get completely resolved in India. Thulasi shows us what is possible, but also grimly reminds us of the limitations of human agency. After all, the structure of society impinges upon that very human freedom craved by the heroine of this engrossing film. It works well in the classroom with Loïc WACQUANT's excellent book titled *Body and Soul* (2004) to discuss Bourdieu's concept of practice theory.

REFERENCES

WACQUANT, Loïc
 2004 *Body and Soul: Notebooks of an Apprentice Boxer.* New York: Oxford University Press.

Frank J. Korom
Boston University

Tim Graf and Jakob Montrasio, editors and directors, *Buddhism after the Tsunami: The Souls of Zen 3/11 Japan Special* (Classroom Edition)
Tim Graf and Michael Zimmer, producers. 2012. 63 minutes. In Japanese and English, with English subtitles. Open access: https://vimeo.com/158309233.

THIS FILM, narrated by co-director Tim Graf, seeks to shed light on the role of Buddhist religious organizations in the wake of the triple disasters—earthquake, tsunami, and nuclear crisis—that occurred on 11 March 2011 (3.11) in Japan. Graf contributed two vignettes related to this subject in this journal (vol. 75, no. 1), a special issue focusing on religious groups' responses to disasters in Asia.

Buddhism after the Tsunami was not Graf's initial research project. He was investigating Zen Buddhism for his PhD in Japan when the earthquake struck at 2:46 p.m., which caused him to rethink his work. He saw that Buddhist organizations were among the first to mobilize a response to the earthquake by raising funds in the streets within days and helping survivors. As he was witnessing "the greatest religious mobilization in postwar Japanese history," he realized that he and his colleagues could help by telling this story.

A number of key themes emerge in the film. One concerns the direct effects of the earthquake and tsunami. Takahashi Seikai (now deceased), who was the head priest of the Jōdo shū (Pure Land) temple Jōnenji, and his daughter Takahashi Issei, then the vice head priest but now head priest, describe in detail life immediately after the disaster occurred. Jōnenji is located in Kesennuma, the city nearest to the epicenter of the quake. While the temple and its newly built main hall survived, 80 percent of the households affiliated with the temple were damaged. The temple provided shelter for over 140 victims, not all of whom were members of the temple.

Locals could not comprehend the extent of the initial damage for almost a week, we learn from Shōji Yoshiaki, head priest of the Jōdo shū temple Unjōji, which is located in the city of Rikuzentakata, one of the most profoundly affected areas. While the world watched images of the tsunami's aftermath, those in the area were without electricity.

The effect on communities is explored in revealing ways. Takahashi Seikai explains how he achieved his dream of building a hall that would withstand earthquakes yet was forced to completely reevaluate his plans—he wonders whether he should ask temple members to pay the donations they had promised to contribute to the new building. He describes how a nearby Shinto shrine had also completed a large new hall just before the earthquake that was funded by donations from the community. Although the shrine's priest and his wife initially opened the hall for the affected community members, they demanded that they leave after two days. Takahashi notes that people were so angry they refused to participate in the shrine's annual festival that October, suggesting that the selfish actions of the priest and his wife were repaid through community anger.

The film also explores the changing nature of funeral rituals. Japanese Buddhism in practice is strongly linked with the dead, and the bonds connecting the living and their ancestors are crucial. Ninety percent of funerals in Japan are Buddhist, and complex rituals have developed over the centuries—temples have been the sites where the rituals are performed. But after 3.11, priests and temples in the area were forced to adjust rituals to the circumstances. There were no coffins available and bodies were simply wrapped in sheets for cremation. People tried to go to temples to cremate their relatives but the temples themselves were unable to provide traditional rituals for the dead. Takahashi Issei explains how the first thing people searched for were remains of family altars, photographs, and mementos of those who had perished—anything that would provide a sense of normality to the rituals that had guided their practice.

Kaneta Taiō, priest of the Sōtō-shū temple Tsūdaiji, discusses the difficulties his fellow Buddhists faced in giving services and how to actually speak to those directly affected. Priests became psychological counselors, dealing with survivors as well as fellow priests who could barely deal with the situation. In a fascinating interview, he discusses the Sōtō-shū organization amid the complex religious foundations of the seaside area and the local beliefs in Sanriku-chō. Sōtō temples in the area are dedicated to the dragon god, the dragon being a symbol of nature that is said to calm the sea.

Media representation of religion is another theme that the film touches on. Like the other themes, it could easily have been extended but the main points are enough for audiences to get a sense of its import. Graf notes that the Western media largely ignored the importance of spiritual support to disaster victims and focused on "Japan's stoic resilience in the face of adversity." This was due, he states, to virtually no reported cases of looting or disorder, and few public displays of grief. By contrast, the Japanese media is given credit for treating the social engagement of religious organizations during the crisis fairly. Traditionally wary of discussing religion—a situation exacerbated by the fallout from the Aum Shinrikyō affair of the 1990s—the media played an important role in showing how different religious groups can work together for communities.

One theme that appears somewhat out of place is that of the inheritance of family graves. Grave succession remains patrilineal in Japan and we see a temple in Tokyo that sold part of its graveyard plot to finance a subterranean memorial hall. This hall houses the remains and memorial tablets of those who joined the temple's "Society of Bonds" *En no Kai* (that is, those who have paid the one-time fee). While it is interesting to learn that the temple is catering to single women and childless couples, for example, who are unable to find graves of their own, this five-minute section is not specifically related to Buddhism's response to the tsunami.

The footage for the film is a combination of visual ethnography taken by Graf, archival news footage, and interviews. There are some exquisitely shot scenes of temples and rituals but occasionally the music overpowers what people are saying, which is distracting because the interviews are revealing and profound. While focusing on just one or two themes may have been more effective, presenting a number of areas opens up the possibility for future discussion on these subjects. Despite this, the film is a thoughtful exploration of complex issues. Graf and his colleagues deserve praise for making the film open access, and I would encourage its use in classrooms.

Benjamin Dorman
Nanzan University

BOOKS

General

Raminder Kaur and Parul Dave-Mukherji, eds., *Arts and Aesthetics in a Globalizing World*

London: Bloomsbury, 2015. 304 pages. Cloth, $112.00; paperback, $37.95; ebook, $24.99. ISBN 9781472519306 (cloth); 9781472519313 (paperback); 9780857855473 (ebook).

THE CHOICE of the title *Arts and Aesthetics in a Globalizing World* by the editors Raminder Kaur and Parul Dave-Mukherji seems to be very unspecific. However, it indicates a complementarity that places arts and aesthetics side by side instead of imposing a hierarchy that separates them as different fields of inquiry. At first glance, the title fits the content and the idea that the world is indeed globalizing. The publication is mainly about open processes, interconnectivity, and dissolving static views of changing value systems in human society. It is the result of a conference based on research collaboration between the Association of Social Anthropologists (ASA) with the School of Arts and Aesthetics and the Centre for the Study of Social Sciences at Jawaharlal Nehru University (JNU) in Delhi. The arrangement of the chapters is suitable for a wide array of readers in academia, and it may also interest the general public interested in anthropology, who will benefit from some very new and some vintage yet still valuable ideas presented in this volume, which is comprised of sixteen chapters.

The introduction by the editors starts with a citation from Jalal ad-Din Muhammad Rumi: "The art of knowing is knowing what to ignore" (1). Out of a large number of panels and plenary sessions, the most convincing chapters present a mosaic of approaches, ideas, and emerging theories. A few aspects, however, appear more frequently and stand for a paradigm shift in research about the role, impact, and function of arts and aesthetics in society; namely, the focus on sensory and material features within the scope of arts and aesthetics connected to local communities and their capability to interconnect with globalizing movements. Connecting the local to the global is a highly interesting point of departure. Some chapters, such as Atreyee Sen's "Slaps, Beatings, Laughter, Adda, Puppet Shows: Naxal Women Prisoners in Calcutta and the Art of Happiness in Captivity" (119–34), or Christopher Pinney's "Hot Bricolage: Magical Mimesis in Modern India" (85–98) are clearly dedicated to this approach, and their contributions to this volume will surely be discussed among scholars in the future.

Despite the innovation of some contributions, there are also less fresh arguments concerning the underlying criticism of Eurocentric assumptions and so-called indigenous artwork. Though both topics are high priority topics for researchers, and no less important than others in the broader context of the anthropology of art, some of the contributions are lacking in updated information on theoretical protagonists and their views. In a globalizing world, the fact of being born in a colonized country or in a colonizing country can no longer be used as an epistemic attribute, for too many social layers of human experiences create ongoing changes that configure with ethnic, national, gendered, and generational belongings. The chapter titled "Of Mockery and Mimicking: Gagnendranath Tagore's Critique of Henri Bergson's Laughter (1911)" by Emilia Terraciano (21–37) reflects upon an assemblage of very detailed historical facts and sources. However, the position of the observer remains slightly static and dualistic. In another chapter, Shiv Visvanathan's "Rethinking Waste: Time, Obsolescence, Diversity and Democracy" (99–118), the author deals with the positions of key figures within their societies regarding the perception of waste as opposed to dirt. Visvanathan similarly moves through his chapter with rich philosophical discussion. In the end, however, a clear direction or position is missing, despite his oscillation back and forth between sharp observation and pluralistic generalization.

Another important topic of the volume is the therapeutic effect of the arts and aesthetics on people's capability in coping with the globalizing world. Though the healing dimension is often an integral part of art analytics, chapters 9 and 13 take very specific views on the subject. Chapter 9 is Andrea Griede's "Rwanda: Healing and the Aesthetics of Poetry." She sets out to explain the value of poetry as a grounded search for metaphors in a traumatized community. Describing the power of words as an extension of self, she argues that they help in overcoming jealousy and loss. In so doing, she offers interesting insights into the aesthetics of local history. Chapter 13 is Susanne Schmitt's "Intimacy Out of Place: On the Workings of Smell in an Exhibition on Human Sexuality" (205–20), which deals with bodily experiences at the Deutsches Hygiene-Museum in Dresden. The creation of cultural and physical contact points is investigated as an aspect of ethnographic relevance in the transmission of sensory experience to museum goers. Interesting insights are offered on smell as an ethnographic category connected to the human body.

The impact of mobility and tourism is the last topic under the umbrella of arts and aesthetics mentioned here. In chapters dedicated to this topic, the rather undifferentiated view of Eurocentric assumptions and categorizations partly continues. In "The Aesthetics of Diaspora: Sensual Milieus and Literary Worlds" (153–68), Pnina Werbner and Mattia Fumanti discuss what they term "vernacular" and "encapsulated" aesthetics. After reviewing a huge amount of previous research, they conclude that these two forms of aesthetics are especially represented by the exile literature dedicated to departure cultures. Soumendra Mohan Patnaik in his "Consuming Culture: The Re-figuration of Aesthetics in Nagaland Cultural Tourism in India's Northeast" (221–40) remains rather modest and secure by limiting his discussion to conventional analyses.

The most innovative contributions, however, seem to be those dedicated to the overarching idea of the publication, which is a rather philosophical and empirical ap-proach to discussing "mediated audiovisuality" in arts and aesthetics. Among this core group is Denis Vidal's very interesting analysis titled "The Return of the Aura: Anish Kapoor: The Studio and the World" (39–60). This is also one of the few chapters diverting from the headline model "x:y," where X stands for an extremely minimized abstract and Y for the primary object of research. It does so by inserting Anish Kapoor, an important and fashionable name that is often cited alongside that of the legendary Homi Bhabha, who is widely cited throughout all chapters. Patricia Spyer's chapter, "Art under Siege: Perils and Possibilities of Aesthetic Forms in a Globalizing World" (73–84), also falls into the cluster of core chapters. Her argument appears compelling, straightforwardly using technical terms within a reflection concerning the narration of experiences. Spyer's chapter leaves the reader with many productive questions.

All of the chapters, including those not mentioned here, deal generously with the relevant scholarly literature. The editors have paid special attention by creating clear structures by thematically grouping the essays. As a whole, the entire publication en-riches anthropological research on art and aesthetics, especially within the context of South Asia, which is indeed appropriate given that the conference upon which the volume is based was held in India. The chapters demonstrate a broad diversity of top-ics regarding art forms, theoretical perspectives, and the role of the human senses. They collectively offer a considerable number of novel insights, while only occasionally adhering to conventional and predictable analyses. In some cases, however, improve-ments could have been suggested on how to apply more differentiated views on the role of individuals in the production and reception of art. Coming back to Rumi, the editors knew well what to ignore.

Gisa Jähnichen
Shanghai Conservatory of Music

Faye Yuan Kleeman, *In Transit: The Formation of the Colonial East Asian Cultural Sphere*
Honolulu: University of Hawaiʻi Press, 2014. 302 pages. Hardback, $52.00. ISBN 0824838602.

WITH *In Transit: The Formation of the Colonial East Asian Cultural Sphere,* Faye Yuan Kleeman adopts an interdisciplinary and multi-textual approach for providing a trans-national history of Japan's "empire-wide cultural sphere" (9), and the multi-faceted ways in which individuals were embroiled within this sphere. By the onset of the Pacific War, this "cultural sphere" had become articulated within government propaganda as the geopolitical construct of the "Great East Asia Co-Prosperity Sphere," the paradig-matic expression of Japanese imperialist ideology. It is this ideological understanding of the Co-Prosperity Sphere that Kleeman wishes to reread, shifting focus to the cultural and personal interactions between Japan and other parts of East Asia prior to, and continuing after, the manifestation of the concept within Japanese state propaganda. As Kleeman reminds us, it was not through state ideology that people chose to participate in Japan's imperial projects; "rather, it was through the lure of desire and pleasure, through their romantic imaginations" (7). Seeking to "transcend previous studies of the Japanese empire as a hegemonic macrosystem with unifying governing principles" (16), Kleeman uses the medium of biography to view Japan's empire as "a fluid, interconnected site that is dynamic, complex, and full of multiple possibilities and conflicted, competing values and ideas" (18). Whether Kleeman "transcends" the existing literature is debatable; however, what is not debatable is that she enhances the existing literature by providing a rich examination of how certain individuals navigated the complex ideological and geopolitical landscape of the empire. Through this "microscale approach" (16), Kleeman is able to explore a wide range of topics crucial to understanding the complexity of Japan's empire and individual interactions within it, including gender, class, racial and ethnic identity, biopolitics, marriage and romance, ideology, cultural representation, imperial cosmopolitanism, and colonial modernity. Among these, the topic of gender is most fully developed in Kleeman's argument, particularly issues of female subjectivity, with all but the first chapter devoted to female subjects.

In Transit is divided into three parts, each containing two chapters, which follow a loose chronological order. An account of Japan's emergence as an empire provides the background to Part I, which examines the Pan-Asianism of the "continental adventurer" (or, *tairiku rōnin*) Miyazaki Tōten and educator-cum-spy Kawahara Misako. Focusing less on Miyazaki's political dealings in China and elsewhere, Kleeman seeks to "bring a cultural dimension to the discussion of Pan-Asianism" (22) through an examination of Miyazaki's incorporation of his political ideals into the performance of traditional narrative chanting, *naniwabushi*.

Chapter 2 continues the theme of Pan-Asianism, but connects with a broader focus of the book: the individual in their relations with the state and its geopolitical interests. Here, Kleeman discusses the exploits of Kawahara Misako, or the "Mata Hari of Japan." Educated by a Sinophile father and motivated by Japan's "civilizing mission" on the continent, Kawahara travelled to China and Mongolia as an educationalist, but ended up working as a spy for the Japanese government in its machinations against the Russians. Kawahara's life history also provides a gateway for exploring gender roles in Meiji Japan. While personifying the ideal of the self-actualizing "New Woman," she was also a traditionalist, and fell into the role of the "good wife, wise mother" in her later life—"two constructions of the feminine that, together, bookended the Meiji period" (45).

Parts II and III continue the theme of gender, but broaden it to include a consideration of ethnic identity during the high period of Japanese imperialism. These parts comprise the bulk of the book and get to the crux of Kleeman's argument. Kleeman examines subjects "who crossed between the metropole and the colonies, blurring the national boundaries and confronting issues of race, gender, and identity" (79).

Chapter 3 covers the life histories of two Japanese aristocratic women: Nashimoto Masako (Ri Masako) and Saga Hiroko (Aisin-Gioro Hiro), who were married off to the loyal courts of Korea and Manchuria, respectively. This chapter provides insights into the biopolitics of empire and the use of private bodies for public deployment by the state. Marriage challenged the Japan-centric cultural assumptions held by these women, and deeply altered their ethnic identities and affiliations. Chapter 4 looks at celebrities, Kawashima Yoshiko (Aixinjueluo Xianyu) and Ri Kōran (Yamaguchi Yoshiko). The lives of Kawashima (a crossdressing Manchu princess and Manchukuo generalissimo who was raised in Japan by a "continental adventurer") and Ri (a Japanese actress who was raised in China and affected a Chinese ethnic public persona) provide a gateway for Kleeman to deepen her examination of gender and ethnic hybridity in the context of Japanese imperialism. Chapter 5 turns to literary representations of Taiwan in the works of Masugi Shizue and Sakaguchi Reiko. Kleeman "explores the intersections of colonialism, modernism, body, transnational mobilizations, and the female writerly subjectivity" (161). The final chapter examines the "transmission of knowledge and modernity through the medium of the human body," with a look at dancers Choi Seunghee from Korea and Tsai Juiyueh from Taiwan (182).

The novelty of Kleeman's work and her largest contribution to our understanding of Japanese imperialism is the biographical approach she brings to the subject matter. Through a series of life histories, *In Transit* explores the fractured identities created by empire, the multiplicity of personalities that it makes possible, the conflicted and competing loyalties it makes inevitable, and how these were formed and remolded over the geopolitical landscape of the empire. Through this focus on individuals and their histories, Kleeman seeks to answer three questions: "What did common people gain from the empire? How were they persuaded to accept the ideology of Japanese imperialism? What sustained their interest in the project of empire building?" (7). While Kleeman provides compelling answers for the personalities she explores, her subjects can hardly be described as "common people"; rather, they were extraordinary. Kleeman's analysis of the "cultural sphere" of Japan's empire focuses on the agents of cultural production within the sphere rather than the consumers. This makes generalizations about the everyday experiences of ordinary individuals—common people—in their consumption of these cultural products difficult. Kleeman's focus on the lives of a limited number of extraordinary individuals thus makes *In Transit* problematic as a general history of "the formation of the colonial East Asian cultural sphere," in the words of the book's subtitle. This, of course, is not Kleeman's objective, which appears to be the opposite: the formation of individual subjectivities within the cultural sphere. This is an objective which Kleeman's work fulfills in a readable, insightful, and engaging manner. Finally, the addition of a conclusion would have been helpful in tying up the multiple themes running through the work as well as suggesting future avenues for exploration.

Danton Leary
Australian National University

Regina F. Bendix, Aditya Eggert, and Arnika Peselmann, eds., *Heritage Regimes and the State*

Göttingen: Universitätsverlag Göttingen, 2012. 413 pages. Paperback, $54.95. ISBN 978-3-86395-075-0.

HERITAGE REGIMES AND THE STATE is a significant, timely volume that features a who's who of contemporary heritage studies. A comparative exploration of the intersection between the international heritage regime and processes of state implementation, it is a product of two European heritage conferences held in 2011, the first at the University of Göttingen, Germany, by the interdisciplinary research group The Constitution of Cultural Property, and the second at the Villa Vigoni in Loveno di Menaggio, Italy, by the French-German-Italian research group, Institutions, Territoires et Communautés: Perspectives sur le Patrimoine Culturel Immatériel Translocal (Institutions, Territories and Communities: Perspectives on Translocal Intangible Cultural Heritage).

The volume sets out to explore the impact of international heritage conventions, particularly the UNESCO World Heritage Convention (1972) and UNESCO Intangible Cultural Heritage (ICH) Convention (2003), upon existing local, regional, and state cultural conservation efforts. The first comparative study of its kind, *Heritage Regimes and the State* presents seventeen case studies across four regions, namely Europe (France, Germany, Italy, Ireland, Lithuania, Russia, Spain, Switzerland), Africa (Mali, Mauritania, Morocco), Asia (China, Uzbekistan), and the Caribbean (Barbados, Cuba). Emphasizing the meta-cultural operations of heritage construction and translation—how cultural monuments, landscapes, or intangible cultural practices are transformed into authorized heritage—it illuminates the diverse ways in which international governance interfaces with state governance, with an international heritage regime serving to create a number of unequal heritage regimes worldwide.

In exploring these issues, authors were asked to consider two sets of questions. The first set of questions concerned heritage nomination processes, selection procedures (including potential exclusion), the actors and institutions allowed to participate in the process, and other elements of heritage governance. The second set of questions concerned the implementation of a successful UNESCO heritage nomination, the actors and institutions given permission to participate in the process, issues surrounding user rights, and the effect of heritage-making on both selected cultural forms and their constituent communities. While each author chose to incorporate the questions most relevant for their particular ethnographic study, the resulting diversity of case studies and reflections well complement one another and provide the reader with crucial insights into the multiple ways in which international heritage policy is being implemented at both state and local levels.

With twenty-three total contributions, evaluating each essay individually is beyond the scope of this review. I will instead focus upon the sections and themes more broadly. In the introductory section, alongside the introductory chapter by the volume's editors that outlines the issues described above, Kuutma's essay further engages the theme of heritage as a process of cultural production through exploring the relationship between heritage, engineering, and arbitration. Supporting the call for multi-sited ethnographic research of heritage regimes, she stresses the importance of considering not only the negative but positive effects of heritage regime interfaces, those "moments of empowerment, real instances of emergent agency, and situations where local actors partake in grassroots policy-making" (33). The next section, entitled "The Reach of (Post-)Colonial Sentiment and Control," considers heritage regimes in a number of postcolonial nation-states, addressing issues such as the colonial conceptual legacy within international, state, and local heritage value systems; the relationship between heritage, hegemony, and global justice; and cosmopolitanism, nation branding, cultural resistance, cultural amnesia, and competing agendas in processes of classification and implementation. The section entitled "Layers of Preservation Regimes and State Politics" spans ethnographic contexts across Europe and Uzbekistan while examining UNESCO nomination processes, the dynamics of inclusion and exclusion, the multiple strategies used by actors in competing heritage regimes, the changing relationship between UNESCO, the state, and local stakeholders over time; the cultural practice of state heritage bureaucracies, the impact that relationships between UNESCO personnel and state politicians have upon artisan communities and the items they produce; and the relationship between heritage and human ecology. The following section, "States and their 'Thing': Selection Processes, Administrative Structures, and Expert Knowledge," considers heritage regimes across Europe and China. It addresses issues spanning changes to national heritage policy and practice following ratification of the UNESCO ICH Convention, increased national interest in and control of previously regional cultures, political and bureaucratic mechanisms shaping national ICH programs, the changing role of heritage and tradition within wider sociopolitical spheres, and how UNESCO ICH recognition is changing the relationship between the state and local economies. Finally, the volume's closing commentaries are made by renowned scholars Donald Brenneis, Rosemary Coombe, and Laurajane Smith, with a final comparative assessment by Chiara De Cesari. These provide a number of insights into the ongoing negotiation processes of heritage regimes themselves, shifting configurations of knowledge and power, the need for an ongoing critical reflection upon the nature of heritage discourses themselves, heritage regimes as emergent regimes of power modeled upon neoliberal governmentality, and the potential impact that academic publications may have on the local cultural understandings within these new regimes.

The single critique I have of the volume is one already acknowledged by the editors in the introduction, namely that the majority of the case studies presented are European. The volume does, however, make an admirable effort to counter the hegemony of Anglophone scholarship by including the work of non-Anglophone scholars, albeit translated into English.

Overall, *Heritage Regimes and the State* represents a major contribution to heritage literature, providing the first in-depth comparative look into the relationship between the international heritage regime and state heritage regimes around the world. It should be of considerable interest to heritage professionals, constituent communities, and scholars across a wide range of fields including anthropology, folklore, archaeology, heritage studies, international studies, and area studies.

Leah Lowthorp
Harvard University

Tiantian Zheng, ed., *Cultural Politics of Gender and Sexuality in Contemporary Asia*
Honolulu: University of Hawai'i Press, 2016. 240 pages. Cloth, $69.00. ISBN 0824852974.

BOOKS ON GENDER and secularity in Asia have proliferated over the past two decades. Most of them tend to be focused on one region or nation, and on one gender or one type of sexuality. In *Cultural Politics of Gender and Sexuality in Contemporary Asia*, Tiantian Zheng offers a collection of articles that address a wide variety of societies, both national and regional—Taiwan, Hong Kong, China and Shanghai, Japan and Tokyo, Korea, India, Cambodia, Pakistan and Punjab, and Thailand. In addition, a variety of gender identities and sexual preferences and behaviors—heterosexuality, homosexuality, men's gender display, and women's gender issues—are all included. This collection will prove useful for students to compare and contrast, for example, state attempts at promoting specific types of sexual behavior, such as sexual purity, marriage and procreation, and controlling bodies across a spectrum of nations and societies.

In the introduction, Zheng explains that as a researcher and professor she has "always lamented the lack of a comprehensive volume that pulls together cultural politics, political economy, gender and sexuality across Asia" (1). In this volume, she has achieved her goal. Many of the authors are anthropologists, or grounded in the anthropological methodology of fieldwork, often over a period of several years. Most of the essays state clearly their period of field research that underpins their findings. The various articles are the stories of real people and their experiences. A dominant theme running through the essays is the question as to what degree individuals have agency as they are enmeshed in particular societies and the prevailing sexual economies.

In the first chapter, "Sexuality, Class, and Neoliberal Ideology: Same-Sex Attracted Men and Money Boys in Postsocialist China," Tiantian Zheng examines the so-called "money boys." She looks at a wide variety of individuals who serve as male prostitutes to achieve wealth and social status, compete in the market economy, and produce wealth. These often poor and rural young men situate themselves as pursuing the entrepreneurial goals of present-day China by achieving wealth through prostitution. If they are young and attractive, they quickly find that paid sex earns them much more money than factory work. In fact, the Chinese government wants its citizens to be heterosexual individuals so as to produce more workers in order to produce economically productive, "responsible and governable citizens" (27). A few of the more sophisticated and enterprising young men do amass enough money to begin independent economic activities and normal, successful lives. Zheng concludes that "[m]oney boys, carrying heavy historical baggage due to their rural migrant status contest social inequality and cultural stigma by valorizing state ideology and claiming themselves as 'normal' Postsocialist subjects" (34).

I found the second chapter by Kevin Carrico, "A Ladies' Academy in Urban China," fascinating in his description and analysis of private purity centers known as Ladies' Academies. In attempting to turn the clock back several centuries, men, in particular, have founded and run these academies, which Carrico characterizes as "the ultimate misogynistic fantasy in which all problems are attributed to women, who are out of their natural place" (51). The "ladies" that these male instructors wish to produce are to be sexually pure, produce children, and remain silent, and these academies, which Carrico characterizes as "male-constructed educational uterus ... emerged primarily from the anxieties, uncertainties, and instabilities of the present. Caught between romanticized imaginings of the past and the stark realities of the present" (53).

A related essay, "Mobilizing the Masses to Change Something Intimate: The Process of Desexualization in China's Family Planning Campaign" by Danning Wang (chapter 5), chronicles the Chinese government's campaign in the 1960s, "in the name of creating a 'healthy and spirited' public atmosphere. From dress codes to public behavior patterns and dating rules, this asexual standard governed all aspects of the freedom of love ... [Consequently,] sex and sexuality became a critical tool in regulating Chinese urbanites" (93). The goal of an associated propaganda effort involved "emphasizing mothers' sacred role in contributing to the modernization of the state and the country, this campaign shifted the focus from women's sexuality in the domain of reproduction" (93). Thus, women's sexuality and their desexualization became a goal for both the Mao-era government, which were then reflected in the private efforts designed to create sexually pure women in Ladies' Academies.

Chapters 9 and 12 look at the role of women in three Asian cities. In her essay "Marriage and Reproduction in East Asian Cities: Views from Single Women in Shanghai, Hong Kong, and Tokyo" (chapter 9), Lynne Nakano makes clear that the state and the family encourage women, in many cases, to marry and have children. She looks at the various forces that attempt to influence who and when a woman marries. Her findings indicate that in all three cities, although they differ to some degree, women themselves make the final choice, including the choice to remain single. However, most women want to marry and have children, but most choose not to do so unless they find the right partner.

In "Racialization of Foreign Women in the Transnational Marriage Market of Taiwan" (chapter 12), Hsunhui Tseng describes and analyzes a phenomenon that occurred in Taiwan in the 1990s in which a booming market in foreign brides blossomed. Beginning with Vietnamese and mainland Chinese brides, the industry began to seek women from Ukraine. Problematizing the issue of race in the latter case, Tseng observes that the phenomenon was short lived and the government attempted to put a stop to the practice. Finally Tseng notes that "an imaginary racial hierarchy among foreign women is pervasive in society, and the transnational marriage market is the venue where cultural racism can most easily be perceived" (218).

Two articles address the ways in which working class and poor men, both physically as well as through male social solidarity and neighborhood organizing, display and preserve their culturally based standards of masculinity. In Xia Zhang's article "Labor, Masculinity, and History: Bangbang Men in Choqqing" (chapter 7), Zhang describes the "bangbang" men, who are rural migrant men at the bottom of the social and economic ladder, who act as porters and casual day laborers. To maintain their masculinity, they vaunt their position as independent actors, who do not have bosses. She concludes, "bangbang work seems to provide these working men more flexibility, dignity, and a sense of control" (134). Zhang provides a useful history of the trajectory of Chinese masculinity, with its binary of scholar/warrior in which the scholar was the more valued individual. Zhang states that the migratory experience "also provides opportunities in certain contexts for them to develop alternative masculine ideals and claim new urban masculine subjectivities" (133).

Madhura Lohokare writes in "Boy II Men: Neighborhood Associations in Western India as the Site of Masculine Identity" (chapter 8) that *mandals* (neighborhood associations), through their political and social activities, provide lower class men with identities. "These activities include celebrating religious festivals and national holidays, feeding pilgrims, organizing blood donation camps, running a gymnasium/library, writing civic messages on notice boards, and organizing minor financial help for neighborhood members" (142). I found this article compelling because it resonated with my studies of urban life in the Muslim Middle East, even existing in Iran when I went to school. Such organizations provide sites of construction of masculinity, and Lohokare notes "the fact of belonging to a *mandal* itself bestows a masculine identity on its members" (143).

In contrast, several of the articles focus on the locus of bars, a popular locus of sexual and sensual interchanges for heterosexual, homosexual, and transgender individuals. As various authors point out, sex does not necessarily occur, but it often does. In "Tonight, You Are a Man!": Negotiating Embodied Resistance in Local Thai Nightclubs" (chapter 3), Danielle Antoinette Hidalgo and Tracy Royce "focus on nightclubbers' embodied performances and productions of sexualities and genders in and through a sexualized nightclub space" (57). They found that, not unlike American and European gay bars, in which the participants unsurprisingly are in a hierarchy of desire, masculinity was celebrated and rewarded. "Those clubbers who possess a trim, cut body adorned with fashionable attire have more erotic capital than men whose clothes or hairstyles are out of date, or those whose bodies are less trim" (60). They describe instances in which these less desirable sex objects intrude in the space of the more desirable others, but after the drag shows, it was the masculine acting men who dominated the bar scene in which "Clubbers who embodied femininity were devalued in the space, as were erotic players who failed to live up to a gay masculine ideal" (68).

Nana Okura Gagné (chapter 4) demonstrates the ways in which Tokyo hostesses, through their training and skills, create an intimate environment in which customers pay for expensive drinks, snacks, and conversations with hostesses but no sexual service is offered on site (75), in contrast to hostesses in China and Korea who do offer sex to their customers. Gagné stresses that the Japanese hostesses offer, through intimate conversation and entertainment, a means of bolstering their customers' masculine images. Following a brief discussion of the historical circumstances of hostess bars from the Edo period, she observes that "[b]y wielding economic capital to purchase the companionship of women at these clubs they promote corporate ideology and 'salarymen masculinity' through conspicuous consumption" (75). The skillful "hostesses distinguish themselves by capitalizing on their strengths—singing ability, conversational skill, or physical appearance—in order to attract customers" (86), and through these activities bolster their customer's positive masculine image.

In "Pleasure, Patronage, and Responsibility: Sexuality and Status among New Rich Men in Contemporary China" by John Osburg (chapter 6), nightclubs appear peripherally, but are one of the sites of places in which nouveaux riches men act out their masculinity through liaisons with younger women, often denigrating their first wives as "relics of the past and representative of a poorer and less sophisticated period both in their lives and in China as a whole" (114). These rich men, by drinking, singing, and being flattered by female companions in nightclubs, are both creating and enacting a particular version of masculinity associated with being a man of status and wealth in post-Mao China (109). In this way, Osburg's article somewhat parallels that of Gagné; however, marriages in Japan tend to stay intact, whereas the Chinese counterpart frequently avoids their home and first wife, except for more traditional family gatherings.

In "Media, Sex, and the Self in Cambodia" (chapter 10), Heidi Hoefinger looks at bar girls (a term with which the author notes the women self-identify (182, note 1), who negotiate the competing identities of modern, glamorous women and traditional women who remain submissive and "close to home." In the bars, "many use sex and intimacy to cement materially fruitful relationships with Western men" (171).

This is a wide-ranging collection both geographically and in relation to the topics addressed. This volume will prove valuable in courses on gender and sexuality, anthropology, and Asian studies.

Anthony Shay
Pomona College

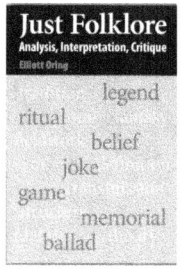

Elliot Oring, *Just Folklore: Analysis, Interpretation, Critique*
Long Beach, CA: Cantilever Press, 2012. xix + 388 pages. 13 photographs. Hardcover, $59.95; paperback, $29.95. ISBN 978-0-9855214-1-7 (hardcover); 978-0-9855214-0-0 (paperback).

IN THIS ANTHOLOGY of largely previously published articles, Elliott Oring confronts many of the most central issues in folklore studies. The eighteen essays spanning his career range from early explorations of whaling songs to recent interrogations of theoretical positions that have, in Oring's estimation, undermined the field of folklore and its standing in the academy. Throughout, Oring's writing is insightful and engaging, bringing to his later essays a nearly encyclopedic knowledge of the history of the discipline. The geographic reach of the volume mirrors Oring's own fieldwork, from the study of Jewish communities in Israel and the United States, to his substantive work in more localized American communities.

The opening essay, "The Arts, Artifacts, and Artifices of Identity" (orig. 1997), emphasizes the role of identity in the study of folklore. The essay provides a potentially unifying perspective to the volume. In his introduction to the opening essay, Oring proposes that "Identity would seem to be a concept that corrals the diversity of definitions and theories [in folklore research] within a comprehensive program of research" (3). He interrogates this proposition, reaching the conclusion that identity is "under theorized" in folklore, thus charting a fertile direction for future study. Indeed, this pattern of identifying a research problem and laying the groundwork for broader disciplinary attention to that problem resurfaces in many of Oring's essays. Consequently, by the end of the volume, the reader has a historically situated and well-documented understanding of several fundamental challenges in folkloristics, as well as a series of potential avenues for further inquiry.

Several of the essays in the first part of the volume deal with specific traditions (2, 3, 4, 5, 6), revealing Oring's ability to ask provocative research questions and reach meaningful conclusions through a rigorous interpretive approach to folk expression. The third essay in the volume is perhaps the most unsettling, with its exploration of the use of gruesome totems among military personnel. Oring's conclusion, that Linton's observation on the analogous nature of "primitive" and contemporary totemism is "on the mark" (54) could be tested with more recent fieldwork. Unfortunately, the retrospective nature of the anthology precludes bringing studies such as this up to date, and one cannot help but wonder the extent to which the thoughtful theoretical perspectives generated by this and other essays could have been more substantively addressed in the short introductory paragraphs.

"Legend, Truth and News" (7, orig. 1990) was written long before the emergence of the Internet, and consequently cries out for someone to extend the observations presented here. The essay moves quickly toward a critique of folklore studies as practiced, and raises profound issues about the relationship between the values of the academic discipline of folklore and the values of the expressive cultures that form the object of study. Oring's conclusion that, "The newspaper stands as a distinct challenge to folklorists to examine their own ideology and their own program" (103) could easily be extended to the Internet and social media. As Oring points out, "if folkloristics ever expects to regain its position as a critical force, it will have to discover a way to look at the center of things without losing a distinctive folkloristic perspective" (103).

A long article on "Legend and the Rhetoric of Truth" (8, orig. 2008), which occupies a central place in the volume, provides a reasonable overview of discussions of the legend genre that have been a mainstay of folklore study since Jacob Grimm made his famous statement in *Deutsche Sagen* about the difference between the fairy tale and legend (1816). Yet Oring's model of the rhetoric of truth in the legend is far too complex and list-like to actually be applied in any meaningful way to a collection. The observations Oring proposes could perhaps be better characterized as a series of features that frequently can be found in legends or legend performances than a comprehensive model of the rhetorical aspects of the genre.

The remaining articles alternate between largely theoretical articles (10, 12, 14, 15, 16, 17, 18), and those grounded in data (9, 11, 13). The theoretical articles are well argued and focus largely on fundamental problems in folkloristics. Oring provides an important discussion of the concepts of devolution and evolution in folklore (10, orig. 1975); a reconsideration of the theoretical underpinnings of Victor Turner's work on symbolism that Oring anchors in the writings of Freud (14, orig. 1993); and a brief meditation on the meaningful nature of the "trivial" (18, orig. 1996). In the only previously unpublished article in the anthology (12), Oring provides an incisive discussion of the fundamental concept of "tradition" in folklore, noting, "Only when the term *tradition* directs folklorists to frame substantive questions, can it gain any conceptual value for the discipline" (239). This essay alone is worth the price of the volume.

Several additional essays (16, orig. 2006; 17, orig. 1998) take direct aim at the "theoretical turn" in folklore that has challenged the very premises of the discipline, leading to an institutional retreat from investment in the field. In his masterful "Missing Theory" essay (15, orig. 2006), Oring notes that "folklore theory" should not be driven by "recourse to abstract statements" (291), a phenomenon that has become far too frequent at meetings and in folklore journals, as well as in the humanities as a whole. Instead, theory, according to Oring, must meet several criteria to rise to the level of actual theory: "It is: (1) interesting (2) plausible (3) generalizable and (4) testable" (291). Folklorists would be well advised to take this advice to heart.

Two of the data-driven articles are of particular note. The first of these (9, orig. 1997) on counting out rhymes offers an excellent example of how interdisciplinary collaboration—here with mathematicians—can extend the scope of folkloristic enquiry. The problem, properly conceptualized, is one of interest both to mathematicians and folklorists, and illustrates how domain expertise from widely disparate fields can lead to significant advances in understanding. The second essay (11, orig. 1978) illustrates how folklore could contribute to experiments that focus on communication and memory. There are significant opportunities to extend the work presented here, given advances in neuroscience and in computation.

My only quibble with the volume is the almost random organization of the essays. While some of the articles are grouped thematically (for example, the two articles on legend), the majority of the articles have little connection to their adjacent articles. If there in fact is an organizational principle, simple section headings would make that more apparent. Although a strictly chronological ordering of the essays would have been equally chaotic, providing a date immediately after the title would allow a reader to try to follow the development of Oring's ideas over time—as it stands, creating such an ordering requires a bit of spelunking in the acknowledgements section of the front matter. This organizational problem is one that haunts most anthologies and by no means detracts from the intellectually stimulating material Oring presents here, particularly those essays that challenge heterodoxy and confront developments in the field that do little to further knowledge. The essays are uniformly well written, and the short introductory paragraphs help situate the essays in the broader disciplinary context. The critical apparatus could be augmented with an index to make the anthology cohere a bit more, but that is a small oversight. The volume should find a home on any folklorist's bookshelf, presenting as it does a one-stop shop for the major articles of one of America's leading folklorists. Instructors and researchers alike will find the comprehensive downloadable teacher's guide online (www.cantileverpress.com) to be particularly useful.

Timothy R. Tangherlini
University of California, Los Angeles

India

Mrinalini Chakravorty, *In Stereotype: South Asia in the Global Literary Imaginary*

New York: Columbia University Press, 2014. xiv + 320 pages. 6 illustrations, notes, bibliography, index. Hardcover, $50.00; e-book, $49.99. ISBN 9780231165969 (hardcover); 9780231537766 (e-book).

THIS IS A PONDEROUS TOME, neither an easy read nor an easily comprehensible anthropological and sociological investigation, but rather is in the genre of theory-laden postcolonial/postmodernist literary criticism. Beginning with the author's acknowledgment of debts to an unusually long list of scholars, associates, and relations who have cajoled, counseled, and prodded her to undertake and complete her enterprise, every chapter of this book is overflowing with innumerable quotations from other texts—ironically dealing with the problems of a notoriously overcrowded subcontinent. Yet this a stupendously scholarly product yelling for readers' attention and accolade. Quite expectedly, the book's jacket is emblazoned with powerfully crafted paeans from her two distinguished acolytes.

This study wishes to evaluate the role of cultural stereotypes in some select Anglophone fictions by South Asian writers in producing the subcontinent's image on the world stage. As a scholar, Chakravorty judiciously distances herself from the camp of stereotype bashers who consider—that is, in her borrowed phraseology, through "ethical reading practice" (224)—and help situate "readers' interests (even in terms of their detachment or disinterest) in relation to worlds of difference" (223). Paraphrased in simple prose, the author maintains stereotypes do not uniformly or always imply disdain but, most of the time, difference, despite globalization. They help us realize that our world is inherently unequal (that is, not the same, though not in any hierarchical or moral sense). Indeed, such a view of a heterodox world has been the staple of postmodern *Weltanschaüüng* forms and this informs the ideological intellectual foundation of the book under review.

Chakravorty's select authors are Salmon Rushdie, Arvind Adiga, Michael Ondaatje, Monica Ali, Mohsin Hamid, and Chetan Bhagat, Rushdie being the most controversial as well as the most feted of them all. She observes that "the multitude exists in Rushdie's *Midnight's Children* "to reify stereotypical images of the subcontinent as teeming, chaotic, heteronormative, excessively consumptive, and fecund—a vision of a people aligned with the goals of a liberal state" (46). The stereotypes about hunger, poverty, and overcrowding in slums in Adiga's *The White Tiger* are discussed in tandem with Mike Davis's box-office blockbuster *Slumdog Millionaire* to highlight the myths about the informal economy of the "third economy" of the "Third World" as a cunning response of the criminal poor to the challenges of burgeoning modernity (47). In Ali's novel *Brick Lane*, Chakravorty considers what happens when the stereotype ("destitution, displacement, tenement housing, and crowds") about a people follows them as they move from the colony to the metropole (48). Hamid's post-9/11 novel, *The*

Reluctant Fundamentalist, in Chakravorty's estimation, exposes "stereotypes about South Asia's place in the world," and forces his South Asian readers to "contemplate [their] involvement in how collectives elsewhere are mirrored in [their] ideas about the globe" (48). A brief concluding discussion of Bhagat's fiction, *One Night at the Call Center*, along with the film and television series, *Outsourced*, makes the point how the odyssey of both the terrorists and the overworked and tired corporate night shift workers affect assumptions "how coercion and free will are globally perceived" (49).

The above, indeed, constitutes a rich fare for commentaries and analyses and they are delivered sumptuously in steroidal muscular prose with copious quotations and footnotes. No wonder the work resembles an impressive dissertation demonstrating the depth and intensity of scholarly research—a magnificent literary overkill. A sober editorial intervention would have helped reduce its gratuitous bulk, the numerous asides in the text, and the long explanatory endnotes for the sake of greater precision and clarity as a monograph.

One should bear in mind that the stereotypes analyzed in the book are not to be understood as fictive or as products of prejudice. Stereotypes cannot arise *ex nihilo* but must refer to some actuality. As the British fantasy writer, poet, and political activist China Tom Miéville has it, "the stereotype exists because it is very often true." In the book under review there is, however, a puzzling elision of some typical cultural stereotypes not always connected to the subcontinent's colonial contact and impact. Although these are not to be found in works used by the author, the title *In Stereotype* does call for a discussion of the more comprehensive and deep-seated cultural and behavioral stereotypes but the author purveys only those that are the usual fare for either Western or based-in-the-West global authors and observers. For example, the stereotypes of social mannerisms such as eating and drinking habits and sense of hygiene and cleanliness of the South Asians in general. Oprah Winfrey's unabashed remark in a tone of muted surprise that "Indian people eat with their hands still" may have been uncalled for in respect of the American visitor's wealthy and educated host family (4) but it was right on the mark.

Thus, the Indian habit of eating with hands, so majestically claimed by a journalist remonstrating against Oprah's remark, cannot overlook or overwrite the brute fact how most Indian males (I speak from my experience in West Bengal, Bihar, and several areas of Uttar Pradesh), with the sole exception of a tiny fraction of the populace, not only use their hand to put food in the mouth but also masticate with their mouth open and "smack, smack, smack," nonchalantly—a grim spectacle that is provocation enough for any unsuspecting stranger amid them or sitting nearby to turn misophonic. Then, at the end of the meal, they invariably lick all five fingers like a child sucking on licorice or an ice cream, until all the food particles are duly gulped. Thus, with his bellyful of succulent lunch or dinner, the happy Hindu Adam lets out a roaring burp signifying total satisfaction. Burping boasts a hallowed tradition that is sanctified in the *Mahabharata* story of Lord Krishna producing a cosmic burp on touching with his divine tongue a fragment of a cooked leaf (*śāk*) from Draupadi's hand as a sign of *tripti*.

Likewise, most women, *mutatis mutandis*, feed their toddlers and even older kids at home as well as in public little balls that are shaped by slowly and meticulously mashing the cooked stuff in their palms and stuffing the child's mouth adorably. Of course, Indian men, adolescent and adult alike, sip their tea or coffee with pronounced slurps—and the noisier the slurp, the more sapid the brew. There are other male habits like yelling over the phone, relieving themselves by the roadside, and expectorating oral and nasal phlegm or bloody red betel juice everywhere on the street, and unabashed nose-picking in public. On the other hand, the Indians' hypersensitive purity fetish makes them use gallons of water to wash away trash, dust, and effluent matter, thus contaminating the entire home as well as the nearby households. There are scores of other stereotypical habits of Indians that exist outside of the frame of experience of the six literati and the author is concerned with the theoretics of the familiar stereotypes in the world.

Another stereotype of South Asia is visual and olfactory: raw sewage and the consequent malodorous air that Indians inhale but to which they are totally blind or anosmic. A blogpost from an Indian website describes the "obvious reality in India—a ghastly spectacle of rows of people defecating daily along any railway lines. Fifty-five percent of Indians defecate in the open every day. More than half the Indians cannot afford a toilet." However, the Indian (especially Bengal and Bihar) countryside stinks not only of human waste but also of cow dung used as cleanser, protective coating, and as holy shit, purifier of the walls and floors of the mud huts. The first prime minister of independent India, Pandit Nehru, proclaimed publicly: "The day every one of us gets a toilet to use, I shall know that our country has reached the pinnacle of progress." The distinguished diasporic literati Naipaul, on his first visit to India, was brutalized by the ubiquitous sight of people defecating everywhere and famously regarded the land of his ancestors as a part of the "turd world" rather than of the Third World.

An important point in respect of stereotypes of the Indians is that they are totally impervious to self-reflexivity about acknowledging their shortcomings which they regard as their sacrosanct cultural heritage and are ever ready to label any queries in this regards as inventions of the benighted outsiders at best or ignorant nitpicking by the arrogant and prejudiced foreigners at worst. Thus, Oprah's innocent but spontaneous remark was received with sneer and mockery by an educated journalist just to prove that the Indians' respect for time-honored practices are and must remain the hallmark of their culture and tradition apotheosized as *sanātana* (perennial), even in an ever-changing, heterogenous, globalized world.

Narasingha P. Sil
Western Oregon University

Kama Maclean, *A Revolutionary History of Interwar India:*
Violence, Image, Voice and Text

London: Hurst and Company, 2015. 342 pages. Hardback, $70.00; paperback, $29.93. ISBN 9780199396115 (hardback); 9780190217150 (paperback).

THE UBIQUITY AND continued appeal in India of the portrait of a handsome, photogenic, and youthful Bhagat Singh with his habitual hat decades after he was hanged, prompts Kama Maclean to venture on an exploratory journey. This is a journey that takes her from the archives and historical sources—including the recently declassified Indian Political Intelligence files in the British Library, London; written records of "oral" testimonies commissioned by the Nehru Memorial Museum and Library, New Delhi, and the Centre of South Asian Studies, Cambridge—into the bazaars of north

Indian towns replete with calendars, lithographs, posters, and other visuals, legends, stories, rhymes, rumors, and "un-archived" histories. The result is a remarkably rich, stimulatingly sensorial, textured account of the activities of Indian revolutionaries in general and the Hindustan Socialist Republican Army (HSRA) in particular, and their intimate links with the Congress in the period between the two World Wars.

Her purpose in offering this combined aural, oral, visual, and written narrative, Maclean tells us, is twofold: an epistemological reconsideration of the impact of the revolutionaries on the nationalist struggle, and a methodological opening up of "history" and historical accounts by means of an effective integration of visual, oral, and un-archived materials in them (1). The book, divided into three parts, eight chapters and an introduction, a conclusion, and an epilogue, sets out to substantiate Maclean's propositions. While Part I examines the interwar period (with primary focus on 1928–1931) from the perspective of the HSRA revolutionaries and their leaders Bhagat Singh and Chandrasekhar Azad, Part II explores the intense but clandestine interaction of revolutionary and Congress politics. Part III engages in a critical reflection of the challenge thrown by revolutionary violence to Gandhism, the colonial state, and the revolutionaries.

Standard histories of the Indian nationalist struggle, Maclean contends, give overwhelming predominance to Gandhi and his ideology of nonviolent agitation that not only displaces the significance of revolutionaries and their "violent" struggle, but also forecloses an examination of the interface and intersections of the violent and nonviolent strands of the struggle. This point, although valid, is not particularly original. It has been made in different ways in "standard" histories, ranging from Sumit SARKAR's classic *Modern India* (1983) to BANERJEE-DUBE's *A History of Modern India* (2015). Irfan HABIB's *To Make the Deaf Hear* (2007) added a valuable analysis of Bhagat Singh's thought and ideology, as well as his role in, and impact on, the nationalist struggle at the time Maclean began her work on the subject. Maclean seems to have been intrigued by the lack of fit between the numerous calendars and posters of Bhagat Singh she saw in the bazars of Amritsar, the success of the 2006 film *Rang de Basanti* that reiterated the nostalgia for and relevance of Bhagat Singh and the revolutionaries, and finally the relative lack of scholarship on Bhagat Singh and his comrades (vii). Even though she acknowledges that revolutionary pressure on Congress leadership is "frequently noted in passing" in important works (7), they amount to no more than a reluctant recognition of violence in the political spectrum on the part of Congress (8). This point about the lack of serious scholarship on the revolutionaries or the Congress-revolutionary interaction seems a bit overstated at times.

The real strength of the book lies not just in what is being said, but also in how it is being said. The unexpected focus on Bhagat Singh's hat, for instance, and the suggestive insights that come out of it; the incisive comment on the irony of the clandestine, censured, secret, and proscribed activities of the revolutionaries versus their planned public display and circulation of studio portraits in the media on the eve of martyrdom and its lasting implications; the unearthing of the important role played by "marginal" yet crucial characters, such as Durga Devi Vohra; the considered comments on the discrepancies in memories of events recounted by revolutionaries; the deft demonstration of tactical and empathetic overlaps in purpose between important Congress leaders such as the senior and junior Nehru and the revolutionaries in the critical years of 1928–1931, and, most significantly, the urgency brought to Congress's move towards complete independence (Karachi Congress) by the literal "explosions" occasioned by the revolutionaries leave us with a lot upon which to reflect.

A Revolutionary History improves and enriches our understanding of the three-way interaction between the British Raj, the Congress under Gandhi, and the HSRA in the crucial and intermediate "interwar" years. It successfully "positions" the role of violence in the freedom struggle by highlighting the porosity of boundaries between nationalist institutions in the context of a broad anti-British sentiment; a porosity that allowed Congress leaders to work secretly with revolutionaries and brought back many of the surviving revolutionaries into the mainstream of Congress politics after the death of Singh and Azad.

Maclean deserves our praise for her skill in digging up clandestine and proscribed histories, secret and elusive collaboration, and comfort and discomfort inherent in the mutual imbrication of violent and nonviolent anti-imperialism, and in presenting them in a richly layered narrative. The most significant contribution of the work perhaps lies in its astute demonstration of the centrality of the "visual" in the "un-archived" material she analyzes, a centrality that transforms our understandings of the past and the present, history and politics, and enables the writing of histories from a "post-subaltern" perspective.

REFERENCES

BANERJEE-DUBE, Ishita
    2014   *A History of Modern India.* Cambridge, UK: Cambridge University Press.
HABIB, Irfan
    2007   *To Make the Deaf Hear: Ideology and Programme of Bhagat Singh and His Comrades.* New Delhi: Three Essays Collectives.
MEHRA, Rakyesh Omprakash
    2006   *Rang de Basanti* (film). Mumbai: UTV Studio.
SARKAR, Sumit
    1983   *Modern India. 1885–1947.* New Delhi: Macmillan India.

Ishita Banerjee-Dube
El Colegio de México

Frank Heidemann and Philipp Zehmisch, eds.,
Manifestations of History: Time, Space, and Community in the Andaman Islands
Delhi: Primus Books, 2016. 187 pages. Cloth, $59.95. ISBN 9384092045.

THE CULTURAL history of the Andaman and Nicobar Islands is a crucial, yet under-estimated, key to understanding British colonial practices, Indian constructions of nationalism, as well as the mobility of people and diasporas in the Indian Ocean. This interesting volume presents original views to make sense of the complexity of the history of the Andaman Islands, and demonstrates a recent growing interest in the academic study of this area. It appears shortly after the similarly structured *New Histories of the Andaman Islands* (ANDERSON, MAZUMDAR, and PANDYA 2016), with which it shares a similar premise and methodological commitments. The contributors to the volume reviewed here remain curiously silent about the other twin publication, perhaps because both books were in press at roughly the same time.

The book begins with two maps, symbolizing the authors' focus on place and space as markers of popular historiographies. It also introduces readers to the particularities of the Andaman and Nicobar Islands, where seventeen different ethnic and linguistic communities coexist in a territory of 8,249 km² (less than Cyprus) divided into 349 islands.

As explained in the introduction, the common thread for the multifarious essays contained in the volume is the concept of "manifestations" of history: manifestations are intended as objects of the present—for example, monuments, flowerbeds, museums, community names, toponyms, and so on—that embody certain historicizations of the past. The process of manifestation indicates a transition from mind to matter, and thus it reveals imaginations and constructions of history physically enacted in a place, or in a community; however, it can also indicate a transition from matter to mind. For instance, as analyzed in Claire Wintle's essay, the politics of the display of material culture behind the glass of a showcase has a specific role in bolstering particular views of history and the present. The history of the ideology behind the display of Andamanese and Nicobarese objects in ethnological collections reveals that museums contributed to the caging of indigenous people into the forced paradigm of primitiveness. The essay by Satadru Sen is equally powerful in deconstructing the discourse on aboriginality. Sen explains how Andamanese tribes came to be known in modern India almost exclusively through British mediation, tinged with exotic representations as primitive people out of time and out of place. Being aboriginals and citizens simultaneously poses a dilemma. Excluded from the nationalist project of inclusion of the folk and tribal elements in the making of the modern nation, tribes of the Andaman and Nicobar Islands are forced into isolation and do not share the same rights enjoyed by the mainland tribal groups (Adivasis), who can access the legal and bureaucratic portal toward citizenship accorded to the so-called Scheduled Tribes.

Oral literature of the indigenous inhabitants is taken as a central reference by Manish Chandi, whose essay on the ethnohistory of some uninhabited Nicobar Islands reflects upon the significance of folktales and legends for environmental sustainability and for regulating the exploitation of natural resources. He underlines the dichotomy between a society where space, land, and resources are the propriety of a collectivity as opposed to an individual owner, and a scheme for development and housing that does not take into consideration emic concepts concerning the use of land.

Apart from giving space to the voices of native storytelling, the book gives a polyphonic presentation of the history of the Andaman and Nicobar Islands as well as their mosaic-like society, presenting the point of view of ex-convicts and early settlers, of British families, of Ranchi contract laborers, and of Tamil repatriate families from Sri Lanka. Kanchan Mukhyopadhyay's essay disentangles the composite category of people formally classified as Pre-42. The Pre-42s are those who inhabited the island before the Japanese invasion of 1942: ex-convicts of the penal settlement, persons deported individually, such as dissenters and freedom fighters, but also entire tribes accused of rebellion, such as the Moplahs of the Malabar Coast, or those of habitual criminal tendencies (for example, the Bhantus of the United Provinces). Decimated by the Japanese occupation, these groups now claim recognition as martyrs and builders of the modern Andamans.

Particularly infamous as *kāla pānī*, the dangerous black waters, the Cellular Jail of Port Blair was the place where political enemies of the British Raj were imprisoned. Prison literature produced in the Cellular Jail, also known as the "Indian Bastille," constitutes an interesting source on the history of pre-Independence Andamans. Jamal Malik examines the Arabic poems composed by the Muslim scholar Fadl-e Haqq during his incarceration, and discusses how his tomb came to be venerated as a Sufi shrine as well as a local symbol for Hindu-Muslim harmony. It also serves as a material symbol of composite and multicultural nationalism.

Often portrayed as a "mini-India" because of the "unity in diversity" of their social puzzle, the Andaman Islands host a diverse range of ethnic, linguistic, and religious groups that, on the one hand, peacefully coexist as equal citizens of the Indian nation, while on the other hand, compete and negotiate for the use, occupation, and ownership of local spaces. Frank Heidemann focuses on the history of the repatriation of Tamil families. Previously displaced and resettled in Sri Lanka as laborers under the British dominion, the government of India had to transfer them back after Independence. Half a million people were thus translocated with little choice and little information in an alien environment located in the middle of the ocean. In Katchal (one of the Nicobar Islands), the Tamil repatriates from Sri Lanka were coercively placed on rubber plantations, occupying a tribal land over which their families had no rights. Tensions and notions of social injustice are often underlined through the comparison with their Bengali neighbors, who are refugees from (present day) Bangladesh that were granted a few acres of land each to cultivate as so-called agricultural pioneers. They now constitute a demographic and linguistic majority.

Similar to the displaced Tamils and Bengalis, the tribal laborers consisting of heterogeneous ethnicity who were hired from Chotanagpur are indistinctly classified as Ranchis (after the city in Bihar). They arrived only to inhabit the islands without any of the supporting measures provided to the other communities, as Philipp Zehmisch shows. These "invisible architects" (122) of the modern Andamans cleared the forest and erected infrastructures that prepared the ground for the settlement of other migrants, but the authorities denied a subject position to those who wanted to remain on the islands. The families who occupied forest lands were thus treated as squatters. Still suffering from little social mobility and unequal representation, the Ranchi community represents the third largest group on the islands, and seeks recognition and visibility at present.

A strong claim that remains consistent throughout the book is the necessity to surpass the assumption that history is a series of chronologically ordered events placed in linear time. In the case of the cultural history of the Andaman Islands, history is better understood when it takes spaces and places, rather than time, as reference points. The identity of communities and their status does not depend on the historical moment of their arrival, nor on their temporal developments, but rather on spatial dimensions: their access and rights in relation to land resources, their ancestral homes and places of origin, and the space they inhabit on the island: *bājār* (urban space), *bastī* (village), or *jaṅgal* (forest). In popular conceptualizations of history, spatial aspects overshadow temporal aspects, for "space matters, time passes" (8). A delicate ecological as well as social area whose history was traced by innumerable actors, from native societies to colonial programs, from immigrants' claims to governmental schemes, trans-disciplinary and innovative historical studies on the Andaman Islands, such as those offered by *Manifestations of History*, are rare and most welcome. While it excels as a volume on history, ethnology, and diaspora studies, a lack of contextualization in the broader sphere of multicultural societies and newly occupied spaces can be noted as one theoretical and methodological oversight of this work. The introductory chapter alludes to this oversight (for example, "we see parallels to other places that have experienced large-scale migration. Societies with a heterogeneous migrant population, such as Israel, Singapore and California, display origin and movement in space as more important than timelines" [3]), but the comparative dimension remains unexplored.

General notions on the history of the Andamans and its infamous Cellular Jail are delineated in the introduction, and then repetitively appear throughout the book. The lack of specific historical information on the domination and domestication of the Nicobar Islands is juxtaposed with a general redundancy in background information on the Andamans, which may help the nonspecialist reader, although the reiteration sounds unnecessary at times. At the end of the core of the book, the afterword, authored by Sita Venkateswar, who worked extensively on indigenous tribes, colonial practices, and ethnocide on the Andaman Islands, reflects on the positionality and subjectivity of the scholar through the lens of *hindsight*, somehow sounding disconnected and self-referential in respect to the overall cohesion of the rest of the volume.

The general theoretical orientation that emerges throughout the book is a fresh perspective on history. Stepping beyond traditional notions of archival material, the essays include as primary sources ethnographies, oral histories, material culture and folk narratives, photographs, and personal correspondence. Successfully fulfilling its declared intentions, the book's underlying methodological premise fills the gap between history and anthropology by giving special attention to the connection between understandings of the past and their significance in the present. Much more than simply "manifestations of history," Heidemann and Zehmisch offer us alternative histories drawing upon identity-making processes that are closely connected to the history of the shaping of a space that rapidly transformed itself from a penal settlement to a global destination of mass tourism. It is now a battlefield for activists and their romanticized vanishing primitives.

REFERENCES

ANDERSON, Clare, Madhumita MAZUMDAR, and Vishvajit PANDYA
    2016   *New Histories of the Andaman Islands: Landscape, Place and Identity in the Bay of Bengal, 1790–2012*. Cambridge: Cambridge University Press.

Carola Erika Lorea
International Institute of Asian Studies, Leiden

Lakshmi Srinivas, *House Full: Indian Cinema and the Active Audience*

Chicago and London: University of Chicago Press, 2016. 315 pages.
Hardback, $112.50; paperback, $37.50; e-book, $37.50.
ISBN: 978-0-226-36142-0 (hardback); 978-0-226-36156-7 (paperback);
978-0-226-36173-4 (ebook).

THE ACT OF PUBLIC spectatorship encodes learned and socially conditioned behaviors that show considerable variation across time and cultural space. Contemporary Euro-American disciplines of film viewing—including the maintenance of silence and composure in a darkened hall and concentration on the images projected on its screen (still regularly reinforced by messages flashed up before the movie begins)—would have seemed bizarrely authoritarian to audiences at, say, Shakespeare's Globe, or to European opera-goers from the beginning of that art form until the latter part of the nineteenth century. It was only then that technology made possible the dimming of halls and bright illumination of their stages, compelling audiences (as some viewers noted grumpily) to concentrate on the staged production rather than on the encompassing, participatory spectacle that had generally included conversation, periodic snacking, the display and observation of fashion—and, of course, intermittent attention to the music, singing, and staging of what was usually a well-known story. That such practices of reception, even in darkened cinema halls of the late twentieth century, remained quite "normal" for a significant segment of humanity has been richly documented by sociologist Lakshmi Srinivas in *House Full*, her engaging study of the "active audience" of South Asian popular cinema. Based on extensive fieldwork, primarily in the late 1990s, in the burgeoning metropolis of Bangalore (now officially Bengaluru) in Karnataka state, Srinivas's book (its Indian-English title phrase appears on signs announcing that a particular film screening is, in American jargon, "sold-out") turns its focus away from the "reading" of films as "texts"—the predominant mode of cinematic analysis, which, she argues, is itself a byproduct of the learned discipline of silent, individualized reading—to look seriously at audience reception and its attendant practices, permitting her to conceptualize and examine the presentation of films as collectively-staged "performance events."

An introductory chapter explains the choice of Bangalore as fieldwork site; admittedly a somewhat anomalous Indian city, it was familiar to the researcher from her youth and, as a decidedly cosmopolitan and multilingual metro, offered her opportunities to sample, refreshingly, the reception of not just one but several cinemas (Hindi- and Kannada-language film events figure prominently, although a number of Hollywood movies that were popular in India—especially *Titanic*—also generate observations, and there are interesting asides concerning the hyper-cinephilic audiences of Tamil- and Telugu-language productions as well). Much of the chapter, however, is devoted to a spirited defense of the researcher's project and approach—"an immersive ethnography of film reception" (4)—and to her well-argued critique of "the mainstream reception aesthetic of niche-marketed Hollywood films in Anglo-American settings and the (Eurocentric) model of film and spectatorship … normalized and generalized as a 'universal' film experience" (9). Srinivas is equally critical of what she calls the "film-centered" readings of most other scholarship on Indian cinema (11), resulting in "preoccupation with the film and its texts and messages," particularly as these are received by a hypothetical "individualized" viewer (13).

Chapter 2 highlights the author's fortuitous interactions with the small but vibrant Kannada film industry, since Bangalore is also "Sandalwood"—the teasing, Bollywood-derived name of its home base. Unexpected research contacts led her to visit film studios and location shoots and to interview producers, directors, technicians, and actors. The result is not only an interesting glimpse of a little-studied regional cinema, but the insight that its practices and products themselves reflect and anticipate the "active audience" that will be highlighted in later chapters. Srinivas's observations of the "constitutive" effect of audience behavior on this niche industry seem equally relevant to the more widely-distributed "blockbusters" of Hindi cinema, particularly those that became dominant from the 1970s on under the genre label "*masālā* film"— a spicy mix of main and sub-plots with varied emotional moods (comedy, suspense, pathos, and so on), interspersed with "item number" song and dance sequences. Such films, with their "loose" narrative structure, deliberate flaunting of cinematic artifice, and even auto-parody and intentional referencing of other films, seem expressly designed for the kinds of raucous audiences and participatory viewing practices that Srinivas's study especially highlights.

Chapters 3 to 5 focus on cinema halls and the practical logistics and social rituals involved in going to them. After providing a guided tour of the "space cultures of cinema" in two areas of Bangalore that boast an unusual number of movie houses (albeit catering to different audience demographics), Srinivas considers the many factors that influence viewers' decisions regarding which films to see—ranging from "theater merit" (which may include such pragmatic perks as functional air-conditioning, unbroken seating and non-smelly toilets, and a good concession stand for the obligatory "interval" snack), to the ease or difficulty of securing tickets (which may involve long waits in unruly queues or, alternatively, paying exorbitant prices to scalpers) and negotiating transportation and traffic, to the choice of "class" of seating—for India's large cinema halls have always been, like so much else in its society, hierarchically structured. Additional attention is given to the sociality and playful quality of most cinema-going, such as the fact that family groups of a dozen or more are common and invariably include small children, that such groups' arrivals in theaters do not always correspond to showtimes, and that their behavior toward other filmgoers may range from warmly interactive to openly antagonistic—the latter casting the theater as a "contested" space.

The book's thick description and scholarly arguments both reach a kind of crescendo in chapters 6 and 7. The former offers vivid accounts of hyperactive audience behavior, which can include loud conversation, the translation of dialogue for a friend into another of India's many languages, crying and playing children, and (especially among young men) peripatetic viewing, horseplay with friends, dancing in the aisles or on top of seats, outbursts of whistling, applause, and mimicry of onscreen action— and much more. The latter chapter focuses on the excitement that often accompanies first-day screenings or re-releases of films by adored stars, and that may include street processions by jubilant, dancing fans accompanied by marching bands, the draping of forty-foot flower garlands on even larger cutout images of the star adorning a theater facade, the ceremonial worship (by a hired priest) of cans delivering film rolls to the theater, and even occasional "lathi charges" by club-wielding police. The role of fan clubs in coordinating this (apparently) chaotic activity—what Srinivas drolly calls "a paroxysm of cinema"—is highlighted, as is the extreme devotion of fans (often lower-class "informal sector" workers) who affirm their willingness to "die for" a star and his family, and who will never miss a "first-day, first-show" screening, even if it means spending a significant portion of their meager income. The frenzied and sometimes scary ambience created by such devotion is vividly evoked, and the author suggests that these carnivalesque events may have roots in traditional folk performance forms such as Ram narrative dramas (*rāmlīlā*) in the north and Yaksha dance performances (*yakṣagāna*) in the south, as well as in religious fairs, temple processions, and indeed the ambience of the crowded bazaar. Though these parallels are interesting, the author's fascination with the "improvisation" and "inversions" of fervent fan behavior (217) seems to sidestep the fact that it, too, surely has "rules"—as does, for example, the (rather similar) performance activity of young Western fans at rock 'n' roll concerts (think: "front-benchers" = "mosh pit").

The book's concluding chapter reiterates its principal arguments, but also, and importantly, discusses changes in exhibition and viewing practices that followed the "liberalization" of the Indian economy in the 1990s, and that led in Bangalore and elsewhere to the gradual closure of many of the thousand-plus-seat theaters that especially favored the economically diverse and "active" audiences featured in the study. India's new film-viewing landscape, especially post-2000, is increasingly typified by mall multiplexes that charge much higher ticket prices for classless but cushy seats in small (two- to three-hundred viewer) halls and that encourage viewing by "homogenized and atomized individuals" (234). Though this transformation is still far from complete (and may never be), it highlights the importance of the author's research not only as sociology and performance study but also as social and cultural history.

Srinivas's writing style is readable and refreshingly free from the sometimes opaque jargon of the text-centered film scholarship at which she regularly takes aim. If there is a flaw in this welcome book (apart from its hyper-abundance of distracting endnotes—which average more than a hundred per chapter), it is that the author's repeated and dismissive critique of much film analysis begins to seem overstated, and even something of a disservice to both popular Indian cinema and its enthusiastic audiences. To be sure, she has a point: audience reception is notably under-researched in film studies (and not just for South Asia), and the agency of the region's exceptionally "social and interactive audience" (13) has been largely ignored. But it is also true that films, as complex textual artifacts, *do* have enduring lives that transcend the ephemeral contexts of their reception, and (despite her examples of people choosing to see movies based on factors other than their content, or of fans who watch every film featuring a beloved star regardless of its quality) that Indian mass audiences, however unruly, are notoriously discriminating about their so-called "formula" films, quickly making some into triumphs and others into flops—usually based on criteria that hinge in some measure on a film's content. Srinivas's presentation, in chapter 7, of the hyperbolic fan-phenomena centered on Dr. Rajkumar, the most acclaimed Kannada-language star of the last four decades of the twentieth century, lacks even a brief introduction to the types of roles and films that brought him such remarkable celebrity, and hence seems oddly decontextualized to a reader unfamiliar with that regional cinema. Moreover, a number of the "active" performance practices that Srinivas richly documents (such as repeat viewing and the consequent ability of audience members to sing and recite along with songs and dialogue, or to enact particular scenes in tandem with onscreen action) all presuppose some degree of attentive film-watching, which in turn depends on the film delivering a "message" that resonates with viewers. The examination of such messages must remain, in my view, a desideratum of comprehensive film studies, though additional and supplemental research on the context of film reception—so excellently pioneered in *House Full*—should be equally welcomed.

Philip Lutgendorf
University of Iowa

Andrew Duff, *Sikkim: Requiem for a Himalayan Kingdom*
New York: Vintage Books, 2015. 380 pages. Cloth, $26.75. ISBN 8184006969.

ANDREW DUFF'S *Sikkim: Requiem for a Himalayan Kingdom* tells the story of political turmoil and personal intrigues that led to the erstwhile Himalayan Kingdom of Sikkim's contested merger with the Indian Union in 1975. Spanning ten chapters, preceded by a prologue and ended by an epilogue, Duff traces the politics, plots, and wider regional and political factors that culminated in the end of the Chogyal kingship, a 333-year-long period of continuous rule. The author's motivation for writing the book under review is in part personal. Duff's grandfather left behind a diary and photographs of a trek he had made across Sikkim in 1922, and so the book is based on Duff's desire to trace his grandfather's footsteps. A central and hitherto unused source are the private letters (written to their parents) of Martha Hamilton and Ishbel Ritchie, both of whom were Scottish teachers and principals at the Paljor Namgyal Girls School located in Gangtok, Sikkim's capital, at the time of Sikkim's merger.

Duff begins with a historical discussion. Sikkim's gradual loss of sovereignty, he recounts, commenced with the arrival of the British, whose authoritative presence was poised towards their "desire to open trade relations and gain political influence in Tibet" (17), which bordered Sikkim. The British never formally conquered Sikkim. Their presence, however, altered political hierarchies in the region, and the Chogyal (king), while officially in charge of his subjects, was "supervised" by a British political officer. In 1935, Sikkim was admitted to India's so-called Chamber of Princes, after which it was recognized as a "special case" (25) because of its strategic geopolitical location couched, as it was, between Nepal, Bhutan, Tibet, and British India.

When the British departed in 1947, Sikkim officially returned from being a protectorate to its prior status as an independent kingdom. Its recovered independence, however, did not last long. Soon, newly independent India started making political inroads, since it saw Sikkim as a strategic territory, given its close proximity to China. As the author writes, "the history of Sikkim's demise could not be seen in isolation" (10) from such factors. In discussing Sikkim's merger, Duff links it both to such wider political developments, as well as to rivalries and intrigues within Sikkim. Some of the external developments include the following: the Chinese intervention in Tibet and, later on, in Arunachal Pradesh; the Dalai Lama's flight to India; the Panchsheel Treaty signed by Nehru and Zhou Enlai; Nehru's demise; the ascension to power of his daughter Indira Gandhi; and the declaration of the Emergency by Indira Gandhi in 1975. According to Duff, all of these events were part of the wider political context in which the merger of Sikkim unfolded.

Duff goes on to discuss the internal affairs of Sikkim after the British withdrawal. What his book showcases, in a way, is the emergence of an identity crisis. While the Chogyal was trying to maintain Sikkim's unique identity as a Buddhist kingdom that is religiously and culturally close to Tibet, during the British era Sikkim's population changed. More and more Nepalese settled in Sikkim, whose language and culture was closely affiliated not with Tibet, but with India. The Chogyal's attempt to safeguard Sikkim as belonging to the Bhutia and Lepcha communities started to create dissatisfaction among the now numerous Nepalese tenants who had been "brought in as part of a mass programme" during the late nineteenth century' (33) by the British from Nepal. Duff calls it the failure of the Chogyal "to fully accept that the ethnic makeup of his country had changed" (119), culminating in the Nepalese settlers resorting to demonstrations, and then insisting on the replacement of monarchy with democracy.

Much more was happening in Sikkim, though, than a demographic transition and an associated demand for political change. There was, for instance, the Chogyal's glamorous but controversial marriage with Hope Cooke, an American citizen, which placed Sikkim in the global spotlight. While some saw their marriage as a "fairy tale," others feared the new foreign Queen, and rumors soon spread that she was a CIA agent (9). Duff too begins to suspect her intentions. He considers her "[o]bsessed with the desire to be a real queen—of an independent nation" (205). He further portrays Cooke as naïve in her actions, "jealous" in her relationship, "insecure" within the family, "unhappy," "emotionally isolated," and "depressed" at times (150).

In describing Cooke's marriage, personality, and her role in Sikkim's politics at the time, Duff mostly relies on her autobiography, *Time Change* (COOKE 1981), as well as the personal letters of Martha Hamilton and Ishbel Ritchie—letters whose contents he subsequently seems to have delinked from their context to match the plot of his book. Duff's focus is on Cooke's relationship with the Chogyal and her role as a controversial political personality. While this is of interest, and much discussed in other treatises on Sikkim, it overshadows many other aspects of Cooke's life in Sikkim, including the various contributions she made to the region. With Sikkim's merger looming, Duff describes Cooke as a "disturbed wife," seeing her role as queen of a Himalayan kingdom evaporate, and as seeking consolation in the barbiturate valium (104). This does not seem entirely fair, as Cooke actively engaged in projects concerning education, cultural preservation, and material history, in addition to being an involved mother (COOKE n.d. [b]).

Cooke's most significant contribution, entirely omitted by Duff, was as the Chairman of the Text Book and Curriculum Committee, in which capacity she oversaw the design, publication, and use of innovative and culturally appropriate textbooks for all of Sikkim's schools (COOKE n.d. [a]). On the whole, Duff paints an overly political and unfavorable image of Cooke. She herself laments Duff's selective usage of materials, saying that, "Duff copied a great chunk from previously published books," and drew heavily on the testimonials of Martha Hamilton. As Cooke writes in her unpublished personal papers archived in Gangtok, "Martha (who never lived to see Duff's book) was his original patron in Sikkim. She would have died twice over if she had read his representation of me...." (COOKE n.d. [b]). Duff, however, cannot be fully blamed for not bringing out new data on Cooke, as he wrote, "I contacted her [Hope Cooke] in 2010. At first, she offered to talk about the 'cultural context' to Sikkim, but then decided (after consultation with her children) that she should leave her 1981 biography (*Time Change*) as her record of the political period" (111).

For the Chogyal himself, Duff also writes about his inability to overcome his ego and the expectations from people around him. "Chogyal often felt insecure and acted indecisively, both as a ruler and a family man" (65). At this point, Duff's book takes on the shape of a *Bildungsroman*, as it concentrates on the "Hamartian flaw," the perplexed individual characters, their psychology, circumstances, fast changing situations—all related to the eventual fall of Sikkim.

Another crucial player in Sikkim's political field at the time was Kazi Lhendup Dorji (later Sikkim's first chief minister), who led the political movement advocating Sikkim's transition to democracy. Like the Chogyal, Kazi Lhendup Dorji, too, was married to a foreign national, his Belgian wife Elisa Maria Langford, who seemed to have envisaged a life at the side of a democratically elected chief minister. This movement for democracy, as Duff explains, was primarily supported by the Nepalese settlers in Sikkim, who had by then multiplied into the majority population. After all, democracy, being a game of numbers, gave them prospects of power sharing in ways that Bhutia kingship did not.

Duff's book is an enjoyable read. However, there are a number of inaccuracies, particularly in historical details, some of which are too important to ignore. For instance, Palden Thondup Namgyal is not the second son of the Ninth Chogyal of Sikkim, as Duff writes, but of the Eleventh. Duff also states certain episodes as being "historical facts" without adequate evidence or references (particularly concerning the marriage of the Chogyal with Hope Cooke). Duff's book, admittedly, does not claim to be an academic treatise, but this does not justify the lack of references in a number of places. His book should thus not be elevated to the status of a core historical source for future researchers.

While most of Duff's chapters seem to be dramatized—and much better written—accounts of what has previously been written about Sikkim's merger, the strength of the book is the lucidity with which Duff tells the story, as well as his stress on the minutiae of the often purely personal jealousies, rivalries, and disputes among the characters, all of which often tend to be overlooked in more formal reconstructions of Sikkim's merger. Duff certainly does not shy away from washing the dirty linen of historical characters in public. What can be taken from Duff's book is that the merger of Sikkim should not be portrayed as a simple or even singular story, but as a myriad of tales and events that jointly culminated in the fall of the Chogyal Kingship.

REFERENCES

COOKE, Hope
    1981   *Time Change*. New York: Simon & Schuster.
    n.d. (a) Development of Curriculum and Textbooks Grades: Kindergarten-VIII in Sikkim
            1967–1973. Paper presented at Columbia University's Teacher's College. Gangtok,
            Sikkim: Namgyal Institute of Tibetology.
    n.d. (b) Personal Papers. Gangtok, Sikkim: Namgyal Institute of Tibetology.

Kikee Doma Bhutia
University of Tartu

Townsend Middleton, *The Demands of Recognition:*
State Anthropology and Ethnopolitics in Darjeeling
Stanford: Stanford University Press, 2016. 278 pages. Cloth, $90.00;
paperback, $25.95. ISBN 9780804795425 (cloth); 9780804796262
(paperback).

SINCE THE TURN OF the twentieth century, issues of ethnicity and recognition have
been a persistent concern in Darjeeling. Ethnic demands for regional recognition were
carried out unabated in the past and are still carried out in renewed forms. In this
regard, the current demands for recognition as scheduled tribes raised by a host of
ethnic associations can be regarded as the latest addition to fervent ethnopolitics in
the region. Drawing on such developments, this timely book by Middleton sheds a
great deal of light on the contemporary ethno-politics in Darjeeling structured around
the quest to become tribal subjects within the official register. Discussing these demands, Middleton highlights the complex interface between state apparatus, local political structures, and postcolonial ethnological practices. He looks at the intersection
between local, regional, national, and global forces, and draws parallels between the
present articulations of identity claims, and the wider politics of recognition unfolding
at the global scale. He calls this discourse of cultural rights "ethno-contemporary" (9),
which reflects the pertinent concern of ethnic groups to use ethnological categories
to redefine their identities, and thereby secure rights and entitlements from the state.

Tracing the contours of these practices, Middleton outlines how ethnological
knowledge is utilized by both the state and ethnic groups to structure the popular
notions of tribes in postcolonial India. He adopts a multi-sided ethnography along
with an in-depth study of state officials and state anthropologists toward understanding this prolonged struggle to attain rights and recognition in the hills. Interestingly,
the book also makes ample use of archival records to outline the historical constitution
of Darjeeling; document-specific interface between people and the state, the present,
and the past; and the dynamic relationship between lived experience, cultural memories, and the classificatory categories of ethnology. The book charts Middleton's long
ethnographic engagements and chronicles the intricate history of the region and the
periodic transformation of identity politics in Darjeeling.

The first chapter foregrounds the discussion on issues of belonging and relates it to
different strands of ethnic demands unfolding since the turn of the twentieth century.
He characterizes the quest to belong as "anxious belonging," which is intimately tied
to "politics to belong" in India (29). Charting the convoluted trajectory of ethnic demands in the hills, Middleton recounts the experiences of the people while providing
a detailed account of the politics of ethnic revival epitomized by current demands for
recognition as scheduled tribes. Taking into account these demands, he shifts register
in order to consider the evolution of ethnological governmentality in India. Drawing
from a rich array of sources, he provides gripping insights on debates surrounding
tribes in colonial India, and its periodic transformation in the postcolonial phase. His
astute rereading of the discourse of ethnology in India throws a great deal of light on
the formation of official categories and its application in shaping ethnic subjectivities.

Following the official and academic discourse surrounding tribes in India, the book charts the convoluted journey of enumerative categories while noting the interconnected history of statist categories and regimes of power. Treating tribes as specific manifestations of colonial and postcolonial modernity, the book discusses in detail the discourse and contours of cultural recognition in India. In this regard the book narrates the interesting case of ethnic entrepreneurs, political leaders, and their quest to register themselves as scheduled tribes in Darjeeling. In particular he cites the role played by the Department of Information and Cultural Affairs (DICA) under the Darjeeling Gorkha Hill Council (DGHC) in framing and augmenting demands for recognition as scheduled tribes. The book provides a fascinating and vivid account of the encounter between aspirant tribal subjects and state anthropologists, and minutely describes how communities are studied through conceptual and ethnological categories framed during the colonial period. Accounting for such practices, Middleton writes, "state ethnography involves practices that surpass the official designs of tribal recognition, as well as contingencies of a more affective register" (116). He captures the power dynamics existing between the anthropologists and the subject, and the emotive content of demands made by the ethnic leaders. He focuses on the performative aspects of identity claims amplified by the relentless quest to assert their indigenous status in the region. Noting this aspect, Middleton writes, "for people of Darjeeling, managing their histories of migration and hybridity was thus a legitimate concern in their attempt to become a scheduled tribe" (130). He characterizes these inventive ways adopted by ethnic minorities as a living example of ethno-contemporary where both ethnic subjects and the anthropologists studying them are caught in the artifice of state ethnography.

One crucial and novel aspect of the book is the way it documents the views of official anthropologists from the Culture Research Institute (CRI). While narrating the inner working of the state anthropologists, Middleton reverses the gaze upon ethnological institutions, and explores the world views of the officials, vividly documenting the ways ethnographic data is modulated and structured at CRI. Middleton characterizes this everyday ritual of state anthropologists as "bureaucratic durée," a protracted temporality that prolongs the process of securing rights and benefits (148). Tracing the undulating trajectory of ethnic demands in the hills, the book shows how people reframe official categories in their quest to reaffirm their authentic tribal identity, and also notes the internal politics operating within ethnic groups and their associations. The book lucidly documents the tensions and the sense of loss felt by the ethnic subjects who are periodically demanded to recast their ethnic habitus by reclaiming a long-lost cultural past. Most importantly, the book highlights the intersection between the tribal recognition movement and renewed demands for regional recognition in the form of the Gorkhaland movement of 2007.

Drawing from his rich ethnographic fieldwork, Middleton argues that the state apparatus fails to recognize the identities and differences of cultural groups that in turn create structures of anxiety relating to belonging in the nation. He argues that the convoluted discourse of ethnology continues to create ambivalence in the steady attainment of rights and entitlements enshrined in the constitution for ethnic minorities. The colonial taxonomies continue to haunt and structure the postcolonial imagination of ethnic groups and boundaries, and so Middleton vouches for a post ethnological future that would rework colonial categories. He states that the ethno-contemporary asks us to reconsider the present predicaments of groups trying to categorize back the identities foisted upon them by the state. Though lacking in a detailed account of ethnic associations and the intersection between ethnicity and class, the real merit of the book lies in documenting the convergence of concerns emanating from struggles for regional autonomy, developmental demands, and the politics of belonging and recognition in the region. The book compels us to think beyond the narrow confines of recognition as defined by the state, and reconsider the possibility of recognizing culture, and thus contemplate a different kind of anthropological future.

Nilamber Chhetri
Maharashtra National Law University

Prabhavati C. Reddy, *Hindu Pilgrimage: Shifting Patterns of Worldview of Shri Shailam in South India*
New York: Routledge, 2014. 237 pages. Hardback, $153.00; ebook $38.00. ISBN 9780415659970 (hardback); 9781315815022 (ebook).

IN THIS STUDY of Shri Shailam, located in Andhra Pradesh, Prabhavati Reddy brings together a variety of historical and ethnographic sources to present a comprehensive account of the evolution of a prominent Shaiva pilgrimage center in South India. The wide arc of materials is crucial to the methodology of the book, which aims to place "texts in an interactive discourse" (15) with each other. The result is an erudite study of several kinds of medieval and contemporary texts (*paurāṇik*, epigraphic, topographic, and popular stories), although this interactive discourse does not characterize the ethnographic process of the book. The book's authoritative account comes from the author's skillful interweaving of written, sculptural, and archaeological texts rather than from a transparent interweaving of voices of living individuals whose devotions and livelihoods tie them to Shri Shailam. Pilgrimage, for instance, is interpreted as a phenomenon of "experience and consciousness" as imaged through texts rather than constructed through the subjective experiences of pilgrims. In another example (chapter 13), we learn that the major festival of Mahashivaratri at Shri Shailam includes a ritual event in which the outside tower of the main temple is draped in white cloth that is woven by the Devanga (weaver) community. At the time that Reddy witnessed it, the head of a Devanga family performed the draping, climbing the tower in the nude. Reddy interprets the ritual in the light of a wonderful story in the Devanga Purāṇa about the competing devotions of a spider, elephant, and snake for Shiva—a story that may have gained credence during Virashaiva patronage of the temple in the fifteenth century. But it is puzzling that save for a few allusions, voices from Devanga families remain indistinct in this interpretation.

The book is organized into four parts. The first part (chapters 1–3) lays out the map of the book itself. A well-grounded description of Shri Shailam, with its older name of Shri Parvata, tells readers that here Shiva goes as Mallikarjuna ("Lord of White Jasmine") and his consort Durga is known as Bhramarambha ("Mother Bee"). Mallikarjuna and Bhramarambha are worshipped with ritual grandeur and sectarian specificity that are part of local traditions, but this localization intertwines with Shri Shailam's location in pan-Hindu, Sanskritic mythology. Thus Shri Shailam is named and praised in the *jyotirliṅga* tradition elaborated in the Skanda Purāṇa, a text that identifies the twelve sites of Shiva's manifestation across India in the form of a *jyotirliṅga*, an unscalable brilliant column of light that for Shaiva devotees demonstrates Shiva's supremacy over Vishnu and other deities. The other pan-Hindu framework into which Shri Shailam has been absorbed is that of the Devi or Goddess tradition. Two particular aspects are embodied in Shri Shailam: one, Durga's manifestation as a formidable giant bee (*bhramara*), and two, Shri Shailam as a site in the *śāktā* network of primary Sati temples. The book provides a table with timelines (80) that helps the reader visualize the development of Shaivite and Shakta traditions at Shri Shailam.

In Part II (chapters 4–6), Reddy proposes that the historical development of Shri Shailam into a sacred site can be understood through a threefold process, which she identifies as idealization, materialization, and sanctification. As an idealized place, Shri Shailam is a product of various Sanskrit and Telugu *sthalapurāṇa*s (place lore texts) that conceptualize it as a site of Shiva and Durga's hierophanies and human encounters with these. A key text is the twelfth- to thirteenth-century *Shrishaila Khanda*, a Sanskrit text available as an unpublished written Telugu manuscript, which maps out the sacred geography of Shri Shailam both as the cosmic mountain of Meru, as well as a *maṇḍala* (geometric diagram) with eight mountains—symbolizing the eight forms of Shiva (the five elements, the sun, the moon, and the human mind—with the Shri Parvata at the center). Reddy shows how several other texts, such as various Shaiva *purāṇa*s and the thirteenth-century *Panditaradhya Caritra*, map narratives and cosmologies onto Shri Shailam's topography and demonstrates how "place becomes a mediating agency" (29) that expresses, over time, layered world views. As a place that undergoes sacred materialization, changing over time (Reddy's observations span fifteen years), Shri Shailam's boundaries of a *kṣetra* (sacred land) expand, making three regions visible. The innermost region is the *axis mundi* (the mountain of Sri Shailam, the temple complex, and immediate township); the middle region contains other local sacred sites and intersections of an important pilgrimage network—the Nallamalla hills that boast of two other famous sacred centers, Ahobilam and Tirupati. Apart from the mountain, Reddy discusses two other topographical features that "materialize" Shri Shailam's sacrality. The river Krishna whose flow around the region's plateau is checked by a triad of hills forms an inland body of water called the *pātāla gaṅgā* (the underworld Ganga). However, when Reddy discusses the subterranean confluence of rivers, it would have helped if she had clearly distinguished between actual geography and ones imagined by *paurāṇik* texts, and further, if she had critically addressed the question of visibility and invisibility in Hindu sacred geography that underlies her findings. Similarly, a reader wishes for ethnographic conversation on the fascinating account of the *sthala vṛkṣa* (place tree) that Reddy provides. Here it is a banyan tree, declared dead in 1985, and "replaced by a new one" (48) by the temple management. (The Hindu Religious and Charitable Endowments Department has since instructed temple managements "to adopt cloning to preserve the *Sthala Vriksham* or tree unique to each temple"; see http://www.thehindu.com/news/national /tamil-nadu/sthala-vriksham-to-be-preserved-through-cloning/article6656463. ece.) Reddy's description of the middle and outer spatiality of Shri Shailam is equally vivid. The sixth and final chapter of Part II illustrates how different sectarian Shaivisms engage this sacred geography through ritual and pilgrimage.

Part III (chapters 7–10) studies the history of Shri Shailam through diverse Shaiva orders over fifteen hundred years, a history that mirrors the development of Shaivism itself. It begins with references to Shri Shailam in the Mahabharata, and takes us through the seventh century, when Kapalikas (esoteric Shaivite traditions) were prominent. Through a visual analysis of the temple enclosure, Reddy shows how Shri Shailam became important for the Kalamukhas and their monastic establishments during the tenth century. Between the twelfth and fourteenth centuries, under the patronage of the Kakatiya kings, Shri Shailam began to crystallize its identity as a Smarta Shaivite center. (Reddy attributes this crystallization to the aforementioned Shrishaila Khaṇḍa, which she discusses in detail.) One of the singularities of this text and concomitant phase in the emergence of Shri Shailam is that it established the manifestation of the great Devi of the Durga Mahatmya as Bhramarambha of Shri Shailam. The diversity in Shaiva "ownerships" of Shri Shailam continued through the thirteenth century through Shaiva Siddhanta lineages, which brought a distinct *āgamik* identity to Shri Shailam through temple building and the establishment of ritual procedures for *liṅgam* worship. Reddy provides complex portraits of the distinctive and influential phase of the Virashaivas after the thirteenth century.

Part IV (chapters 11–13) concludes with a modern history of Shri Shailam, which Reddy traces against key political developments of the eighteenth and twentieth centuries. After discussing Shri Shailam's dilapidated fate in the twilight of the Vijayanagara dynasty and during the British colonial regime, Reddy brings us to the most modern era of Shri Shailam's history when the Endowment Department of Andhra Pradesh (EDAP) took over the temple's management. The temple complex and township have since been systematically transformed through architectural rearrangements and new annual festival regimens, creating in effect a Shri Shailam that continues to consecrate a divine realm of timeless myths but also to cater to a civic realm of state-directed imperatives for reaping a tourist economy. The major festival tradition of Mahashivaratri displays the intermeshing of the divine and civic agenda.

This magisterial study of Shri Shailam, even with its ethnographic limitations, adds a wealth of information to the archive of Hindu pilgrimage studies—where studies of Shri Shailam are scant. It persuasively demonstrates that a diachronic, layered, and intertextual reading can widen our understanding of the enmeshed theologies and politics of ancient sacred sites.

Leela Prasad
Duke University

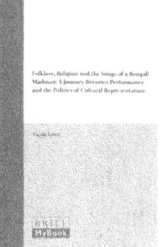

Carola Erika Lorea, *Folklore, Religion and the Songs of a Bengali Madman: A Journey between Performance and the Politics of Cultural Representation*

Leiden: Brill, 2016. xviii + 334 pages. Cloth, $163.00/€145,00; e-book $163.00/€145,00. ISBN 9789004324701 (cloth); 9789004324718 (e-book).

IN THIS WORK, Carola Erika Lorea documents the life, songs, and legacy of a widely popular, but academically unexplored, songwriter and guru of Bengal, Bhaba Pagla, whose songs are now mostly sung by the well-known mystic minstrels called Bauls. This is the first English book on Bhaba Pagla. It studies song-texts and their lives, not from the usual textual perspectives, but as contextual realities, best understood as performances. Through detailed ethnographic research and a consideration of theoretical literature, especially on performance, the work shows with clarity and deftness what a very close-grained ethnographic work, rather than a textual one, and performance-oriented study, rather than a treatment of texts and traditions as fixed phenomena, can do to our understanding of culture. The work thus critically engages with very important terms that are essential to the discourse of popular culture: for instance, orality, texts, folk, tradition, literacy, and orthodoxy. These are the key strengths of the book.

The work addresses the problem of the absence of Bhaba Pagla in the academic works on Bauls, and tries to locate the problem in much broader discursive questions about the representation of appropriate markers of authenticity of the "folk" and "tradition." The author discusses the life and migration of Bhaba Pagla, his songs, the varied contexts of their performance, and debates on technology impacting these songs, to critique the discourse on folk religion and culture in Bengal. The work is based on readings of the poet's texts, including the very rare ones; long ethnographic work with musicians and performers, and practitioners and gurus of Bhaba Pagla's lineage in various temples and ashrams of West Bengal; in-depth interviews; and participation in a great number and variety of performance contexts. Scholars of South Asian religions, culture, folk studies, and ethnomusicology will find the book helpful in innovative ways.

In the first chapter, the author directly addresses the problem of Bhaba Pagla's absence in the literature on Bengali folklore. In a very comprehensive way she looks at the history of ideas constituting the image of the Baul in popular culture. Lorea explores a variety of images, such as the defiled body substances used in Bauk rituals, Tagore's romanticized wandering minstrel on one end of the spectrum, to the practitioners of materialism and subversive agents of history on the other end. A significant number of such features have been identified through the centuries as markers of the "authentic" Baul. The poor rural practitioner of religion and music, in most instances, has thus been represented as an exotic figure. The author argues against these fixed definitions of authenticity, and says that Bhaba Pagla went amiss in the literature, since he did not squarely fit the images of authenticity. He followed and espoused both exoteric rituals in public and esoteric practices (of Bauls and other popular religious groups) in private, and acquired a varied following among different castes and classes. She notes that a number of factors, such as sustenance and self-defense, influenced Bhaba Pagla's strategies of maintaining a fluid identity, which must be analyzed, rather than being taken as proof of his not being an authentic Baul. Indeed, the author questions the authenticity of categories generally, and instead foregrounds the need to study a phenomenon contextually in order to understand the formation of such categories in the first place.

The second chapter focuses on the persona of Bhaba Pagla, his lifestory constructed from hagiographies and other narratives, and the oeuvre of his songs, to think about questions of genre and the oral-literary divide in studies of popular traditions. The author suggests that Bhaba Pagla's songs are most heterogeneous, and can easily traverse different musical types such as, folk, Baul, *śyāmāsaṅgīt* (songs addressed to the mother goddess). In tune with the first chapter, she argues that one must not fix the idea of genre, as that in turn would also lead to other essentializations. It is more important to analyze the politics of representation involved in identifying genres. While *sādhansaṅgīt* (songs of devotion) would be the most appropriate genre of the poet's songs, his patriotic songs are also important. The omission of the latter in discussions and performances reflect the workings of the same notion of authenticity in defining a Baul. The chapter also makes a critical contribution to studies of performance theory and folklore theory, by arguing that the life of a composition is a long one, from the moment of conception to performance, and thus most often, traverses many possible points between orality and literacy. She thus questions the oral-literate binary in folklore studies.

The third chapter has interesting descriptions of very different kinds of musical gatherings (informal/semi-formal/formal, ritual/commercial, staged concerts, festival renditions, fusion music, and so on) in which Bhaba Pagla's songs are sung. The author analyzes how different kinds of song texts, tunes, and modalities are chosen, according to complex relations among performers, audiences, and settings. The author thus suggests that the esoteric-exoteric complex in popular religious traditions of Bengal may also be understood in relation to varied performative contexts. The second theme that the chapter develops is the role of folklore in cohering shared identities, in this case, among expatriated performers from Bangladesh, especially those from the lower castes. Bhaba Pagla becomes not only the religious guru, but also a general cultural hero, whose songs evoke the nostalgia inevitably associated with migration, and who is himself an icon of successful resettlement—with status, popularity, and legacy.

Chapter 4 builds on different themes, such as the need to rethink the oral-literate divide and the tendency to view the singer Baul as inauthentic, to engage critically with another discourse about technology destroying the world of the so-called authentic Baul. In an interesting analysis, the author argues that technology has both negative and positive effects on Baul music. Technology, for example, not only falls short of total intrusion into the Baul song performances and their ritual lives but also facilitates innovation. She also argues that technological vocabulary (such as "mobile phone") aids in religious expressions. Technical vocabulary associated with modernity is thus creatively appropriated in songs and sermons. In a provocative argument, she suggests that these terms help disciples understand complicated religious issues. In other words, technology and the terminology associated with it now play the role of the best communicative medium in rural Bengal. Given such changes, what then happens to general questions concerning the folk, the popular, and the village? These themes could have been further developed in the book.

Indeed, while the main contribution of the book is that it thinks about categories such as the folk in terms of their form, rather than their content, further analyses could be developed to critique the nature of relations among the "folk" and the "popular" on one hand and tradition, modernity, heritage (of religious music as a genre), technology, and performance on the other. These themes are discussed in the individual chapters, and often in original ways, but the connections among them could have been made more conceptually.

While Lorea's theoretical arguments could be pushed further, the book is an excellent ethnography, with original perspectives. It will help scholars refine their folklore research, especially concerning the religious and performative traditions of Bengal, in new ways.

Sukanya Sarbadhikary
Presidency University

Indonesia

Jennifer A. Fraser, *Gongs & Pop Songs: Sounding Minangkabau in Indonesia*
Athens, Ohio: Ohio University Press, 2015. xv + 270 pages. Notes, bibliographical references and index. Hardcover, $75.00; paperback, $ 29.95. ISBN 978-0-89680-294-0 (hardcover); 978-0-89680-295-7 (paperback).

INTERNATIONAL ethnomusicological studies on Indonesian traditional music, especially those dealing with idiophone musical instruments, have concentrated mainly on Javanese and Balinese gamelan. For centuries, Western scholars gave the outer islands such as Nusantara much less attention than other regions until the appearance of Jennifer Fraser's book. Fraser became fascinated by *talempong* after travelling to West Sumatra, the homeland of the Minangkabau, the last remaining prominent matrilineal society in a twenty-first century world dominated by patriarchal societies. Fraser spent a year in 1998 studying at the Academy of Indonesian Traditional Music (now Higher Institute of Indonesian Arts, STSI) in Padang Panjang under the Dharmasiswa exchange program sponsored by the Indonesian government.

Since then, Fraser seems to have fallen in love with *talempong*. Her interest in this Minangkabau traditional gong-chime ensemble, however, differs from that of other foreign anthropologists, who are more interested in the Minangkabau ethnic group's matrilineal kinship system, especially its coexistence with Islam. Nine years later, Fraser's strong fascination with *talempong* bore a dissertation entitled "Packaging Ethnicity: State Institutions, Cultural Entrepreneurs, and the Professionalization of Minangkabau Music in Indonesia," submitted to the University of Illinois at Urbana-Champaign. *Gongs & Pop Songs* is adapted from her dissertation, which she calls "a culmination of two years of research in West Sumatra lasting over a sixteen-year period" (ix).

In *Gongs & Pop Songs*, Fraser, now an associate professor of ethnomusicology and anthropology at Oberlin College, explores the transformation of Minangkabau *talempong*. She traces in detail how *talempong* music "has changed over the last sixty years and how it was transformed in response to a number of different forces, including political events, the institutionalization and the related professionalization of the arts, and the pressures of a free-market economy" (216).

The book consists of six chapters accompanied by audio and video examples, as well as images that are available online (listed on 255–58). Chapter 1, "Ethnicity, Gongs, and Pop Songs" (1–36), is an overview of the main chapters of the book. It shows how *talempong* "is shaped in different styles that come to articulate different understandings of Minangkabau ethnicity" (35–36) by sketching its position in Minangkabau traditional arts and society. The chapter also explores *talempong*'s recent incorporation in Minangkabau pop songs as a consequence of the professionalization and monetization of Minangkabau music that, in turn, has brought about changing perceptions of it. The author also provides theoretical considerations using a cognitive perspective on ethnicity to define who the Minangkabau are. This introductory chapter offers the core ideas of the book: "the ways [*talempong*] music expresses ethnic sentiments and the ways that expression is shaped by social, political, economic, and cultural currents at the local, regional, and national level" (36).

Chapter 2, "Talempong and Community" (37–88), describes *talempong* practices in the *nagari* (village federation) of West Sumatra. In the *nagari*, the author found two original *talempong* styles: *talempong duduak*, which is more likely to be performed by women, and *talempong pacik* or *talempong bararak* which is mostly performed by men. Both are "broad stylistic categories that transcend differences in performance practice from one *nagari* to the next" (49). The author describes in detail how to play both *talempong* types and the different melodies each contains. However, the repertoire of *talempong* practices in this *nagari* has changed with the passage of time. For example, "the musicians in some *nagari* choose to incorporate pop songs and *dendang* [any indigenous Minangkabau song composed in *pantun* verse] into the repertoire of both *talempong pacik* and *talempong duduak* ensembles" (64). But most of them are still performed in their original function: as music to enliven the celebration of weddings (*baralek*). The author extensively describes the processions and cultural significances of this major rite of passage in Minangkabau life (67–80). Though weddings are the most frequent occasions for *talempong* performance in the *nagari* under investigation, the music is also performed in other ceremonies and communal events, such as a child's first ritual bath, circumcision ceremonies, and *batagak panghulu* (installation of a lineage leader). Sometimes *talempong* is also performed at sports events, festivals, and government functions outside of the *nagari* (80). The *talempong pacik* seems to have been performed to accompany villagers while working voluntarily (*gotong royong* or *kerja bakti*) to build or restore public facilities (ANONYMOUS 1953). The last part of this chapter discusses the monetization of *talempong* in the *nagari* along with the increasing influence of money culture in Minangkabau society, which, to a certain extent, has decreased the sense of communalism.

The author mentions that the monetization of *talempong* has engendered newer styles of such Minangkabau ensemble music. Chapter 3, "Institutionalizing Minangkabau Arts" (89–132), explores these new styles and processes and the principal factors that engendered them; namely, the formal training that has occurred since the 1960s in Minangkabau arts at special schools. The author looks at how educational institutions (such as the STSI Padang Panjang, the Indonesisch Nederlandsche School [INS] at Kayutanam, and the High School of Indonesia Traditional Arts [SMKI] in Padang) and various performing arts troupes (*sanggar seni*) have become a primary factor in driving the transformation of Minangkabau indigenous *talempong*. These educational institutions are credited with standardizing *talempong* music and other Minangkabau indigenous art genres.

The two remaining principal chapters trace various new performance styles of *talempong*, as a consequence of the institutionalizing of this genre of music. The musicians graduating from such educational institutions for the arts, and those who work with them, have created new styles of *talempong* musical performances, which are shaped in professional performing arts troupes or musical groups. Chapter 4, "Performing Talempong" (133–75), looks at educational practices for *talempong*, especially at STSI Padang Panjang. It details the emergence of a new idiom: the diatonic *talempong*. This experimentation, carried out by ASKI instructors, has subsequently developed into *orkes talempong*. The author analyzes ethnomusicologically the musical structure of ornamentation of the *orkes* and the melody of its prominent piece "Kumbang cari" (not "Kambang cari" as incorrectly written somewhere else in the book, just as *jengkel* occurs instead of *jengkol* [pungent nut] on page 14).

In chapter 5, "Talempong in the Market Place" (176–215), the author continues her focus on modern diatonic *talempong*, and compels her to look closer at the practice of this new genre in the context of "money matters: how concerns of the market shape the arts [including talempong] or, put another way, how arts are modified and framed in order to be viable in the market place and respond to the needs of the paying clientele" (176). Looking at the effects of the free-market economy on the arts, in which artistic and cultural goods are exchanged for economic capital, especially at a time when tourism is an important source of revenue under the government's policy of regional autonomy, this chapter traces the emergence of Minangkabau *sanggar*, which is now established both in the homeland (West Sumatra) and in the *rantau* (migration areas outside West Sumatra), the origin and musical characteristics of new styles such as *talempong goyang* and *talempong kreasi baru*, as well as their economic significance.

In the concluding chapter, "Multiple Ways of Sounding Minangkabau" (216–24), the author underlines two important points as logical consequences of the transformation of *talempong* due to the institutionalization, professionalization, and monetization of the arts in Indonesia. First, the teaching of Minangkabau indigenous arts by formal educational institutions has lowered the quality of indigenous arts, so the preservationist objectives of these institutions have failed. According to the author, the Institute of Indonesian Arts in Padang Panjang, the leading higher education institute of arts in West Sumatra, has done more to undermine than to preserve Minangkabau indigenous arts, including *talempong*: "First, by decontextualizing these arts and stripping them of embedded value systems; second, by pedagogical approaches to teaching these practices that dilute their aesthetic content; third, by producing a class of musicians who dismiss the value of rural practices and the accomplishment of indigenous practitioners; and last, by encouraging the development of indigenous arts and the creation of new musical styles nominally predicated on them" (219). Second, the transformation of *talempong* has changed this music from a sub-local musical practice to a new form that transcends *nagari* affiliations, therefore symbolizing a pan-Minangkabau identity. Like the commercial recordings of Minangkabau pop music (SURYADI 2014), these new *talempong* styles have actively fostered and created ethnic sensibilities, Minangkabau-*ness* in this context.

This book is academically rich, and with its sophisticated and insightful interpretations, it is a truly worthy scholarly contribution to the understanding of the dynamics of local culture in contemporary Indonesia. It will be a valuable resource for ethnomusicological and ethnographic studies of Indonesian regional pop music.

References

Anonymous
1953   Seni suara Minangkabau [Minangkabau vocal arts]. In Z. Moechtar & Aman St. Sinaro, eds., *Pantjaran Budaja: Buku Batjaan mengenai Kebudajaan untuk Sekolah Landjutan Atas di Indonesia* [Wellspring of culture: A cultural reader for Indonesian high schools], 63–65. Jakarta: Penerbit "Siliwangi" N.V. (Reprinted from *Pewarta Djakarta*, no. 17, 1951.)

Suryadi, Surya
2014   The Recording Industry and "Regional" Culture in Indonesia: The Case of Minangkabau. PhD dissertation, Leiden University.

Surya Suryadi
Leiden University

Henry Spiller, *Javaphilia: American Love Affairs with Javanese Music and Dance*
Honolulu: University of Hawai'i Press, 2015. 278 pages. Cloth, $42.00. ISBN: 978-0-8248-4094-5.

Falling in love with exotic cultures—including their sounds, aesthetics, foods, belief systems, and people—is not for everyone. In fact, for some "exotic lovers," the fact that they are in the minority, running against the populist tide, is exactly part of the appeal. Difference captivates them, and even becomes their calling card of just who they are or imagine themselves to be, such that their taste for the exotic can be seen as but one part of a generalized psyche built on self-fashioned distinctiveness. Ethnomusicologist Henry Spiller's 2015 book, *Javaphilia: American Love Affairs with Javanese Music and Dance* addresses this phenomenon, focusing on four American aficionados ("javaphiles," as Spiller calls them) of the music and dance of Indonesia: singer Eva Gauthier (1885–1958), dancer/painter Hubert Stowitz (1892–1953), ethnomusicologist Mantle Hood (1918–2005), and composer Lou Harrison (1917–2003). Spiller's book tackles the big questions not only for ethnomusicologists, but also for anthropologists and (non-Asian) Asianists, as well as others more loosely espousing consumerist appetites surrounding exotica. The big questions are these: what is the appeal of the exotic? For whom? Under what sociopolitical conditions? How? And with what kinds of repercussions, not so much in the place of origin, as in the place of newfound reception? Those repercussions include individual lives, careers, creative arts, and serious scholarship.

Spiller focuses on the "-philia" nature of the attraction. These are more than passing interests, but abiding passions that create professional and personal identities for those involved. By calling this attraction a "love affair," Spiller gets at not only the headiness of the thing, but also its structural positionality: the exotica—here, gamelan, the traditional metallophone-based orchestra of Java—as a temptress, a seductress, a feminine bundle of brown wiles that lures the masculinized, white adventurer. This love affair is overdetermined in racial, class, national, and gendered terms. Spiller goes one step further; he suggests that the encounter is not by happenstance, but part of a personal quest: the adventurer seeks that which is missing or deficient in his regular life. Gauthier was an unsuccessful operatic mezzo-soprano; Stowitts grappled with his homosexuality; Hood harbored conflicting interests in spirituality and scholarship; Harrison faced criticism from the field of "serious" avant-garde music for his predilection for "pretty music." In short and concrete terms, gamelan music and dance provided these four javaphiles with the missing puzzle piece in their personal, artistic, and professional lives.

Spiller analyzes a basic tripartite trope in each of his case studies: disenfranchisement by and from mainstream American society—"discovery" and personal reinterpretation of Javanese arts as a means of filling the disjuncture—reincorporation into mainstream American society through a newly reconfigured self, based in part on Javanese arts. In this way, the javaphiliac approach is far less concerned with Java itself, and far more concerned with cultural appropriation for personal ends, coalescing in what Spiller calls "self-fashioning"—that is, the creation and assertion of a public identity of one's own making. This trope sounds highly critical, asking scholars, artists, and "exotica" aficionados alike to turn the mirror of analysis upon themselves. To his credit, Spiller does this in a section entitled "Javaphilia and Me," analyzing his own involvement with gamelan music and dance, from his days as an undergraduate at the University of California at Santa Cruz, through his professional career as a specialist in Sundanese dance.

In many ways, this book's strength is also its weakness. Challenging Asianists (and others) to unpack their motives, interests, and even passions regarding "Asia" is a complex endeavor. Spiller brings insightful analytical tools to bear, such as "dicent authority" (borrowed from ethnomusicologist Thomas Turino), the external credibility that derives from direct contact with a source culture. Dicent authority gives these javaphiles the veneer of authenticity outside of Java, in particular within the context of a relative lack of widespread knowledge in America of Indonesia and its people and culture. Note, however, the need for an authenticating filter from the javaphiles' very outsider status. In short, by this external construction, people indigenous to "exotic" cultures need not apply. Their authority is typically mounted on the backs of biology, even if they have never touched a gamelan instrument or attended a *wayang kulit* (shadow puppet play).

The category of Javaphile, then, automatically sets up a racialized binary: outsider versus insider, foreigner versus native, lover/fan versus indigene. It is the external status of the javaphile that assumes the internal as already-knowing, as if gamelan music and dance coursed through their blood. Spiller's analytical scheme does not attend to the anomalies in this binary: for example, the foreigner who has long "gone native," living in Indonesia for decades, perhaps marrying a Javanese musician, perhaps giving birth to children whose lives are interwoven within Javanese social threads. What happens when javaphilia captivates an outsider so thoroughly?

Spiller astutely notes the doubled position of javaphiles: on the one hand, they identify with the exoticized Javanese in contesting mainstream Euro-American culture; on the other hand, they participate in the very project of imperialism in exoticizing Javanese culture itself. Further, dicent authority positions them to fashion not only themselves, but Javanese culture itself, as presented to Euro-American audiences. Java's very remoteness, its lack of familiar presence in Euro-America, allows these javaphiles to manipulate "Java" at will, for their own purposes.

These are all important insights and teach us a lot about this set of case studies. Spiller meticulously documents the details of these javaphiles' lives and activities, and builds a convincing argument. (In fact, some of those details may well be lost on the non-javaphiles among his readers. But for those who occupy the world of diasporic gamelans, this book contains tantalizing details with familiar names, incidents, and concerts.) Notably, this book was honored by the Society for Ethnomusicology as the 2016 recipient of the Bruno Nettl Prize, awarded annually since 2012 for contributions to the history of the field of ethnomusicology.

Yet, a reader is left with the impossibility of the task of asking, why? How to truly know motivations? How to fully understand the why of a person's proclivities, including one's own? This sounds more like the stuff of deep psychology, well beyond the training of most scholars. As any ethnographic researcher can tell you, just taking people by their words or actions is certainly not enough. Nor is it enough to examine the social conditions and contexts of –philias. What draws some people—and not others—to exotica? This may be an impossible task. How to know beyond conjecture? What draws certain people to particular exotica? Answering this question may be more feasible, but ultimately still an enigma. Some people credit past lives with their present proclivities. This only points to the enigmatic quality of the "why" endeavor.

However, even if this book is not able to truly answer its own questions, Spiller should be credited with addressing this large issue in a thoroughgoing manner. By provoking the discussion, Spiller's book challenges us to spin that mirror upon ourselves and pay heed to the self-fashioning from "exotic" materials that has become naturalized as part of many of our selves and scholarly careers.

Christine R. Yano
University of Hawai'i

Japan

R. Keller Kimbrough, trans. with an Introduction,
Wondrous Brutal Fictions: Eight Buddhist Tales from the Early Japanese Puppet Theater
New York: Columbia University Press, 2013. 288 pages, appendixes, glossary, bibliography. Cloth, $55,00/£38.00. ISBN 978-0-231-14658-6.

KELLER KIMBROUGH's *Wondrous Brutal Fictions* is a translation of eight works conventionally described using the term *sekkyō*, a pseudo-religious "medieval and early Edo-period 'sermon-ballad' storytelling genre" (268) focused on karma, Buddhist merit, and the divine origins of Buddhist icons. Kimbrough brings English-language readers lively, engaging renderings of representative titles from the genre, filled with instances of miraculous births, gloomy sequences about children separated from their families, solitary wanderings, torture, disfiguration, death, and eventual redemption through Buddhist merits. The book includes reproductions of more than fifty illustrations—some printed and some done by hand, some of scenes within the stories themselves, and some of theatrical presentations—taken from a variety of sources including literary works and *shōhon* ("true texts"), which purported to reproduce performance manuscripts used by professional chanters. *Wondrous Brutal Fictions* is a welcome addition to a small body of English-language translations and studies of *sekkyō* and early puppet theater that includes DUNN (1966); MATISOFF (1978), her detailed and thorough treatment of *sekkyō* as a genre (1992), and her later scholarship on specific titles such as *Karukaya* and *Oguri*; ISHII (1989); and MORRISON (2006) and her recent articles on the topic. Its publication makes it possible for the first time to fully integrate *sekkyō* into classes on premodern Japanese literature and theater from several different perspectives: as part of the broader performative and literary landscape of the sixteenth century, as one popular descendent of medieval performed narratives (*katarimono*), as an instance of the manner in which lay priests used religious elements in entertainment, and as a way of approaching early-Tokugawa puppet performance and the issues surrounding its textual circulation in early modern Japan.

Wondrous Brutal Fictions opens with a helpful introduction that traces the evolution of *sekkyō* from medieval "street-corner *sekkyō*" (*kado-sekkyō*) to an early modern theatrical spectacle staged in urban theaters. Kimbrough shows that in various regions the old *sekkyō* of the sixteenth century were typically chanted under an umbrella "to the rhythmic accompaniment of *sasara*, a kind of notched bamboo scraper" at "bridges, crossroads, and the grounds of temples and shrines" (1), until during the seventeenth century the form found its way into urban theaters as a type of puppet performance accompanied by the *shamisen*. In the mid- to late-seventeenth century, *sekkyō* assumed a place "in the major urban centers of Edo, Kyoto, and Osaka as thriving, competing genres of puppet theater, each with its own repertoire and distinctive linguistic conventions" (2–3), only to disappear in the mid-eighteenth century as it was gradually absorbed by *ko-jōruri*, or early puppet theater—a term referring to *jōruri* theater prior to the emergence of the canonical playwright Chikamatsu Monzaemon (1653–1725). *Sekkyō* thus belongs to a broadly defined genre of early-Tokugawa puppet theater, but was in practice distinguished from *ko-jōruri*: *sekkyō* productions were marked as such, featured chanters who specialized in the art, and drew on a repertoire with distinct linguistic characteristics and to some extent themes, even though the uniqueness of *sekkyō* gradually gave way as the genre imitated and absorbed the conventions of *ko-jōruri*. As Kimbrough explains, "*sekkyō* survives in a limited number of seventeenth- and early-eighteenth-century woodblock printed *shōhon* 'true texts,' which date from the age in which *sekkyō* had begun to move into urban theaters and to be influenced by the *ko-jōruri* puppet theater" (268). The translations are thus based on particular iterations of *sekkyō* works that occupy a particular position in the history of the genre's development.

The eight *sekkyō* works shed new light on nearly a century of early modern theatrical productions that preceded the Genroku period (1688–1704) and Chikamatsu Monzaemon, whose plays have profoundly shaped our understanding of early modern theater history. Kimbrough's translations, in fact, point to the survival and indeed popularity of tropes and sensibilities from the late medieval period even in urban centers during the seventeenth century, in the roughly nine decades before Chikamatsu began creating his tightly woven *jōruri* texts centering on urban struggles between private feelings and duties in the contexts of a highly stratified feudal society and a monetary economy. Almost all these *sekkyō* texts are set in locales far removed from urban centers, and the translations are replete with scenes of tearful family separations and the lonely travels of protagonists living in extreme poverty. In *Sanshō Dayū*, two young children are sold and separated from their mother and must endure being forced to labor as slaves. Aigo in *Aigo-no-waka* eventually commits suicide after being brutally beaten by his relatives and wandering in the mountains, living a miserable life as a beggar. In *Shintokumaru*, the protagonist, abandoned by his parents, lives as a blind, disfigured beggar, and Oguri in *Oguri* returns from hell on a cart as a "hungry ghost" (*gaki*) and has to rely on volunteers to pull him where he wants to go. These *sekkyō* works exhibit an enduring early modern fascination with karmic tragedy that supersedes human agency (as opposed to the man-made tragedies that often dominate views of early modern theater), as well as with brutal, solitary itinerancy and work at the bottom of the social ladder, perhaps reflecting the experiences and world views of the outcast itinerant performers who chanted *sekkyō* on the roads. In his introduction, Kimbrough also emphasizes the particularly brutal nature of the tales, highlighting their copious depictions of violence and torture alongside the celebration of "psychological strength and the power of the human will" (17). The almost overly sentimental subject matter, the crude violence, and the harsh views of life in rural areas, combined with the strength of character that allows the protagonists to endure hardships, speaks volumes about the tastes of early modern urban audiences in the mid-seventeenth century, before Chikamatsu's time. It is telling, in this sense, that *sekkyō*'s influence lasted longest in Edo, a city that brought people from all regions and backgrounds together.

The study of *sekkyō* helps connect important tropes in later puppet theater such as the famous "travel sequence" (*michiyuki*) and "scenes of lamenting" (*shūtanba*) to their early modern social environment in much more grounded terms. All eight *sekkyō* works translated in this collection include travel-guide-like lists of the places characters travel to in dismay, perhaps indicating that one of their important functions was to cater to travelers who heard the tales on the streets, or that these works helped map certain geographical spaces. In later *jōruri*, traveling still played an important function, but it had undergone a sort of conceptual transformation so that it highlighted characters' emotional and dramatic states. One example of this is the list of bridges that the lovers cross before their double suicide in a celebrated scene in Chikamatsu's *Shinjū ten no Amijima* (Love suicide at Amijima, 1720); this scene helps the lovers and the audience watching them reflect on their lives and on their symbolic descent to hell. *Sekkyō* also favored tearful and sorrow-filled moments of separation among family members, while later works for the puppet theater found it more fruitful and poetic to create drama in the context of amorous relationships. Noting these differences also helps us revisit and confirm the nature of the distinctiveness of the early modern experimentation and innovation that gradually took form in later puppet theater, allowing us to reexamine well-known early modern plays and the manner in which they built on earlier theatrical materials.

As I have noted, *sekkyō* originates in the sixteenth century, but the large majority of surviving texts are from the time after *sekkyō* was transformed into a type of puppet performance in the early modern period. It is significant that most texts date from a period when *sekkyō* was going through something of a revival, and that most were published via the new medium of commercial woodblock printing. Kimbrough is well aware of the early modern textual identity of *sekkyō*, but also of the potential it has to be read as an embodiment of traces of medieval chanted narratives. He has thus made eclectic editorial choices, working not from a single collection of annotated transcriptions as his source text but from various major collections such as the *sekkyō* volumes in the Iwanami Koten Bungaku Taikei (SHINODA and SAKAGUCHI eds., SNKBT 90, 1999), the Shinchō Nihon Koten Shūsei (MUROKI ed. 1977), and Tōyō Bunko (ARAKI and YAMAMOTO eds., Tōyō bunko 243, 1973), cross-referencing these typeset texts with facsimile editions and/or with a secondary text. Kimbrough's translations thus derive from a variety of different types of texts, ranging from the woodblock printed *shōhon*, which is most closely connected with the theater, to hand-copied books with lavish illustrations known as *Nara ehon* (Nara picture books) and rare picture scrolls, the texts of which are often included today in literary anthologies. While Kimbrough does not discuss his editorial principles in detail, it seems that when possible he has chosen texts that retain phrasing and formats typical of older *sekkyō*, while at the same time avoiding early editions that have large omissions or missing parts. For this reason, he sometimes includes texts that might be thought of as "readerly versions"—texts that are included in literary anthologies today with *monogatari* or *shōsetsu* in the title—when they are thought to retain traces of the characteristics of older *sekkyō* or earlier *shōhon* texts. This is the case, for instance, with the source text of Kimbrough's translation of *Sayohime*, which is a *Nara ehon* at Kyoto University printed in transcribed form in SHIMAZU ed., (1928) and in transcribed or facsimile form in other *sekkyō* collections. The degree of care Kimbrough invested in selecting the best text for translation is evident from the impressive appendix he includes categorizing extant *sekkyō*, showing how some were marketed as *shōhon* while others were sold as illustrated popular fiction. Kimbrough provides bibliographical notes and information about the texts' location in archives, as well as lists of available modern transcriptions, annotations, or facsimile reproductions. Kimbrough surveyed each textual variant in order to create a sort of archetypical text that shows as much as possible a fairly early style of the work while simultaneously avoiding omissions or incompleteness.

At the same time, it is interesting to observe that the order in which Kimbrough presents the *sekkyō* he has chosen to translate seems to echo the gradual changes that took place in the textual circulation of *sekkyō* in terms of language and subject matter. Kimbrough writes:

> In light of the seventeenth-century history of *sekkyō*, the works translated in this volume are perhaps best understood as occupying points on a continuum between "pure" *sekkyō* and *ko-jōruri*, with *Karukaya* (1631), *Sanshō Dayū* (ca. 1639), and *Shintokumaru* (1648) representing a relatively older form of *sekkyō*; the six-act *Aigo-no-waka* (ca. 1670) representing the genre of *sekkyō-jōruri* (*sekkyō* under the heavier influence of *ko-jōruri*); and *Amida no munewari* (1651) and *Goō-no-hime* (1673) representing *ko-jōruri*. The undated *Oguri* and *Sayohime* manuscripts represent an early- to mid-seventeenth century form of *sekkyō*, but as either illustrated transcriptions of *sekkyō* performances or novelistic adaptations of *sekkyō shōhon*. (9)

While early publications of *sekkyō* works were simply divided into three books or parts, as we read through the collection we find that the texts start adapting the six-act style common in published *ko-jōruri* plays. The framing device featuring place names and the association of the protagonist with important Buddhist icons, which was typical in early *sekkyō* such as *Sanshō Dayū* and *Karuyaka*, was similarly replaced later on by, for instance, the name of the emperor to designate a historical era in *Aigo-no-waka*—a framing device typical of later puppet theater. In addition, battle scenes more suited to *shamisen* accompaniment than *sasara* begin to crop up in the later tales, indicating in another manner the gradual transformation that *sekkyō* underwent as it absorbed influential theatrical themes and styles.

Naturally, editors must always make certain sacrifices in order to produce texts suitable for use in undergraduate and graduate classrooms. The flip side of a readable, typical text is the smoothing out of certain irregularities that are specific to individual texts or books. Kimbrough mentions in his introduction that "there is nothing to distinguish the pre-1658 *sekkyō shōhon* (*Sanshō Dayū*, *Karukaya*, and *Shintokumaru*) from the non-playbook manuscripts included here (*Oguri* and *Sayohime*)" (10), and that "the extant *shōhon* and illustrated manuscripts give little indication of what an actual performance may have been like" (10). There is a certain truth to this, but at the same time certain performative codes were important to *shōhon* from at least sometime in the seventeenth century. Chanter's names were often written at the beginning of *shōhon*, including those for *sekkyō*, sometimes in characters even larger than the title of the work. For instance, the 1639 book that forms the basis for the translation of *Sanshō Dayū* opens with a big announcement that this is "The Release of the Greatest Sekkyō Chanter Yoshichirō's 'True Text'" (Tenkaichi Sekkyō Yoshichiro shōhon hiraku), while the 1648 *Shintokumaru* book also opens with "The 'true text' of the Greatest Sado Shichidayū" (Tenka musō Sado Shichidayū shōhon). These statements clearly marked the performative identity of the text, and must to some degree have conditioned the experience of the reader, even though they represented a commercial strategy initiated by the bookstores in collaboration with the theater, rather than the other way around. The decision not to include this information certainly is not unique to this collection of translations: even in Japanese critical editions, different editors make different choices about whether to reproduce or omit such statements. In this case, Kimbrough's decision not to include information about chanters was most likely inspired by a desire to give appropriate weight to consistency and readability, since some of the *sekkyō* source texts he used were themselves published as "readerly" works. Even in the case of *shōhon* texts, there are irregularities: many texts omit any reference to a chanter or simply note at the end that it is a chanter's "true text" without giving the chanter's name (this is the case, for instance, with the source text that Kimbrough used for *Aigo-no-waka*). Kimbrough still marks the performative identity of *sekkyō* by including as an appendix a detailed list and profiles of early modern *sekkyō* chanters. This allows him both to give each translation in *Wondrous Brutal Fictions* a smooth, readable feel and to make the book useful for scholars who are interested in the extra-textual world of performance and its social contexts.

The publication of translations like *Wondrous Brutal Fictions* both helps expand the field of Japanese literature as it exists in English-language contexts, and makes it possible to think in the context of Japanese studies about the fleeting nature of performance, and about the embodiment of performative materials in textual form at specific periods in history. On some level, even published *sekkyō* texts partake in a specifically performative fluidity. For instance, the text Kimbrough used as the source for his translation of *Oguri* notes at the end that Oguri is the human form of Aizome Myōō of Kitano Shrine, which is incongruous with his identity as the son of Shō Hachiman Shrine, mentioned in the opening. This has been regarded as a compromise in which associations were provided to link Oguri to the place in which the *sekkyō* was being performed, and so that the content of the text reflects spontaneous changes that found their way into the textual forms *sekkyō* assumed (TOKUDA 1976; ARAKI 1998). The absence of information about the performance that prompted this insertion—the inaccessibility of the vanished moment in which it occurred—is a challenge all of us studying performance must face. That challenge is relevant beyond the fields of performance and theater studies, however: the attempt to question the stability of texts and to learn, through them, more about things texts themselves may not be able to tell us is very exciting, and has the potential to lead to important contributions to the broader field of Japanese studies.

In sum, *Wondrous Brutal Fictions* is both the product of a careful, scholarly approach to selection and editing and an eminently readable and approachable translation that can be used and enjoyed in both undergraduate and graduate classrooms. Along with important translated anthologies of premodern theatrical works (see TYLER 1993; BRAZELL ed. 1998; KEENE 1998; and BRANDON and LEITER, eds. 2002–2003, to list just a few examples), I believe *Wondrous Brutal Fictions* will be widely used in the study of late medieval and early modern theater and literature, helping to expand the range of what is possible in the study and teaching of premodern Japanese theater, literature, and culture.

REFERENCES

ARAKI Shigeru
    1998   Sekkyō no seisui. In *Jōruri no tanjō to ko-jōruri*, Iwanami Kōza Kabuki Bunraku, vol. 7, 71–93. Tokyo: Iwanami Shoten.

ARAKI Shigeru and YAMAMOTO Kichizō, eds.
    1973   *Sekkyō-bushi*. Tōyō bunko 243. Tokyo: Heibonsha.

BRANDON, James R., and Samuel L. LEITER, eds.
    2002–2003   *Kabuki Plays on Stage*. 4 vols. Honolulu: University of Hawai'i Press.

BRAZELL, Karen, ed., and James T. ARAKI et al., trans.
    1998   *Traditional Japanese Theater: An Anthology of Plays*. New York: Columbia University Press.

DUNN, Charles James
    1966   *The Early Japanese Puppet Drama*. London: Luzac.

ISHII Nobuko
    1989   Sekkyō-bushi. *Monumenta Nipponica* 44: 283–307.

KEENE, Donald, trans.
    1998   *Four Major Plays of Chikamatsu*. By Chikamatsu Monzaemon (1653–1725). New York: Columbia University Press.

MATISOFF, Susan
    1978   *The Legend of Semimaru: Blind Musician of Japan*. New York: Columbia University Press.
    1992   Holy horrors: The sermon-ballads of medieval and early modern Japan. In *Flowing Traces: Buddhism in the Literary and Visual Arts of Japan*, James Sanford, William LaFleur, and Masatoshi Nagatomi, eds., 234–62. Princeton: Princeton University Press.

MORRISON, Barbara S.
    2006   Body Rhetoric: Women en Route to Salvation in *Oguri* and *Pilgrim's Progress*. PhD dissertation, University of North Dakota.

MUROKI Yatarō, ed.
    1977   Kaisetsu. In *Sekkyō shū*. SNKS (Shinchō Nihon koten shūsei), 393–423. Tokyo: Shinchōsha.

SHIMAZU Hisamoto, ed.
    1928   *Kinko shōsetsu shinsan*. Tokyo: Chūkōkan.

SHINODA Jun'ichi and SAKAGUCHI Hiroyuki, eds.
    1999   *Ko-jōruri, sekkyō shū*. SNKBT (Shin Nihon koten bungaku taikei), vol. 90. Tokyo: Iwanami Shoten.

TOKUDA Kazuo
    1976   Sekkyō toki to shoki sekkyō bushi no kōzō. *Kokubungaku Kenkyū Shiryōkan kiyō* 2 (March): 19–46.

TYLER, Royall
    1993   *Japanese Nō Drama*. London: Penguin Classics.

Satoko Shimazaki
University of Southern California

Rebecca Suter, *Holy Ghosts: The Christian Century in Modern Japanese Fiction*
Honolulu: University of Hawai'i Press, 2015. 194 pages. Hardback, $45.00. ISBN 978-0-8248-4001-3.

ONE OF THE MOST difficult tasks for a student of Japanese history is to truly understand the ebb and flow of Japan's contacts with the outside world. There appears to be a struggle within Japanese society whether Japan should retain its own "unique" culture or whether it should be engaged in a form of "hybridization" of its cultural norms with worthy elements of foreign cultures. At times Japan closes itself off from the outside world, while at other times it appears to open itself up to foreign influences.

Rebecca Suter visits this question in great detail in *Holy Ghosts*. Her focus is the so-called "Christian century of Japan" (1549–1638) when Japan made its first real contact with the West with the arrival of Jesuit missionaries, the final Christian revolt, and the formal ban on Christianity by the new Tokugawa Shogunate. She is particularly interested in the repeated appearance of the "Christian century" in modern Japanese fiction and how modern writers such as Akutagawa Ryūnosuke, Endō Shūsaku, and others have handled Japan's reaction to penetration by foreign cultures. She argues that although the topics of these stories focus on this earlier period, these writers are really debating Japan's position in the modern world.

Throughout her work Suter has discovered a tendency by domestic and foreign media "to characterize Japanese culture as exceptional/exceptionalist" (108). The term *Nihonjiron* is based on the presumption that "the Japanese constitute a culturally and socially homogenous racial entity, whose essence is virtually unchanged from prehistoric times down to the present day," and that they "differ radically from all other known peoples" (108). Suter notes that in many *Nihonjinron* texts, Japan and the "West" are dissimilar in every possible way, but with the idea that in discussing Euro-American stereotypes, Japan is portrayed as "superior, rather than inferior, to its Western counterparts" (109).

Suter begins her analysis with a look at the late Meiji and Taisho literary authors who used the "Kirishitan" to reflect on the "complexity of Japan's relationship with the West." She focuses on Akutagawa's collection of stories *Kirishitan mono*, published between 1916 and 1927. Suter feels that these stories highlight "the cross-cultural negotiation in which Jesuit missionaries and Japanese converts engaged during the early stages of the Christian century provide a powerful analogy for the combination of fear and desire toward the West that Japan was experiencing in the modern age, and demonstrate how the same dynamics apply to all cultures when they are faced with an Other" (170). These writers also reject the Western self-identification with "science and rationality" and their depiction of Asian cultures as "superstitious" and "primitive." Japanese writers of the period, Suter notes, often portray European culture as being "irrational" and "emotional," thus deflating the Western idea of the West's "civilizing mission," which included Christian missionary objectives. These writers thus invert the idea of "Orientalism" so that it is Asia that now appears primitive and superstitious. These stories, concludes Suter, oblige us to "rethink conventional notions of East-West relations and mutual representations" (170).

The second half of the book focuses on postwar literature, with a more intense reaction to the West from those writers who express a fear and loathing of things foreign—two sentiments dominating the thinking of *Nihonjinron*. "Thus from the 1960s to the mid-1990s representations of the Kirishitan in the realm of fiction transformed them into a symbol of the danger, rather than the excitement, of cultural hybridization, and presented them consistently in a negative light, as inherently evil characters" (171). One finds in these writings an incessant demonization of the Kirishitan characters.

There was yet another transformation in literature in the late 1990s and early 2000s. During this time, Suter notes, "the Kirishitan began to participate in the dynamic play of gender and cultural subversion that is the staple of the genre of *shōjo* manga and related subcultural practices such as Lolita fashion. The queer Kirishitan became the harbinger of a critique of Japanese heteropatriarchy and, at the same time, marked the transition towards a new model of interaction with foreign culture, a third way beyond the assimilation/rejection dichotomy that had characterized their previous incarnations" (171).

Reading Suter requires considerable stamina. Her stilted, excessively detailed, and very dry writing style is often hard to digest, but the content of her scholarship is both profound and groundbreaking. The depth and quality of her research is impressive. Her thesis that an examination of "Kirishitan" literature also reflects Japanese attitudes towards Japan's contacts and relations with the West is strongly supported through her analysis of writers like Akutagawa and Endō. Any serious Japanese historian or anthropologist would surely gain new insights through Suter's work.

Daniel A. Métraux
Mary Baldwin College

Korea

Laurel Kendall, Jongsung Yang, and Yul Soo Yoon,
God Pictures in Korean Contexts: The Ownership and Meaning of Shaman Paintings
Honolulu: Hawai'i University Press, 2015. 176 pages. Hardback, $54.00; paperback $29.00. ISBN 97808248-47647 (hardback); 9780824847630 (paperback).

THIS DELIGHTFUL yet compact book reports a collaborative project between Laurel Kendall (a long-established and well-known observer of Korean shamanism who works as chair of anthropology, and as a curator at the American Museum of Natural History), Jongsung Yang (formerly at the Korean National Folk Museum of Korea, and now director of the Museum of Shamanism), and Yul Soo Yoon (the founder and director of the private Gahoe Museum in Seoul). With the benefit of Kendall's elegant narrative style, the three authors explore how interest in and the valuing of shaman paintings evolved as Korean urban development and modernity embedded folklore in nationalist discourse. They reject the old anthropological structural-functionalist discourse that separates magic from religion, and instead reference Europe and America's twentieth-century discovery of primitivism through the work of Picasso, and the subsequent public displays of modernist art in Europe and America alongside traditional artefacts sourced from the global south.

KENDALL first bought a painting in the 1970s during fieldwork (which led to her 1985 and 1988 monographs). Previously, as a Peace Corps volunteer, she had hung prints of shaman god paintings on the wall of her boarding house room. At that time, most Koreans felt uneasy about displaying objects once venerated as the houses of gods, and few perceived that such folkloric depictions could have artistic value. Since then interest has shifted over time, and the authors explain this by utilizing Bruno LATOUR's (1993) sense of purification through naming, and Arjun APPADURAI's (1996) discussions of the social life of objects, to theorize about how this has occurred. Citing Michael TAUSSIG (2009), they note that purification is seldom complete: objects considered primitive, in this case shaman paintings, still, as objects, retain "a frisson of magic" and traces of their past. However, unlike the distant lens through which Europeans and Americans view primitivism, Koreans have a more intimate nostalgia for a past that remains close: their recent ancestors valued shaman rituals, and regarded the very air as being populated by myriad gods. This nostalgia accords a purity lacking in modern life, an idea Kendall discussed in her account of Korean village spirit poles, *changsŭng* (KENDALL 2011). Also, sitting alongside this volume, two articles by KENDALL and YANG (2014; 2015) sketch out the "Picasso Face" and the ambiguities of materiality and religion inherent in shaman paintings.

All three authors have personal baggage to account for arising from their collecting activity. This becomes clear in the brief biographies incorporated into chapter 1. Kendall notes how the shaman she closely observed during fieldwork would refer to her grandfather and grandmother as gods residing in the images pasted to the walls of her shrine. At the time, the cheap prints that adorned the walls of their residences hardly interested Kendall. However, she goes on to explain how and why she came to study the costumes and altar fittings in ways that readily relate to her more recent concerns for god paintings: "By following objects, I came to understand relationships … between the client's family, their own potent gods, the shaman, and the gods in the shaman's own shrine" (13).

In contrast, Yang was interested in shamanism as a youth, and was apprenticed to a shaman for six years. Even though he never went through the initiation ritual that would mark his acceptance as a shaman—instead opting to travel to America for doctoral studies at Indiana University—he did have the chance to observe how the costumes, paintings, and paraphernalia of deceased shamans would be burned or buried. He began collecting these objects, thereby preventing their destruction and loss. This in turn required reassuring those concerned that he would take responsibility for the spiritual power attached to them. In so doing, he acquired the collection that is today showcased in the Museum of Shamanism. In his turn, upon graduating from university, Yoon trained with the folklorist and founder of the celebrated Emilé Museum, Cho Cha-ryong (Zo Zayong), learning to value the peculiar Korean identity inherent in folk paintings. He explored the relationship of shaman paintings to other folk art and, indeed, to the broader corpus of Korean art. His collection of god paintings became part of the Gahoe Museum that he curates. The two collections of Yang and Yoon provide most of the illustrations in the book.

Starting with the Picasso epiphany—the discovery of primitivism or, in Korea, the realization that folk paintings have value as art—folklorists began to collect and deal in shaman paintings. The popular discovery in 1963 of ten old paintings hidden in a cave by the Cheju island folklorist Hyŏn Yong-jun marked the starting point. He had wanted to acquire some of these paintings, but the shaman who used them to house her gods refused. After her death, he found the paintings bundled up on a ledge high in the cave. Then came the folklorist Kim T'ae-gon, currently at Kyunghee University in Seoul, who documented all things shamanic—rituals, texts, paraphernalia, and the like—and who collected paintings that became the subject of the first landmark text on the subject, published in 1989. Cho Cha-ryong had long encouraged the embrace of folk paintings, but Yoon notes in his brief biographical statement that foreigners came to appreciate shaman paintings before Koreans. Hence, we read that two paintings were displayed in a 1983 exhibition curated by a foreigner, despite protests from Korean officials (indeed, the National Museum of Korea still has no shaman paintings in its collection, and I note that the large collection owned by the British Museum in London remains hidden from public view). By the 1980s, though, the "critical scaffolding" (60) for appreciating the shaman paintings was in place, and the prices demanded for them rose. Dealers and professors "abducted" paintings, often offering half-hearted supplications to mollify concerned shamans. Collecting peaked in the 1990s, just when interest in folklore itself began to wane among Koreans, along with the demise of journals featuring it, such as *Saemi kippŭn mul* (Water from a deep spring), *Chŏnt'ong munhwa* (Traditional culture), and *Konggan/Space*, although it never embraced shaman imagery.

The authors discuss the way that shamans procure paintings, and how they hold rituals to animate them. They observe that in the past, faded, water damaged, and moth- or mouse-eaten paintings would be periodically replaced with new items purchased from the specialist shops along Seoul's central thoroughfare, Chongno, or produced to order from specialist artists. By the 1960s, bright colors had become normal, and prints became available. More recently, China has become the supplier of mass produced paintings, impacting the ability of local artists to compete. Barely any shops remain in Chongno, and those artists who do continue with their craft might produce a painting incorporating a vision that a commissioning shaman has of a specific god, while lesser artists might take a pre-stencilled drawing and fill it in, adjusting the details to suit a client. Two artists are interviewed, along with the proprietors of a couple of the remaining specialist shops. Still, discussion of decline is said to be "modernity talk" (96), and evaluating the veracity of what "conversation partners" detail is resisted on rather nonacademic grounds that it is "impossible to know," or because there is "no independent confirmation."

All three authors, ultimately, have vested interests in shaman paintings as art. But, as Walter Benjamin balances the ubiquity of mechanical reproduction against the incorporation of auras, so the book is clear and vague about the purity of the art that it seeks to champion. There is a sense here in which academic discourse refuses to be silenced by the practices of collecting. Throughout, considerable attention is given to theoretical literature, but this only increases the uncertainty, and quite deliberately so. Hence, taking from Patricia SPYER's "deliberately oxymoronic" characterization of the "border fetish" (1998), and from other more recent literature still, the bridge between a painting animated by a god and a painting given value as an object of art is said to be unstable (67). When two paintings fell off the wall of a shrine and landed on top of each other, the interpretation given held that two gods had quarrelled. A painting is animated only when a god enters it in a ritual dedicated to this happening. If the god refuses to do so, cases are reported where the painting will be returned, as if unused, to the shop or artist from which it was bought. Again, cautionary tales are offered that tell of deaths and accidents that followed the mistreatment of a painting. Attention-seeking gods reject being housed in single paintings that depict multiple gods—paintings designed to fit the cramped conditions of urban apartments. And yet, when a shaman dies or stops giving rituals and leaves nobody to inherit a painting, the interpretation is that the god does not want to stay, and so a painting can be given to a museum. "They go completely away, they fly off. [A museum is] a place where they cannot reside," (123) remarks one shaman, providing reassurance for Yang and Yoo's collection activities. "Has the museum become the twenty-first-century equivalent of a mountain burial, a pure and somewhat distant place where sacred things might be interred?" (125) ask the authors. At this point, those familiar with Hollywood's *Night at the Museum* films might want to remember that the museum featured is where Kendall works, the American Museum of Natural History, and wonder what to make of the resulting ambiguity. And the concluding paragraph to the book leaves the ambiguity hanging: a shaman gives a painting to the collectors, remarking how the god known as the General wants to go to a museum because he has work to do there. Do the gods continue with their work, in the Museum of Shamanism, in the Gahoe Museum, and in other collections of shaman paintings?

REFERENCES

APPADURAI, Arjun
1996   *The Social Life of Things: Commodities in Cultural Perspective.* Cambridge: Cambridge University Press.

KENDALL, Laurel

1985   *Shamans, Housewives, and Other Restless Spirits: Women in Korean Ritual Life.*
        Honolulu: University of Hawai'i Press.

1988   *The Life and Hard Times of a Korean Shaman: Of Tales and the Telling of Tales.*
        Honolulu: University of Hawai'i Press.

2011   The *changsŭng* defanged: The curious recent history of a Korean cultural symbol.
        In *Consuming Korean Tradition in Early and Late Modernity: Commodification,
        Tourism, and Performance*, ed. Laurel Kendall, 129–48. Honolulu: University of
        Hawai'i Press.

KENDALL, Laurel, and Jongsung YANG

2014   Goddess with a Picasso face: Art markets, collectors and sacred things in the circu-
        lation of Korean shaman paintings. *Journal of Material Culture* 19: 401–23.

2015   What is an animated image? Korean shaman paintings as objects of ambiguity.
        HAU: Journal of Ethnographic Theory 5: 153–75.

LATOUR, Bruno

1993   *We Have Never Been Modern.* Trans. Catherine Porter. Cambridge, MA: Harvard
        University Press.

SPYER, Patricia, ed.

1998   *Border Fetishisms: Material Objects in Unstable Spaces.* New York: Routledge.

TAUSSIG, Michael

2009   *What Color is the Sacred?* Chicago: University of Chicago Press.

Keith Howard
School of Oriental and African Studies, University of London

Tibet

Karl E. Ryavec, *A Historical Atlas of Tibet*

Chicago: University of Chicago Press, 2015. 216 pages. 121 color
plates, 36 halftones, 2 tables. Cloth, $45.00; e-book, $27.00. ISBN
9780226732442 (cloth); 9780226243948 (e-book).

ACCURATE MAPS OF Tibet have long been conspicuous by their absence. Travellers
in remote areas of the plateau may still experience that unsettling feeling of realizing
their map is wrong, while scholars, particularly those working on historical texts, are
often unable to precisely locate places mentioned in their sources. The impediments to
toponymical precision are many. They include the propensity for places to have names
in three or four different languages at any one time and for toponyms to shift with
migrating social and ethnic groups. In addition, the boundaries of political units have
shifted over time, and in the case of many historical frontiers imprecision in definition
has been diplomatically valuable under traditional mandala or "ritual state" systems.
Political and cultural considerations have hindered scientific mapping, as has the rug-
ged terrain, and to those difficulties the use of different transcription systems in ren-
dering toponyms into European languages has further confused the reading of such
maps. While the cartographical output of certain scholars has been of considerable
value—one thinks of Guntrum Hazard on Yarlung dynasty sites and John Bellezza

on archaeological sites in Ngari, for example—in general cartography has lagged far behind other areas of Tibetan studies.

We can, therefore, welcome the publication of Karl Ryavec's *A Historical Atlas of Tibet*, a reference work that any scholar in the field will want to have at hand. It includes a total of forty-nine maps of political, cultural, and religious sites across most of the Tibetan Buddhist world, including sites in Mongolia and Manchuria, along with maps of such aspects as major Tibetan Buddhist monasteries in Beijing in the Yuan and Ming periods, language and population distribution, natural resources, and land cover patterns. The maps are annotated with relevant details and accompanied by an explanatory text that effectively serves as a concise and well-balanced history of Tibet. This work is clearly a labor of love and the author has also ventured beyond the cartographic and historical remit, with agreeable, if not original digressions into areas such as Tibetan currency, caterpillar fungus (*yartsa gunbu*), cultural artefacts, and long-distance trade items. It includes a variety of historical and contemporary photographs that mean the work will also appeal to the "coffee table" market, and there is a good general index, although understandably it does not include all of the sites indicated on the maps, and cannot avoid the transcription issue.

There is a good regional balance in the maps between western, central, and eastern Tibet, and it is organized into sections on the prehistoric and ancient periods, the imperial period (ca. 600–900 CE), the "period of Disunion" (900–1642), and the Ganden Podrang Period. In general the maps are clear, with A4 size pages and paper quality enhancing that clarity. A word of caution, however, to those contemplating purchasing the electronic edition; it may prove impossible to read much of the map detail in that format.

There are few obvious errors, at least in the sections this reviewer is qualified to comment upon. Ngari does not include the source of the Ganges (as stated on page 14); maps eighteen and thirty-one show a Hindu temple at Gangotri for which there is no evidence in the relevant periods; and the formal Tibetan toponym of Mount Kailas(h) is Tise (*Ti se*) rather than the more colloquial *Gangs Rinpoche* given here. In addition, given the political implications, the statement that the TAR "roughly" equates to the area of traditional Tibet (4) might have been better replaced by a map showing the actual differences.

Given the pioneering nature of this work, there are naturally some reservations concerning its scope and contents. The author notes (120) that a revised and expanded edition is intended in the future, and this should include resort to the British-Indian maps in the Oriental and India Office Collection of the British Library, which the author does not appear to have directly utilized. These shed considerable light on southern Tibet at least, and would enable the provision of more detailed large-scale maps of those areas. In addition, maps of historically relevant areas of the greater Tibetan cultural world to the south and west of the plateau—Ladakh, Sikkim, Bhutan, and so on—might be added, and consideration given to the inclusion of some examples of indigenous cartographical representations.

Despite such reservations, this is a reference work that will repay detailed study. The author's modest hope that it will be of "some value" is more than fulfilled.

A. C. McKay
International Institute for Asian Studies, Leiden

Ana Cristina O. Lopes, *Tibetan Buddhism in Diaspora:*
Cultural Re-Signification in Practice and Institutions
London and New York: Routledge, 2015. 276 pages. Cloth, $153.00;
ebook $38.00. ISBN 9780415719117 (cloth); 9781315738147 (ebook).

WHEN A FULBRIGHT grant in 2006 to do research in China allowed me an entrance onto the Tibetan Plateau, an area inhabited by more ethnic Tibetans than in Tibet proper, I paid special attention to Buddhist monasteries and local devotion to the Dalai Lama. When I entered monasteries I was surprised to always find photographs of the Dalai Lama. When I asked monks why they dared to show the Dalai Lama's photo, they replied that Chinese authorities would leave them alone as long as they went on with their lives and did nothing to provoke the Chinese.

My own feelings about the Chinese presence in Tibet were mixed. Tibetan university students whom I interviewed said that in traditional times Tibet, despite the glory of their civilization, was weak because of its deep isolation from the rest of the world. Although they deeply resented the presence of Chinese in their land, and hoped the day would come when Tibet would enjoy some degree of independence, they also credited China with opening Tibet to the modern world. At the same time, they feared that the growing presence of Chinese in Tibet would eventually doom Tibetan civilization through a process of deep assimilation.

Many sympathetic people outside of China have carried on a long campaign demanding an end to the Chinese occupation of Tibet, but I always tell them that it is no more than a pipedream. I ask them to consider a very similar parallel in the United States. The Navajo nation once ruled a large area of what is now the American southwest, but by the end of the nineteenth century the United States had taken over the region. There are still tens of thousands of Navajo in the area, but there is no way that the U.S. will return all this land to Native Americans. By the same token, the Chinese will never surrender Tibet.

Anthropologist Ana Cristina O. Lopes, a research associate at the University of São Paulo, Brazil, has written a fascinating book, *Tibetan Buddhism in Diaspora*, that offers bright hope for the survivability of at least some aspects of Tibetan civilization. Her thesis is that the "imperialist ambitions of China, which invaded Tibet in the late 1940s" (1) led to the diaspora of tens of thousands of Tibetans, and, as a result, "sparked the spectacular spread of Tibetan Buddhism worldwide, and especially in western countries" (1). Vajrayana, once an obscure branch of Buddhism hidden away in the Himalayas, did not die with the coming of the secular Chinese. Rather, it has taken on a spectacular new life with followers and communities throughout the world. Once a form of Buddhism tied mainly to ethnic Tibetans, it has become a global force with great influence in such activist arenas as world peace and environmental preservation. It is a perfect case study of how a certain cultural tradition can adapt itself to new contexts with a global following.

Lopes begins her monograph with a detailed study of the rise of modern Tibetan civilization where successive Dalai Lamas wielded both religious influence and political power. We then get a detailed look at the Chinese invasion of Tibet, and the violent suppression of Tibetans throughout the 1950s and 1960s. But what seems like the hopeless destruction of a great civilization finds new life in the massive Tibetan diaspora that included the 1959 escape of the current (fourteenth) Dalai Lama to India. Lopes writes the following:

> In many senses, the transformation undergone by the Dalai Lama—from religious and secular leader of a relatively isolated country to one of the most renowned religious figures in the world—can only be understood when contextualized within the broader phenomenon of the Tibetan diaspora. Over the last 50 years, the world has witnessed the spectacular dissemination of the Tibetan Buddhism, a religion that, until very recently, figured in the Western imagination as a mystical sect of lamas living in a magical universe.... Today, hundreds of 'flesh and bone' lamas travel around the world, founding dharma centers dedicated to the practice and study of Tibetan Buddhism. In the publishing market, dozens of titles explaining the principles, philosophy and history of the religion are launched annually. In universities, American universities in particular, chairs of Tibetan studies are being created. Finally, the numbers of Western followers of that religion is well beyond hundreds of thousands and continues to grow... [T]he life and activities not only of the Dalai Lama, but of other exile lamas too, strongly inflect the effects of globalization... [C]onstant travel, the creation of Buddhist centers in multiple countries, and a strong presence on the internet and in the publishing market characterize the interaction of Tibetan lamas with their disciples around the world.... The transnational religious field of Tibetan Buddhism involves the formation of a 'network of objective relations...' by its global and fragmentary characteristics. (84–85)

One cannot, however, separate Buddhism in Tibet from politics. As Lopes notes, the interchange between Buddhist lamas and western disciples leads to strong support in the West for the political liberation of Tibet.

Lopes goes to great lengths to explain how both the Dalai Lama, who won the Nobel Peace Prize in 1989, and other Tibetan Buddhist lamas and monks, have brought forth many of the principles of their religion—such as peace, tolerance, and justice for all—and have succeeded in transforming the fight for the autonomy of Tibet into a generalized fight "for a more equitable and peaceful existence in an ode to nonviolence that echoes the seminal words of Mahatma Gandhi" (94). This drive for peace, or demilitarization, is also critical for the preservation of the environment. The Dalai Lama himself has said, "Demilitarization will free great human resources for protection of the environment, relief of poverty, and sustainable human development" (97).

Lopes in her *Tibetan Buddhism in Diaspora* goes into far greater detail on the worldwide role of Tibetan Buddhism than can be discussed here. Her book is crammed full with interesting arguments and information. It is brilliantly researched and clearly written. The author's goal to investigate the "process of cultural re-signification" of Tibetan Buddhism in the context of its diaspora is clearly met.

Daniel A. Métraux
Mary Baldwin College

CONTRIBUTORS

Ishita BANERJEE-DUBE is Professor of History, Center of Asian and African Studies, El Colegio de Mexico (Mexico City), and editor of the series "Hinduism" with De Gruyter Open. Her research interests straddle themes of religion, law and power, time and history, food and identity, and gender and nation in modern and contemporary eastern india (Odisha) viewed from the perspectives of subaltern, postcolonial and feminist studies. Her publications include *A History of Modern India* (Cambridge University Press, 2015).

Kikee Doma BHUTIA is a PhD student in the Department of Estonian and Comparative Folklore, University of Tartu, Estonia. Before joining the University of Tartu, she worked as a Research Assistant in the Namgyal Institute of Tibetology, Sikkim, India, where she holds a research affiliation. Her PhD research revolves around belief narratives of mythic histories of Sikkim, particularly through the windows of prophesies, pilgrimage, and patronage.

Margaret CHAN is Associate Professor, Theatre/Performance Studies (Practice), School of Social Sciences, Singapore Management University. Her research interest is spirit possession and Chinese popular religion. She is the author of *Ritual is Theatre, Theatre is Ritual: Tang-ki spirit medium worship in Singapore* (Wee Kim Wee Centre, SMU and SNP Reference, 2006).

Nilamber CHHETRI teaches Sociology at Maharashtra National Law University, Mumbai. His research interests include the politics of social and cultural identities, scheduling of tribes, practices of state classification in India, and issues related to ethnic minorities and the politics of recognition in South Asia. He has contributed research articles and reviews to journals such as *Asian Ethnicity*, the *Sociological Bulletin*, *Contemporary South Asia*, as well as others.

Caroline CHIA's doctoral dissertation examines the use of literacy and script in temple theater pertaining to the Hokkien and Henghua communities in Singapore. Her book chapter, "*Potehi* in Singapore," appears in *Potehi: Glove Puppet Theatre in Southeast Asia and Taiwan* (Kaori Fushiki and Robin Ruizendaal, eds., Taiyuan Publisher, 2015). She recently worked as a Research Fellow at the Center of Chinese Studies (CCS) in Taipei.

Benjamin DORMAN is a Senior Research Fellow at the Anthropological Institute, Nanzan University, and co-editor of *Asian Ethnology*.

Levi S. GIBBS is Assistant Professor in the Department of Asian and Middle Eastern Languages and Literatures at Dartmouth College, where he teaches Chinese language, modern literature, culture, and folklore. His research focuses on the history and dynamics of Chinese folk song performance and collection as they relate to conceptions of the "folk," social change, and regional identity. His current book project explores the life and songs of the "Folk song king of Western China" Wang Xiangrong, examining the role of "song kings" in connecting people, places, past and present. He recently served as Associate Editor and Book Review Editor for *CHINOPERL: Journal of Chinese Oral and Performing Literature* and Senior Convener of the Transnational Asia/ Pacific Section of the American Folklore Society.

Walter HAKALA is Assistant Professor of South Asian languages and literature at the University at Buffalo, SUNY. His recent book, *Negotiating Languages: Urdu, Hindi, and the Definition of South Asia* (Columbia University Press, 2016) was awarded the 2015 Edward C. Dimock, Jr. Prize in the Indian Humanities by the American Institute of Indian Studies.

Keith HOWARD is Professor of Music at SOAS, University of London. He has written and edited nineteen books, including *Korean Musical Instruments: A Practical Guide* (Se-Kwang Music Publishing Company, 2015), *Music as Intangible Cultural Heritage: Policy, Ideology and Practice in the Preservation of East Asian Traditions* (Routledge, 2012). He has been a regular broadcaster on Korean affairs for BBC, ITV, Sky, NBC, and others.

Catherine INGRAM is a postdoctoral fellow at the Sydney Conservatorium of Music, University of Sydney, Australia, and visiting expert with the Chinese Music Ecology Research Team, Shanghai Conservatory of Music. Since 2004 she has conducted extensive research on Kam musical culture, and her forthcoming monograph focuses on the contemporary performance of Kam big song. She has published on many aspects of Kam singing and culture, and is also co-editor of *Taking Part in Music: Case Studies in Ethnomusicology* (Aberdeen University Press, 2013).

Gisa JÄHNICHEN is currently teaching and researching at Shanghai Conservatory of Music on ecomusicology and the performing arts of Southeast Asia. Her recent publications include *Studies on Musical Diversity: Methodological Approaches* (Universiti Putra Malaysia Press, 2011), *Studies on Music and Dance Cultures in Laos* (Books On Demand, 2013), and numerous journal articles. She is chief editor of *Studia Instrumentorum Musicae Popularis* (New Series), a Study Group book series of the International Council for Traditional Music.

Frank J. KOROM is Professor of Religion and Anthropology at Boston University and co-editor of *Asian Ethnology*.

Danton LEARY is a PhD candidate in the School of Culture, History and Language, the College of Asia and the Pacific, the Australian National University. His research comparatively examines Japanese and Australian colonial policy in the Pacific under the League of Nations mandates system. He is coeditor (with Pedro Iacobelli and Shinnosuke Takahashi) of *Transnational Japan as History: Empire, Migration and Social Movements* (Palgrave Macmillan, 2016).

Carola Erika LOREA is a scholar on South Asia currently working as a research fellow at the International Institute for Asian Studies in Leiden. She recently published *Folklore, Religion and the Songs of a Bengali Madman: A Journey Between Performance and the Politics of Cultural Representation* (Brill, 2016).

Leah LOWTHORP is an Associate of the Harvard Folklore and Mythology program, and Mellon/ACLS Public Fellow at the Center for Genetics and Society. Her work ranges from taking a postcolonial approach to UNESCO intangible cultural heritage and the politics of culture in India through the lens of Kutiyattam Sanskrit theater, to examining how biopolitical narratives circulate. She has published in the *Journal of Folklore Research*, *Western Folklore*, and *Indian Folklife*, among others.

Philip LUTGENDORF is Professor of Hindi and Modern Indian Studies at the University of Iowa. He has published extensively on popular culture and narrative traditions, and especially on performance practices centered around the epics *Ramayana* and *Mahabharata*. He maintains a website devoted to popular Hindi cinema (https://uiowa.edu/indiancinema/).

A. C. MCKAY is the author of a number of works on the history and culture of the Indo-Tibetan Himalayas. His most recent publication is *Kailas Histories: Renunciate Traditions and the Construction of Himalayan Sacred Geography* (Brill, 2015).

Anne E. MCLAREN is Professor at the Asia Institute, University of Melbourne, where she teaches Chinese language, literature, and culture. A specialist in the vernacular narratives, classical novels, and popular culture of late imperial China, she is the author of *Performing Grief: Bridal Laments in Rural China* (University of Hawaiʻi Press, 2008), *Chinese Popular Culture and Ming Chantefables* (Brill, 1998), and numerous other studies.

Daniel A. MÉTRAUX is Professor Emeritus and Adjunct Professor of Asian Studies at Mary Baldwin University. He has written many books, book chapters, and articles on modern Japanese and East Asian history and religion. His most recent publication, *How Journalists Shaped American Foreign Policy: A Case Study of Japan's Military Seizure of Korea in 1905*, is forthcoming from Edwin Mellen Press. His current research focuses on the Wakamatsu Tea and Silk Colony Farm, the first Japanese settlement of Japanese in North America in 1869.

Leela PRASAD is Associate Professor of Religious Studies at Duke University, and studies ethics and religion through narrative, broadcast media, performance, and art. Her first book, *Poetics of Conduct: Narrative and Moral Being in a South Indian Town* (Columbia University Press, 2007) won the American Academy of Religion's "Best First Book in the History of Religions" award.

Sukanya SARBADHIKARY is Assistant Professor at the Department of Sociology, Presidency University, Kolkata. She is the author of *The Place of Devotion:*

Siting and Experiencing Divinity in Bengal-Vaishnavism (University of California Press, 2015), among other publications.

Anthony Shay is Associate Professor of Dance and Cultural Studies in the Department of Theatre and Dance at Pomona College in Claremont, California. He is the author of six monographs, the latest of which is *The Dangerous Lives of Public Performers: Dance, Sex and Entertainment in the Middle East* (Palgrave Macmillan, 2014). He is currently writing a book about Igor Moiseyev and the Moiseyev Dance Company, the first state-supported folk dance company in the world.

Satoko Shimazaki is Associate Professor of Japanese literature and theater at the University of Southern California. Her research focuses on early modern Japanese theater and popular literature, the modern history of kabuki, gender representation on the kabuki stage, and the interaction of performance, print, and text. She is the author of *Edo Kabuki in Transition: From the Worlds of the Samurai to the Vengeful Female Ghost* (Columbia University Press, 2016).

Narasingha P. Sil retired from Western Oregon University in 2011 as Professor Emeritus of History. He has published numerous monographs, scholarly articles, book reviews, and encyclopedia, including *William Lord Herbert of Pembroke (c. 1507–1570): Politique and Patriot* (Edwin Mellen Press, 1988), and *Crazy in Love of God: Ramakrishna's Caritas Divina* (Susquehanna University Press, 2009).

Surya Suryadi is Lecturer in the Department of Languages and Cultures of Southeast Asia and Oceania, Leiden University. He is the author of *Syair Lampung Karam: Sebuah dokumen pribumi tentang dahsyatnya letusan Krakatau 1883* (Komunitas Penggiat Sastra Padang, 2010).

Timothy R. Tangherlini is Professor in the Department of Asian Languages and Cultures, University of California, Los Angeles. Along with Stephen Epstein, he has produced two documentaries on the independent music scene in South Korea. His book publications include *Sitings: Critical Approaches to Korean Geography* (with Sallie Yea; University of Hawai'i Press, 2007).

Jiaping Wu is a Senior Lecturer at the School of Education and The Arts, Central Queensland University, Rockhampton, Australia. He is a human geographer and a member of the Kam nationality of China. He has published widely on China's urbanization and regional issues, including in his native region of Guizhou.

Christine R. Yano, Professor of Anthropology at the University of Hawai'i, has conducted research on Japan and Japanese Americans with a focus on popular culture. Her publications include *Tears of Longing: Nostalgia and the Nation in Japanese Popular Song* (Harvard University Press, 2002), *Crowning the Nice Girl: Gender, Ethnicity, and Culture in Hawaii's Cherry Blossom Festival* (University of Hawai'i Press, 2006), *Airborne Dreams: "Nisei" Stewardesses and Pan American World Airways* (Duke University Press, 2011), and *Pink Globalization: Hello Kitty and its Trek Across the Pacific* (Duke University Press, 2013).

Emily Yu ZHANG is a native of Jiashan, Zhejiang province, China. She completed a Masters degree in the study of Chinese oral traditions at East China Normal University (ECNU), Shanghai. In May 2011 and May 2014, together with Anne E. McLaren, she carried out field trips to the Lake Tai region to interview singers and folklorists. She has recently taught Chinese at a college in Aarhus, Denmark.

www.ingramcontent.com/pod-product-compliance
Lightning Source LLC
Chambersburg PA
CBHW081146280526
45787CB00008B/3243